The Ultimate Actualist Convention

THE ULTIMATE
ACTUALIST CONVENTION

A Detailed View of Iowa City Actualism
in the 1970s & 1980s
and Its Migration to the San Francisco Bay Area

Edited by
Morty Sklar, Cinda Kornblum & Dave Morice

The Spirit That Moves Us Press
Established 1975

Jackson Heights, Queens,
New York City

Library of Congress Cataloging-in-Publication Data

Names: Sklar, Morty, 1935- editor. | Kornblum, Cinda, 1950- editor. | Morice,
    Dave, 1946- editor.
Title: The ultimate actualist convention : a detailed view of Iowa City
    actualism in the 1970s & 1980s and its migration to the San Francisco Bay
    area / edited by Morty Sklar, Cinda Kornblum & Dave Morice.
Description: Jackson Heights, Queens, New York City : The Spirit That Moves
    Us Press, [2017] | Series: The spirit that moves us ; volume 15
Identifiers: LCCN 2016053899 | ISBN 9780930370589 (alk. paper)
Subjects: LCSH: Actualism (Literature)--United States. | American
    literature--20th century--History and criticism. | Literary
    movements--United States--History--20th century. | Iowa Writers' Workshop.
Classification: LCC PS228.A28 U48 2017 | DDC 810.9/0054--dc23
LC record available at https://lccn.loc.gov/2016053899

In Memoriam

Allan Kornblum Darrell Gray Anselm Hollo David Hilton
Jim Mulac Kay Amert Howard Zimmon Glen Epstein
David Sessions John Birkbeck John Sjoberg

Missing in Action Audrey Teeter

Also from The Spirit That Moves Us Press

1977–The Actualist Anthology, edited by Morty Sklar & Darrell Gray

1980–Editor's Choice: Literature & Graphics from the U.S. Small Press, 1965–1977, edited by Morty Sklar & Jim Mulac

1987– Editor's Choice II: Fiction, Poetry & Art from the U.S. Small Press, 1978–1983, edited by Morty Sklar & Mary Biggs

1991– Editor's Choice III: Fiction, Poetry & Art from the U.S. Small Press, 1984–1990, edited by Morty Sklar

1983–The Casting of Bells, poetry by Jaroslav Seifert, who won the Nobel Prize in literature the following year. Translated from the Czech by Tom O'Grady & Paul Jagasich

1984–Nuke-Rebuke: Writers & Artists Against Nuclear Energy & Weapons, anthology edited by Morty Sklar

1988–Men & Women: Together & Alone, anthology edited by Morty Sklar & Mary Biggs

1996–Patchwork of Dreams: Voices from the Heart of the New America, anthology edited by Morty Sklar & Joseph Barbato

1985–Here's The Story: Fiction with Heart, edited by Morty Sklar

1989–Speak To Me: Swedish-language Women Poets, in Swedish and English facing pages; Edited by Lennart Bruce & Sonja Bruce

1980–The Farm In Calabria & Other Poems, by David Ray

1988–How In The Morning, poems 1962–1988, by Chuck Miller

1977–The Poem You Asked For, poems by Marianne Wolfe

2000–The Day Seamus Heaney Kissed My Cheek in Dublin, poems by Bob Jaco

1981–Cross-Fertilization: The Human Spirit As Place; poetry, fiction, art edited by Morty Sklar

1982–The Spirit That Moves Us Reader, collected from Volumes 1—6 of The Spirit That Moves Us regular issues, with reproductions of the covers, and a complete index.

Not everything is included here. Write for our catalog.

Acknowledgements

We wish to thank many and various people for their help
in making us aware of many developments, occurrences and people
prior to, during, and after publication in Iowa City of our
1977 *The Actualist Anthology*.

Our main connection to the "unknown" was David Schein.
Thank you, David Larew, for creating our website.

Thank you my Marcela of twenty-five years, for more than your share of
cooking, cleaning, and never once looking askance at me for the time I
have spent on this book.

Thanks to the following for your financial assistance, as we were no longer
eligible for grants. Listed here are two categories plus Other.

Honorary Publishers: Allan and Cinda Kornblum
Elizabeth Toth (1928–2016)
Patricio Bruno

Copy of the Book:
Cyndi and Dean Larew, David Larew, Al Buck, Joye Chizek, Howard
Sloane, Marcela Bruno, Mitch Rosenthal, Patricia Aakre, Stuart Abraham,
David Wilk, Jim Hanson, Howard Josepher, Warren Woessner,
Roy Beuscher, Nancy Hoving, Richard Peabody

Other:
Angela Sobrino, Barbara Yates, Kim Chapman, Steve Lavoie, Rick and
Debbie Vogel, William Karnett, Joseph Barbato, Tom Walz, Jim Falconi,
Walter Ditman, Sandi Rose, Bill and Cristina Weiner, Patricia Salek, Lisa
Hoffman, Patricia O'Donnell, Tom Leverett, Milagros Stevens, William
Karnett, David Olive, Anonymous

"She's brimful of poetry—actualized poetry—if I may use the expression."
 Thomas Hardy in *Tess of the D'Urbevilles*

"Sam Phillips, founder of the label Sun Records, didn't care much about making flawless recordings. Instead, the man who discovered Elvis Presley, Jerry Lee Lewis, Johnny Cash, Howlin' Wolf, Charie Rich, Roy Orbison and a host of others rejected perfection in favor of spontaneity and individualty."
 —from *Sam Phillips: The Man Who Invented Rock 'n' Roll*,
  by Peter Guralnick

"That's the poet's business—not to talk in vague categories, but to write particularly, as a physician works upon a patient, upon the thing before him, in the particular to discover the universal."
 —William Carlos Williams

≈ CONTENTS ≈

Foreword by Fred Chappell

Introduction by Cinda Kornblum

Publisher's Musings by Morty Sklar

I. ACTUALISM

II. BIOGRAPHIES, POEMS & PUBLICATIONS

IOWA CITY ACTUALISTS

SAN FRANCISCO BAY AREA ACTUALISTS

A 19-PAGE FULL-COLOR INSERT WITH 33 PHOTOS AND ILLUSTRATIONS IS INSERTED BETWEEN SECTIONS II AND III.

III. ACTUALIST PERFORMANCES and CONVENTIONS

IOWA CITY

FOREWORD BY FRED CHAPPELL

Actualism may be regarded as less a movement than an attitude, characterized primarily by generosity of spirit. Openminded, rebellious, joyful, dedicated, deranged, searching, and self-satirizing, Actualism included such individuals as David Morice, Allan Kornblum, Michael Lyons, Darrell Gray, John Batki, George Mattingly, and of course Joyce Holland. Perhaps Jaroslav Seifert and Whoopi Goldberg should be mentioned, so they won't feel left out. Many readers may well feel that they were left out of a riotous, funny, colorful party they had not known was taking place. But if they had known, they were welcome to join-in—as long as they did not drag with them a cumbrous baggage of petty rules and protocols. They could even write sonnets, if the spirit moved them.

Blithe minds are not famous for longevity. I think it is fair to say that Actualism, as an entity, is deceased. But the qualities it embraced and embodied are too strongly parts of the American personality to disappear. Some literary movements arise and then are gone forever. Vorticism, propounded mainly by Wyndham Lewis, is an example. But Imagism, as practiced by Amy Lowell and Ezra Pound, entered into and transformed the total geist of modern poetry. It became so pervasive that its special usages cannot now be separated from common usage.

The influence of Actualism upon our contemporary literature is as pervasive as it is untraceable, even though it gave rise to poetry presses and literary journals by the dozen. Its ambitions have been realized not only by Actualists but by scores of other writers, deliberately or unknowingly.

This volume is a montage: memoir, history, celebration, homage, elegy, portrait gallery, and timescape. And a high old time, an old-time high.

About Fred Chappell: (from William Styron) "An immensely gifted, exuberant, versatile writer who should be ranked among our important contemporary voices."

Fred Chappell is a poet, novelist, essayist, and retired professor who calls poetry "the noblest secular endeavor that the human mind undertakes."

INTRODUCTION BY CINDA KORNBLUM

"It doesn't just seem like a lifetime since you walked into Jack Marshall's poetry class with a toilet seat around your neck—it HAS been a lifetime. For a couple of apparently crazy-ass hippies, we both wound up working pretty damned hard in our respective fields, theater and small press publishing. And now we are respected elders. Rather strange, no?"

My husband, Allan Kornblum, wrote this in an e-mail to David Daf Schein when he was writing a biography of Darrell Gray for inclusion in an earlier version of this book. Allan and I had known Darrell for many years, but Darrell was such a philosopher, he rarely included factual details in his discussions. Allan spent weeks and weeks searching the internet, digging through old files, and contacting old friends to fill in gaps in Darrell's life story.

After that dip into the past, one thing led to another. Allan was going through intravenous treatments for Chronic Lymphocytic Leukemia, many of which involved long hours sitting with him in stark clinic rooms. Those were hours I could spend reading, reminiscing, and shaping the material the contributors had supplied. Once Allan passed away, I kept finding more photos, correspondence, newspaper clippings, and other bits of Iowa City history to add to the book. I was hooked and determined to see this book published to share with those who hung out in Iowa City in the good old days, who participated in the Actualist events in Iowa City and the Bay Area, and who helped spark the energy the Actualists thrived on.

Actualism sprang out of a variegated and flourishing community of writers and artists who converged in Iowa City over a period of ten-to-fifteen years. Most were drawn by the Iowa Writers' Workshop, some by the International Writing Program, and some to the Introduction to Typography course in the School of Journalism and Mass Communication, and some just wandered into town.

The first section begins with a piece by Dave Morice and one by Allan Kornblum which include their recollections of the day Darrell Gray created the Actualist Manifesto, followed by pieces that give somewhat of an overview of Actualism in Iowa City and the San Francisco Bay Area.

The second section includes the individual biographies, poems and publications of the Actualists and the community that inspired them. Some began in Iowa City and migrated to the Bay Area and elsewhere. Many more could and should be added. It was a magical mix of poets and writers, artists, actors and playwrights, teachers, musicians, publishers, translators and booksellers. For now, we encourage everyone to personally reach out and capture the stories of the Iowa City and Bay Area Actualists and to fill the margins of this book with additional names, corrections, notes, and quotes as needed.

The third section covers the Actualist events and antics in Iowa City and the Bay Area, and the fourth focuses on the stories of two of the publishers closely associated with this group of writers.

Iowa City in the early 1970s

This was before the military draft and the Vietnam War ended, before Coralville became anything more than a "strip" of businesses along U.S. Highway 6, before Urban Renewal took out old houses with apartments and replaced them with hotels and living units, and before personal computers and cell phones. Students hung out at Coffman Union in the "Gold Feather Room" where White Rabbit played endlessly on the juke box and where people heading to the east or west coast offered rides on the "Ride Board." There were anti-war demonstrations on the Pentacrest, adjacent to Iowa City's downtown with the stores and buildings that had been there since the town was built. The apartments above (many $50 single rooms) had bathrooms down the hall and quirky radiator and plumbing configurations. Telephones were nice when you could afford one but it was easy to rack up $300 long distance phone bills in the days of the "Ma Bell" monopoly. Instead of calling, we would walk from bar to bar or apartment to apartment to find each other. Sometimes the friend wasn't home but a party would be going on in another apartment in the building. Evenings were a serendipitous string of encounters, often ending in the wee hours of the morning. There were two Hamburg Inns, but after hours we would find someone with a car to drive us to the Skelly Truck Stop at the junction of Highway 6 and Interstate 80.

When George Starbuck was director of the Iowa Writers' Workshop, he established a vibrant group of faculty including Ted Berrigan, Anselm Hollo, Jack Marshall, Kathleen Fraser, Michael Dennis Browne, and William Price Fox. Some of the Actualists were in the Graduate Writers'

Workshop while others were undergraduates taking creative writing classes from workshop faculty. Over time they became less interested in learning how to write a carefully crafted "workshop poem" as they were into getting together to learn from one another—discussing other writers and new books, sharing poems, organizing readings, publishing magazines, and having a great time.

Thesis requirements seem to be a recurring theme in the biography section. Dave Morice and Sheila Heldenbrand each worked for a while as "thesis checkers," which included the task of measuring the margins with a ruler. Lloyd Quibble had problems with his title-less concrete poetry. Dave Morice wanted to submit a published mimeographed book but when he found out he would need to re-type it, he substituted a much, much shorter published book of only 81 words. I am also aware of a playwright (not naming names, but he later developed a national reputation as "Dr. Science") who, in desperation, used Wite-Out Correction Fluid to delete the last lines on each page to meet the margin requirement.

In 2008 Iowa City was designated a City of Literature by UNESCO (United Nations Educational, Scientific and Cultural Organization). The annual celebrations have focused on graduates of the Writers' Workshop but little had been said or written about the group who called ourselves the Iowa City Actualists. Although several received MFA's from the Workshop, their names do not appear in the Wikipedia "List of Writers' Workshop People." Yet their influence spread with the dispersal of Actualists across the country and through publications of the presses spawned by the movrment.

This book is our contribution to Iowa City's literary history, and we hope you enjoy the stories and photos we have shared, explore the holdings of the University of Iowa Special Collections, and explore the other sources noted herein.

PUBLISHER'S MUSINGS, BY MORTY SKLAR

Greetings, Dear Reader, and welcome to our labor of love. Had I been asked to publish this book, it would have been easy to decline, my having been eighty years of age and with an autobiographical novel to complete, and so on. And there are two other books I would have considered were I twenty years younger. So how did I get into this? Nobody talked me into it, and I didn't even become passionate about it until little by little it grew in length and depth, as did my relationships to the contributors including my co-editors. The directions and expanse of Actualist activity has been an unexpected education for me.

The idea for it arose after Iowa City was named a City of Literature by UNESCO (United Nations Educational, Scientific and Cultural Organization), and when yearly celebrations came about the people who were featured were those who were associated in some way with the university's Writers' Workshop. What about the community of poets, other writers, and small independent publishers who thrived in Iowa City, many of whom had been in the workshop—as students or teachers, and became alienated from it for reasons mentioned by many contributors to this book?

Thus the idea to bring attention to a community of writers who came to call ourselves the Actualists. *The Actualist Anthology*, co-edited by Darrell Gray—the namer of Actualism—and myself was published by my The Spirit That Moves Us Press in 1977. When Darrell moved to the San Franciso Bay area, many there were inspired and motivated to bring about Actualist activity, a good amount of which was theater.

The book grew to where it would have been too expensive to have someone typeset, format and print. Allan Kornblum, may he rest in peace—friend, and publisher of The Toothpaste Press and then Coffee House Press—told me he missed doing page-layout for books, as he was semi-retired, and I asked him if he missed it enough to do this book, and without hesitation he said yes. And I replied, "Then I'll publish it."

It wasn't long after that he passed away, and I spent much time between finding a good page-layout application (the one I had used last was in the year 2000) and in attempting to apply for grants, for which it turned out my press was now too far out of the loop.

Along the way we found—or they found us—a lot more contributors of work, most from the west coast, and it got to the point that even if I wanted to quit, I didn't want to disappoint our contributors.

Just as the title for this book is quite long, so is the name of my press, which I chose for my magazine in 1975 with the remembrance of what my mother had told me—that if the spirit moves you to do something, then do it. And thus this book.

The current Executive Director of City of Literature, Iowa City, John Kenyon, became very interested in the Actualists and has told us we could have a book launch at the October 2017 City of Literature celebration.

Enjoy.

I. ACTUALISM

The Origins of Actualism
by Dave Morice

One warm spring afternoon at the apartment I shared with Allan and Cinda Kornblum at 214 East Court Street, Darrell Gray, Anselm Hollo, Allan Kornblum, George Mattingly, and I were talking about the Writers' Workshop. Anselm said that we should start an alternative workshop—a writing program of our own. However, such ventures took a lot of capital, and we had no money to spend on challenging the world famous Writers' Workshop.

Then Anselm brought up a most intriguing idea: "You know, I think you guys have a poetry movement going on. The energy is there. All you need is a name for it." Darrell puffed on his pipe, gazed at the ceiling, and said, "Yeah, that's a good idea, a poetry movement."

George groaned. He wanted freedom from formal rules and obligations. "Poetry movement?" he said. "Next thing you know we'll be issuing membership cards."

Darrell smiled, nodded, and said, "Ah, that's a good idea, too."
The next day, Darrell and I went over to Audrey Teeter's house. Audrey wrote poetry and hung around with the writers of our group. She hired Darrell and me to paint her trellises. Darrell seemed preoccupied as we sloshed the paint on the wood. When we ran out of paint, he went into her garage to get a new bucket. When he returned, he hurried up to me and said, "I've got the name for our poetry movement. ACTUALISM." And Actualism it was, and Actualists we became.

Actualism had an open-door policy, which made it easy to join. Basically all you had to do was go to 214 East Court, climb up the steps to the second floor, take a few steps down the hallway, and open the door to the living room. Then you stepped into Actuality.

One thing was missing: a manifesto. In December 1972, Darrell and I went to his apartment to write some collaborative poems. He sat down at his typewriter and began—and he continued writing by himself instead of letting me join in. With joyful enthusiasm, he looked up and said, "I'm writing the Actualist Manifesto!" As he tapped the keys, I took a nearby

1

sheet of typing paper and drew a picture of him typing the Manifesto. Later I drew the words of the Manifesto swirling around his head.

After several minutes of intense writing, he plucked the paper out of the typewriter and handed it to me. I read it and said, "This is great. Can I include it in the next issue of Gum?"

"Sure," he said. I felt like a cub reporter scooping the other literary publications.

My poetry magazine, *Gum*, measured one-fourth the size of a sheet of typing paper. Because of its size, I published mostly short poems. This time, I would roll out the red carpet for the manifesto on a 4.25 x 11 foldout that was published in *Gum* 9.

ACTUALISM—A Manifesto

Actuality is never frustrated because it is complete.

The purpose or "intention" is to complicate matter.
A material paraphrase is a complication.

Or as Guillevic says, "The problem is to do to things
what light does to them."

Typing through sunglasses is, of course, an alternative.

There is no room for alternative illusions. There is
barely room for the table and bed.

The World has changed its mind. Ice cream is on sale.

Concentration is a problem for those obsessed with
process. For those obsessed with stasis, the opposite
of concentration sets in, and there is a seeming dispersal
throughout all the sensory regions.

Where is the missing balance?

Actualism is to Chemistry what Fatalism was to the
Middle Ages.

Actualism poses the question, "Of the seven openings
in the human body, why are five of them located
above the neck?"

Thoughts are concrete things.

Things are characterized more by their conditions
than their conditions are characterized by them.

"The useless is not horrible until it is bandaged
with truth."

Why belabor the impossible?

Defining Actualism

I have no idea how to define Actualism, so instead I'm listing my thoughts on what enabled the movement to thrive. These thoughts don't necessarily represent those of the other Actualists, some of whose are expressed elsewhere in this book.

1. Actualism brought poetry out of the closet. Instead of classroom meetings, the Actualists held reading series, conventions, marathons, parties, etc., and engaged the town in expanding the idea of poetry.
2. Actualism, because of its challenge to the Writers' Workshop, gained literary power that had never existed before among poets who weren't affiliated with the Workshop. Just as there is strength in numbers, there is also strength in letters.
3. The Actualists published a wide range of literary magazines to get the word out, some of which I name on a following page.
4. Many of the mags were printed using state-of-the-art mimeograph machines in the University of Iowa's Student Union. This device allowed anyone to become a hands-on editor. The "mimeograph revolution," which began in the Beat era of the 1950s, brought poetry publishing to the people.
5. In *Gum* 8, John Sjoberg wrote, "We aren't students anymore." The master-apprentice view of literature, so cherished by the Writers' Workshop, was not a part of our show. Or, rather, we were masters and apprentices of each other.
6. We often wrote about everyday objects and events, turning them on the wheel of inspiration, mixing the metaphors as they went around and around.
7. The Actualists had a fantastic time celebrating life, liberty, and the pursuit of poetry. This was during the hippie movement. In breaking away from the old school world, we mocked the gravity of the Writers' Workshop.
8. We were discovering new ways of creating poetry, we were learning about the literary world, and we were "getting the news out," as Allan Kornblum put it when he issued his mimeo magazine, *Toothpaste*.
9. Actualists infiltrated the community of Iowa City. There was no elitism, no ivory tower in our workshop. Our classrooms were our apartments,

4

especially the one at Court Street. In the living room, a typewriter sat on a red hassock, inviting everyone to write.

10. Collaborative poems brought us closer together and expanded the number of people who considered themselves Actualists. We got to know each other's writing styles and techniques. Our relationships were partly built on our writing.

When Actualism was blooming in Iowa City in the 1970s, we wrote a lot of collaborative poems. Collaborations, it should be noted, have been around for quite a while. The Dadaists and Surrealists in the 1920s and the Oulipo in the 1960s both explored the idea of collaborative writing and drawing. In fact the Dadaists invented a collaboration game called "The Exquisite Corpse." The Oulipo were a group of mainly French-speaking writers and mathematicians who experimented with constrained writing where certain limitations are set, such as writing a poem without using the letter "e."

I made it a practice to save the signed collaborations as well as the unsigned orphans that were looking for a home. I put them all into a storage box, put the storage box in the attic and then I forgot about them for more than thirty-five years. In 2010 I found the storage box, which contained over 220 pages of work from the days of wine and Actualism. Some of them were unsigned, but 194 pages bore the names or initials of two or more people—there were 247 people who had written in those collabs.

As time went on, other poets joined the movement. We held Actualist Conventions, which were multifaceted celebrations of the freedom the Actualists felt in writing poetry and exploring other artistic adventures. The first took place on March 10, 1973.

The Actualists published many literary magazines, among them: *Suction* (ed. Darrell Gray), *Toothpaste* and *Dental Floss* (ed. Allan Kornblum), *Search for Tomorrow* (ed. George Mattingly), *P. F. Flyer* (eds. Steve and Sheila Toth), *The Actual Now and Then* (ed. Cinda Kornblum), *The Spirit That Moves Us* (ed. Morty Sklar), *Gum* (ed. Dave Morice), *Matchbook* (ed. Joyce Holland), *Candy* (ed. P.J. Casteel).

George Mattingly (Blue Wind Press) published the *Actualist American Poetry Circuit Readings for 1973-74*, a promotional booklet that presented thirteen Actualists: Darrell Gray, Sheila Toth, Anselm Hollo, Steve Toth,

George Mattingly, Joyce Holland, John Sjoberg, Josephine Clare, Tim Hildebrand, Morty Sklar, Allan Kornblum, Chuck Miller, Dave Morice.

Allan Kornblum (Toothpaste Press) published a large collection of mimeograph and letterpress magazines and books. He was the premier publisher, the master craftsman of Iowa City Actualism. Most of his 100 or so productions were letterpress books, which he put out tirelessly.

He and his family moved to Saint Paul, Minnesota in 1985, where he reorganized the press, changing its name to Coffee House Press.

Morty Sklar (The Spirit That Moves Us Press) and Darrell Gray Su*ction*) edited *The Actualist Anthology*, which Morty published from his press in 1977. The first major collection of Actualist writing, it presents poems, biographies, bibliographies, photographs, and other works by fourteen Actualists: Allan Kornblum, Chuck Miller, Anselm Hollo, Cinda Kornblum, Morty Sklar, John Batki, Darrell Gray, Jim Mulac, David Hilton, Sheila Heldenbrand, George Mattingly, John Sjoberg, Steve Toth, and Dave Morice. The cover, by Patrick Dooley, depicts mug shot drawings of the Actualists in a grid. This book drew the early Actualists together and gave Actualism a permanent place in literary history.

Darrell Gray: A Great Adventure
by Allan Kornblum

I've been involved in literary publishing for some forty-four years, and in that time, I have met few people with more enthusiasm for poetry or more devotion to the muse than Darrell Gray and Anselm Hollo, my late mentors and dear friends. And even though neither of them cared a whit about baseball, they call to mind one of the classic clichés of the sport: the baseball season is not a sprint, it's a marathon. If you let yourself get too excited or too low over a few wins or losses, you won't make it to post-season play. Perhaps being read after one's death could be compared to the post-season, but of course there are no winners or losers, and there is no World Series of poetry. One could say that Anselm ran a marathon, and Darrell blew everything he had on a sprint. One could also say the analogy is completely ridiculous, and yet….

Like all poets, Darrell noticed details and sometimes brooded over them, such as sharing his birthday, April 20th, with Adolp Hitler. On the other hand, he was charmed to have been born "on the cusp" between two astrological signs, Aries and Taurus, although he never ascribed any importance to it. (He once showed me a poem he wrote called "On the Cusp," but I have no idea what became of it.) Considering his delight in details, he sure didn't leave many facts about his personal life behind. Legends aplenty abound, but no one really knows about his childhood.

He was definitely born in 1945 in Sacramento, California to a single mother, who later married a man who formally adopted him. However when it comes to his adoptive father's occupation—well, some believe he was an accountant, a highway patrolman, a landscaper, or just an ordinary gardener mowing lawns and trimming hedges, but no one is certain. Darrell once told me that on his mother's side he had an Uncle Farrell and an Uncle Harrell, but no one can confirm it, so this might have been a late-night tale, told on a whim and enhanced by a few puffs of smoke. I do know that families sometimes get a little crazy with alliterative names, however, so it's possible. Warren Woessner, who published Darrell's *Essays & Dissolutions*, has two brothers—Walter and Wilbur, as a for-instance.

I believe Darrell's family moved back to California during his high school years, but I'm not sure when or where. He did go directly from high school to University of California, Hayward, and despite attending college near the heart of the movement to "turn on, tune in, and drop out," he graduated in four years. It was at Hayward that Darrell met David Hilton with whom he formed a lifelong friendship.

In his senior year Darrell applied to and was accepted by the University of Iowa Writers' Workshop for their M.F.A. program. Today, just about every university has a creative writing program, as do most colleges with a reputation for liberal arts, but in 1967 such programs were few and far between, and acceptance by the Iowa Writers Workshop bestowed quite the cachet back then. As it turned out, Darrell attended during a period marked by a power struggle between the confessional poets and somewhat looser and perhaps more celebratory poets like George Starbuck, Jack Marshall, and two of his major influences, Ted Berrigan and Anselm Hollo. By the time he graduated in 1969, Starbuck and Berrigan had been forced out, and perhaps in protest Darrell often claimed that although he had attended classes, he never actually received his M.F.A. However a phone call to the Writers' Workshop confirmed that he did go through the program in two straight years, and graduated and received his degree with most of the rest of his incoming class.

After graduating, Darrell moved to Colorado for a while, futilely applied for a few college teaching jobs, and briefly sold encyclopedias and insurance door-to-door. During this period he also became a Krishna devotee for a time, and after reading a somewhat academic translation of the Vedas, he tried rewording them to give them the expansive feel he thought they deserved. Unfortunately his version has long since disappeared.

Next, Darrell tried using his poetry chops in what was probably the most ridiculous job of his life when he moved to Kansas City, Missouri to work for Hallmark Cards. As anyone who ever met Darrell or read his poems would have guessed, that didn't last long. And so sometime during the fall of 1970, a little over a year after leaving, he returned to Iowa City, which was when and where I met him. I had moved to Iowa in July 1970, and by fall I had already mimeographed the first issue of *Toothpaste* magazine, and met Dave Morice and George Mattingly. It was George who called to tell me Darrell had moved back to town, and brought me over to Darrell's apartment for an introduction. I have no record or clear memory of that afternoon, but George has written a marvelous account of his own first meeting with Darrell that accurately captures a feel for those days gone by, and he has graciously granted permission to share it:

"I was introduced to Darrell in autumn 1968 by dorm mate John Deason and his friend Marc Harding, who was sharing a ramshackle farmhouse near North Liberty with Darrell and Merrill Gilfillan. One Indian summer afternoon Marc drove us in his not-so-late-model land yacht out to the farm for a party. Darrell was sitting in an armchair, its stuffing bulging out, wearing an off-white shirt, well-worn sport coat, slacks, and his favorite shoes, Hush Puppies. He was puffing on his pipe, while leaning his head toward a speaker pumping out Steve Miller Band's *Children of The Future*. Handed a joint, he put down his pipe on the arm of the overstuffed chair and took a deep toke. 'Greetings,' he said, with a shy smile, pushing a wavy bang out of his eyes, 'You're here.' I'd been wondering what a real graduate of the Writers' Workshop would say to me. Now I knew."

I can see George way back then, suddenly realizing all the permutations of Darrell's simple statement: "You're here." The billions of people who had been represented by "you" over the tens of thousands of years since humans had acquired the gift of speech. The short verb, "to be," which has generated unending philosophical speculation over the nature of existence.

And with the word, "here" George had been placed in a location that could easily have been anywhere. Meeting Darrell made you suddenly aware of language in ways you had never imagined.

Because I came of age during the hippie era, I have always been hesitant to speak of people with auras—the term was so overused in my youth. But when Darrell spoke about poetry, turned you on to new writers, or read his poems or poems by others, he very visibly glowed with a contagious energy that was immediately communicated to all present. Never had I met anyone, nor have I met anyone else since, who so fully embodied such a sense of the powerful potential for magic in the written word.

Anselm Hollo, who was born in 1935—fifteen years before me—served as my elder mentor, and he too delighted in turning others on to writers he loved. But although Anselm had merely come to America from Finland, he seemed to have come from much further away, and with his wolf-like face and earth-shaking basso profundo laugh, he seemed much larger than life. One of Anselm's poems was called "Any News from Alpha Centauri?" and I wouldn't have been surprised if someone told me he had actually been born there. It seemed natural for someone so astounding to be a poet.

Darrell, however, was only four years older. We'd grown up eating the same food, going to the same movies, listening to the same music, and so perhaps he was better able to make the literary life seem like an ongoing, eye-opening expedition that I too could join, a gift for which I have forever been grateful. I know many others who felt the same way about him. That's what led George to publish Darrell's first trade book, *Something Swims Out* in 1972 under his Blue Wind Press imprint, followed in 1974 by his second book, *Scattered Brains* that Cinda and I published as the first full-length Toothpaste Press title.

Between that first meeting and his permanent departure to Northern California in 1974, Darrell and I shared more than a few amazing adventures. During the summer of 1971 we accompanied Anselm on a long drive to Allendale, Michigan for an incredibly comprehensive poetry festival that actually had a right to call itself "national." Ted Berrigan and Robert Creeley, two of the featured poets, were as close as brothers with Anselm, and as a result Darrell and I spent a lot of time with them during that week. Through Anselm we also met Joel Oppenheimer, Paul Blackburn, and Philip Whalen. Other featured poets included Gregory Corso, Robert Bly,

Robert Kelly, John Logan, Diane Wakoski, Sonia Sanchez, Tom Weatherly, Jackson MacLow, Jerome Rothenberg, and Al Young. I was all of twenty-two, and that week hanging out with Anselm, Berrigan, and Creeley was enough to make my head spin. We also met Morty Sklar at the Allendale festival, a refugee from New York City, crossing the country on his motor-cycle, looking for a new direction in his life. He wound up moving to Iowa City as a result of a chance encounter with a woman he met that week, Audrey Teeter, and he eventually became an important part of the Actualist community.

From September 1971 through the end of July 1972 Cinda and I shared the second floor of an old Victorian house on East Court Street with Dave Morice. Dave had a small bedroom across the hall, and Cinda and I shared a larger bedroom adjacent to a comfortable, spacious living room that practically became a clubhouse for our group of poet friends. Endless collaborative poems were written there by sliding an overstuffed hassock—which served as the perch for an old Remington typewriter—from one seedy Salvation Army armchair to the next. The bedroom Cinda and I shared was separated from the living room by glass double-doors, so we had to wait until the last guest left if we wanted real privacy. One rare

13

evening Cinda and I looked around and realized we had no guests. We looked at each other, and being a young couple in love, we retired early, enjoyed an uninhibited figurative roll in the hay, and fell asleep. Hours later, when I heard the sound of typing in the next room and I slipped out of bed, pulled on my jeans and went to the living room where I found Dave and Darrell at 3:00 am completing a twenty-five page collaborative poem—complete with a cover drawing, which they called "Second Winds." After they read the poem to me with gusto, Dave realized how late it was and went off to bed, but Darrell was still awake and ready for more. I remember his turning to me and saying, "Let's surprise Dave and write a few sonnets together. Between the wine, other intoxicating substances, and the heady creative mood in the air, I felt that night as if I could write about anything, no matter how ordinary, and make it sound fantastic. Six full hours later we completed a sequence we called, "Good Morning: Fourteen Sonnets," each with the traditional fourteen lines, albeit without rhyme or meter. When Dave and Cinda woke up, Darrell and I read the sonnets to them, and needless to say Dave was surprised. Then I went back to bed for a few hours, and Darrell finally went back to his apartment and got some sleep. I felt honored when a few years later, G.P. Skratz published the sonnets in a little booklet.

During that year on East Court, Darrell, a frequent visitor, dropped by one notable afternoon and asked if we had a long strip of paper and a pile of pages cut to the size of Dave's 4¼ by 5½ inches mimeo magazine, *Gum*. He took them and the typewriter to a desk in the bedroom Cinda and I shared, and started writing. A half hour later he emerged with "The Actualist Manifesto" on the long strip of paper, and over a dozen "Actualist" poems on the *Gum*-sized pages. Within a month or so other poets became involved and before long we were all Actualists (whatever that actually meant) on our way to our first convention. A few years later, Darrell co-edited *The Actualist Anthology* with Morty who published the book under his Spirit That Moves Us Press imprint in 1977.

Darrell also played a role in a very personal experience by serving as our witness when Cinda and I went to the Iowa City Clerk's Office to get our marriage license. As he peered from behind one of those old bank teller window cages, the clerk asked Cinda and I a few routine questions about date and place of birth, and then abruptly turned to Darrell and barked out, "Now are you prepared to witness that you have known these two people for more than a year and that they are not brother and sister?" We were all stunned by the absurdity of both the question and the overall moment, but poor Darrell was the one on the spot, and at first he didn't know what to say. "Uh, yes, or uh, no, uh, yes I know them, and uh, no, they're certainly not brother and sister," he stammered, looking totally flustered. He knew he had appeared more than a bit uncertain, and was hoping the clerk had believed him. All turned out well in the end, of course.

After we got married, we moved to a large old house in West Branch, ten miles east of Iowa City. Every few weeks, Cinda would pick up Darrell on her way home from her job at the University Hospital, he'd join us for dinner, and we'd talk and write poetry long into the night. Darrell slept over on a spare mattress, and Cinda brought him back to Iowa City the next day. When Jim Mulac began renting a spare room in our house, he too fell under Darrell's spell and began writing collaborative poems and plays with us, and performed in two plays during the second Actualist convention. But we all had a hunch that Darrell wasn't going to stay in Iowa forever.

Finally, in the late fall of 1973, using money he received when the City evicted him so they could bulldoze his house and put up a new building, he bought a Greyhound Bus ticket and moved to California with Patricia O'Donnell, and together they shared an apartment on Divisadero Street in San Francisco. Alas, the relationship didn't last. When contacted, Patricia said she knew very little about Darrell's family. She did suggest visiting his parents once, but he told her he found visits too embarrassing, and was particularly disturbed by his mother's habit of dressing her dog in baby clothes.

Although his relationship didn't go as planned, Darrell was well received upon his return to his home state. He discovered his reputation had preceded him, and before long California became the new center of Actualism. More conventions and a variety of publications followed, several from Alastair Johnston's Poltroon Press.

Wreck O' Lections

Collaborations between Darrell Gray & Alastair Johnston
With Content Adjustments by Anselm Hollo & Alice Kornblum
TRANSITIONAL FACE
1982

From Alastair Johnston's Afterword: "Although 'officially' diagnosed an agoraphobic, Darrell Gray did venture forth on occasion. In August 1978 he invited me along on what he described as a poetry reading tour to the Midwest. We set off on a hippie bus ride along Interstate 80 and landed on the unprepared but gracious Kornblums in West Branch, Iowa. They were already entertaining a Finnish poet of repute and his lady. For a couple of weeks these collaborators circled the typewriter nightly talking, drinking, and listening to old Buddy Holly records. Surveying the accrued manuscript afterwards, the Finn remarked: 'You could edit them down and make them fairly spectacular.'

Darrell lived and breathed poetry. To be around him was to be involved in an ongoing collaboration. If this slight work recaptures some of his spirit, I trust the reader will find that excuse enough for its existence."

But while it was possible to get by in Iowa City with very little money, the Bay Area was less

16

forgiving. Darrell managed to survive through emergency grants, mental disability payments, and occasional gigs as a private tutor and substitute teacher. But as difficult as it may have been to pay the bills, somehow, Darrell found it easier to purchase liquor out West. Although he told himself the mental disability money he managed to obtain was the result of a clever scam, in truth, he simply couldn't hold a job for more than a few months, and most lasted only a few weeks. Darrell's poetry continued to soar through the cosmos, but he was never did learn how to keep his feet firmly planted on the ground.

As we now know, alcoholism is a disease, not a behavior problem or a sign of loose morals as people once believed. Some manage, with great effort and support, to control their genetically acquired urge to drink, but Darrell was driven to ignore efforts to help by some secret source of pain. I remember dropping by his apartment one time, before he moved west, and I saw that glow in his eyes that meant he was excited about a poem. Sure enough, he insisted that I sit down and listen as he read a sonnet by Heinrich Heine that ended with two rather chilling lines: "Sleep is good; and Death is better, yet / Surely never to have been born is best of all." Then he repeated the last few words again—"never to have been born is best of all." —and damn if he didn't sigh with longing. I was willing to follow him almost anywhere he led into the land of literature, but I could not understand a desire never to have even existed.

Some very good people in California made noble efforts to intervene and supply desperately needed support, including G.P. Skratz and his wife, Linda, Alastair Johnston, David "Daf" Schein and Bob Ernst (two Iowa theater people who formed the heart of a Bay Area group called the Blake Street Hawkeyes), and even Whoopi Goldberg—they all took him to a hospital at one time or another, ultimately to no avail. He finally departed from this realm of existence for good sometime in late August 1986, and was discovered a few days later by his landlord. The poetry community didn't learn about his fate until October. At the time of his death, his parents were living in Medford, Oregon. Because Darrell had never revealed that he was a poet to his parents, they had no idea that he owned anything worth saving. Thus, when Darrell's landlord asked if they wanted his possessions, they told him to just get rid of everything. Many of his unpublished manuscripts were fortunately recovered from a second-hand bookstore by his friends.

I once asked Darrell what he knew about his birth father, and I was really startled by his response. "He was probably just an irresponsible drunk," he said, his voice practically quivering in anger. "And I was probably the result of some drunken weekend," he continued, bitterly. Then he paused, looked at me, and added, "Sorry if I sound unfeeling." Unfeeling? Not by a long shot. Much could be made of that exchange, but I'm not about to play amateur psychologist and ascribe his own drinking to some over-simplified anger at his father. Nor will I repeat any of the far too many sad stories about his drunken escapades during his last few years. I actually did recount one on a recent phone call to George, and he said he knew those stories too, but that wasn't the way he wanted to remember his old friend. I regarded that reply as excellent advice.

I do want to remember Darrell's response one evening when I told him I was about to plunge into a book by the Italian poet, Eugenio Montale. "Wonderful!" he exclaimed, his round moon-shaped face beaming with pleasure and approval. "You are about to embark on a great adventure," he concluded. As anyone who ever met him will attest, every minute spent with Darrell Gray at his best, was an amazing adventure, and I will be forever grateful for having had the opportunity to be part of it.

See Darrell's Selected Poetry in the next section following Anselm Hollo.

Actualism—As Movement, Restaurant and Song
by Victoria Ramirez

Victoria (in her words): A wandering scholar of sorts, the author taught literature and writing in England, Algeria, Nigeria, and Japan. Her U.S. gig has been in Utah at Weber State University where she's been a professor of literature and creative writing for over a decade. Before that she got to know her Own True Actualist, who inspired her to pen this piece. She looks for Actualists everywhere and is happy to report she sometimes finds them. If she's lucky.

In a northern Nigerian drinking parlor, alfresco and on the edge of the Shara, I was enjoying a liter of Star Beer when a ragged Hausa man with a traditional banjo, entered and started singing. I leaned towards my semi-drunk neighbor and asked about the man's song. He answered it was a praise song for a wealthy patron also seated in the drinking parlor. Though my informant didn't translate every word, he précised the performance by saying the singer was extolling the wealthy man's generosity to the poor, his faithfulness to Allah, and his total and enduring distinction. He also informed me that the song would have been of a different sort were the patron to withhold his "dash"—that is, reward—for the singer's effort. At that time such itinerant bards roved throughout the Sub-Saharan band from Cameroon to Senegal, following the ancient routes of Hausa cattle traders.

19

This incident reminded me of how poetry, spoken or sung, had been virtually absent from our culture for the last few centuries. Caedmon, the reputed maker of Anglo-Saxon song, lived at a time when folks performed poetry covering a variety of topics for sheer enjoyment—their own as well as their audience's. But Caedmon had been dead for over a thousand years, and people today could hardly imagine a world in which poetry existed in everyday life, just for the fun of it, after the day's work was done. That was back in the late 1980s, and I'd been away from academia for a decade living overseas and teaching English as a Second Language. My college Norton Anthology pretty much had ended with T.S. Eliot, but in the last ten years the publication industry had exploded with new writers, many unheard voices whose gender, race, or ethnicity had formerly disqualified them from serious consideration.

Some of those new voices hailed from Iowa City, where a little-known group of poets called Actualists lived and wrote in the 1970s and 1980s. The more I learned about Actualism through the poems, the more I became charged with the sense that poetry as living art was not yet extinct. I was rescued from the ennui I felt when reading canonical poets or those chosen to grace the pages of *The New Yorker* or *The New York Review of Books*. Reading Actualist poetry kindled a renewed passion for lyrics, and I put down my Yeats to see what was happening outside my window.

What is Actualism? In his "Origins of Actualism" Dave Morice insists that Darrell Gray came up with the tongue-in-cheek notion of Actualism as a literary movement. Allan Kornblum's own remembrance is of a group of writers who supported each other and shared a sense of camaraderie. If that makes up a literary movement, so be it. "I still remember that light in Darrell Gray's eyes, a combination of inspiration and amusement. Which is how I remember Actualism as well—a combination of inspiration and amusement." Chuck Miller recalled that these writers were interested in "the 'actual' in some sense, some sense of the real, whatever that might boil down to."

Steve Toth remembered the term "Actualism" from a book on spiritualism he'd read, and so thought the movement "started out as a parody. Kind of fitting." George Mattingly recalled that the group needed a name for a reading circuit brochure called *The Actualist American Poetry Circuit*.

20

Mattingly adds, "Ironically, the direct mail appeal for readings—the reason we invented a name for our group in the first place—never worked. But the name stuck." The elephant and the blind men come to mind....

Darrell Gray, apparent founder and Actualism's most vocal theoretcian, defined it in a number of ways. In his *Essays & Dissolutions*, published by Abraxas Press, he says "I want to emphasize that Actualism is not an 'aesthetic' movement in the usual sense of the word. It owes nothing to literary history that it could not find elsewhere, least of all aesthetic theory or literary criticism." This proviso is so important it appears again in the preface to *The Actualist Anthology*, edited by Morty Sklar and Darrell Gray: "The word 'Actualism' may strike the reader as just another ism, but in historical terms it is much more than that. It is a community, not always with similar interests, but always a community. The poet's sense of his/her writing becomes a part of that community."

Morty also said recently: "I recall that Darrell asked me if I wanted to read my poetry at the March 10, 1973 Actualist Convention, and I asked, 'Isn't that just for Actualists?' and he replied, 'Well, you're an Actualist.' I felt as though I were knighted."

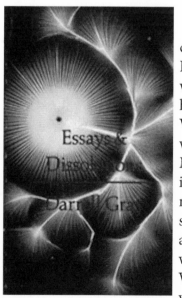

The poets who comprised this community came from across the U.S., from Finland and Hungary. Most were in their 20s, though a few were in their 30s in the 1970s. Some Actualists had attended the University of Iowa Writers' Workshop and its M.F.A. program in poetry, while others had nothing to do with it. The M.F.A. in poetry was, however, the sun that initially drew so many young poets to its stunning light. The metaphor of the Iowa Workshop as center of a solar system, and the Actualists as inhabiting lesser worlds, works best if we imagine that poets not officially part of the Workshop wrote in its shadows. As a person who lives and gardens under relentless Utah skies, I know how sun can scorch seedlings and prevent adequate growth. Yet the Actualists flourished as a community of engaged and connected

21

writers precisely because they lived and worked in cooler, shady spots.

Besides comprising a community of poets whose writing sense, and friendships, bestowed membership in this group, Sklar claims in "What Actually is Actualism" (*Zahir* #9/Summer 1977) that Actualists shared a "basically open, generous and positive approach to our art…so that even when bad times are central to a work, something inspiring/moving can occur." Additionally, Actualists were "concerned with connecting with the reader on some level." In his "Actualism: The Movement as Restaurant" (*Cross-Fertilization: The Human Spirit As Place*, The Spirit That Moves Us Press, 1980) Sklar recalls arriving in Iowa City and finding the "Actualist Community" even if Actualism wasn't associated with the movement in the beginning. "So, everything was there first, then was named."

Whatever the movement's origins, the idea of an Actualist poem's potency derives, Gray claims, from its intimate connection to "acting" or "action," and life itself, when he says, "If we derive joy from a particular Actualist work, it is not because the feeling was somehow embodied in its theme, but rather that the work directed us outward and toward conditions that make joy possible." Gray adds that Actualist poems reflect "a condition where being and doing are the same." Thus, the time and space limitations within which poems exist are extended into the life of the reader: "Discovery does not end in the Actualist work—its essence, both temporally and spatially, is not a hermetically closed vessel that one must return to for regeneration of the magic and delight of its existence."

*   *   *

Actualism-as-song demonstrates an affinity for the word as spoken, and for the concreteness of language alluded to by Gray. The poetry's images are powerful and discovery-generating not because they are the stuff used to create potent symbols. On the contrary, the particular and concrete are what symbols arise from. The movement's conscious emphasis on the "actual"—meaning "real," "present," "current"—connects the Actualist use of the particular to its expressed affirmation as embodied in the poetry. Moreover, the Actualists' dedication to poetry as a spoken, performed artistic medium produces a lyrical style that favors ordinary speech, and accessible imagery and ideas.

Take the following poem by Anselm Hollo:

> ELEGY
> the laundry-basket is still there
> though badly chewed by the cat
> but time has devoured the cat
> entirely

The reader easily contemplates the basket, paradoxically aided by its very lack of description. We are allowed a mere hint of the basket's sad state, a result of obsessive cat-chewing. But the image of the dilapidated object invokes the deceased cat—perhaps many a cat we have known whom time has "devoured." The laundry basket hauls with it notions of time and de struction and the quirkiness of life, at one moment proffering asendency, only later to snatch it away. "Elegy" goes beyond mourning for by-gone pets or laundry baskets; it serves as forecast of what awaits us all. With one concrete image Hollo writes a lament for the living.

Or take Cinda Kornblum's "The Honeymooners," which begins, "When a youngster / I thought they were saying 'celery' / not 'salary.' " Childhood innocence—and ignorance—yields to the knowledge and judgment arising out of maturity, where college finally "solved the celery question." For the poet, and many of us, lack of a salary is made concrete when a limp stick of celery is "the only food still in the refrigerator/at the end of the month." The humorous celery/salary mixup, born of naiveté, is itself an embodi-ment of our collective ignorance of the marital state before we wed, hinted at in the poem's title.

We may seem to have wandered, like that Hausa bard, from the ini-tial thesis of this essay, which is Actualist poetry's dependence on the spoken word, and on its rhythmic and repetitious components in song. Actualist poetry's relative syntactical simplicity and its reliance on concrete, easily-grasped images, contrast with the flagrant erudition and linguistic complexity of much canonical poetry prior to the 1970s. Imagine trying to process "Prufrock" as oral poetry: the average listener would be hard-pressed to absorb or understand most of it upon recitation. For while some of "Prufrock's" imagery is concrete, much of it is not; nor does the poem follow clear narrative lines.

Despite the presence and prestige of the Iowa Writers' Workshop, it hosted few opportunities in the city for the public to participate in the art or aims of the program. Actualists filled the gap, offering citizens myriad events and opportunities for encountering poetic expression. To that end individual Actualists arranged readings at different venues, and sponsored multi-media events that brought together various artists with an Actualist sensibility. Sklar obtained funding to sponsor Poetry-with-Drawings in the Buses. As Dr. Alphabet, Dave Morice brought poetry to people of all types and ages, and performed in such public events as Poetry Marathon Number 1, and Mile-Long Poetry Marathon. The Spirit that Moves Us Press sponsored Actualization events, which brought together poets, film makers, graphic artists, and musicians. These happenings appealed to various audiences, and did so in part because of Actualism's conscious connection to "action" and spoken poetry.

What a contrast between Actualist poems and, say, "The Wasteland," where before we reach its first section, "The Burial of the Dead," we encounter Latin, Greek, and Italian. Later on we must deal with German, sort out a reference to "Mylae," and translate a line of French. Though parts of Eliot's meant-to-be-read work are reflective, the reader senses its retrospective tone, and feels a distancing from the speaker in the poem, and his or her perceptions:

Summer surprised us, coming over the Starnbergersee
With a shower of rain; we stopped in the colonnade,
And went on in the sunlight, into the Hofgarten
And drank coffee, and talked for an hour.
Bin gar keine Russin, stamm' aus Litauen, echt deutsch.

We experience no such distance with Steve Toth's "The Turquoise Mechanic's Son," which surreptitiously invokes the reader/listener:

i am the turquoise mechanic's son
sitting in the drive eating donuts.

Near the end the poet draws us in, linking the poem's speaker with its listener:

> all around me joyful
> we are going for a joy ride
> sound of joy when the engine turns over.

Vernacular rhythms also characterize Sheila Heldenbrand's "God Said to the Angels," humor arising from the poem's recognition of our human condition in the face of deity—characterized as something like a mob boss. When the angels give God the wrong answer to "should I make man?" God burns them. The short poem resolves the standoff when God asks another set of angels, and "They said, sure." The poem's style and content allow for accessibility, while its theme, bluntly stated, offers the audience a chance to meditate on the quirky, tyrannical, and at times, insecure nature of God as Old Testament figure.

Darrell Gray best sums up the gap between canonical modernist poetry still taught in colleges in the 1970s, and the Actualists' approach to lyrical expression. In "An Old Southern Critic Takes a Look at My Poems," Gray ends the piece:

> I quote one poem, "Baffling Turns," in toto:
>
> *Asleep at 60 mph.*
>
> No doubt the poet here has in mind
> how much eludes him. Or, as Allen Tate succinctly said:
>
> "For where Time rears its muted head and all appalls
> We know not where we stand nor where we fall."

*　　*　　*

The Actualists weren't self-made; like all artists they owe a debt to those writers, mainstream and otherwise, who came before them. Just as Sklar's speaker in "Ma" invites his mother to "Come with me / come on, sit on my shoulders and see / the world you gave me," so the Actualists could invoke writers such as William Blake, Robert Browning, and Rainer Maria Rilke, but also Walt Whitman, William Carlos Williams, William Burroughs, Theodore Roethke, Robert Bly, and notably, Frank O'Hara. O'Hara's name comes up again and again when individual Actualists speak of their influences. As influential member of the New York School—an informal group of artists who looked to contemporary avant-garde movements for inspiration—O'Hara had impacted Actualist poet and teacher Anselm Hollo with his Personism, O'Hara's name for his particular poetic style.

As Actualism carries in it the idea of "acting/action," so O'Hara's Personism underscores its lyrical focus—that of one's personal experience relayed to another. After the high-Modernism of the mid-20th Century, Personism—like its young relative, Actualism—brings back into focus both human connection, and the lyric as expressed utterance. And like the Actualists, O'Hara's writing aims to capture life's immediacy, and to fashion poetry "between two persons instead of two pages." As with artists in the New York School, Actualist poets invoke a broad range of influences: political activists, the Mayan Codices, jazz musicians such as Monk, Parker, and Mingus; Jack Kerouac, Walt Whitman and Dr. Williams; grain elevators and "the earthy farmer's fields" of the American Midwest; Woody Allen, Ted Berrigan, Edgar Masters, Herman Hesse and Henry Miller, and any writers who like George Mattingly wish to "masterfully fuse lyricism with stunning metaphysics articulated in fresh vernacular American English."

For Cinda Kornblum, one of two women poets published in *The Actualist Anthology*, influences include "Iowa rhythms" and "hot summer nights."

Chuck Miller's "How in the Morning" echoes Personism as he casts his words between the poem's speaker and its addressee. The use of "you" in the poem can refer to the poet, or to someone listening, or to someone else the speaker has in mind. At the end, though, the "yous" have gathered force, and work to invoke us in a way that connects us with the speaker and the poet:

and so the morning comes grey over the hills
you drop the washcloth on your cold feet
and fumble with the delicate
birds of morning
opening their cages.

Sklar's "Modern Times" articulates in "fresh vernacular American English" his meditation on our contemporary world. The poem plays on the wording of "The Star Spangled Banner," which immediately addresses itself to a second person. Inspired by the occasion of a leaky faucet, Sklar intones,

> Oh Goofy,
> tapdancing in the kitchen
> in the moonlight
> of streetlight
> Oh dripping faucet
> song of environmental unconcern
> beauty of waste
> we sing.

*   *   *

Darrell Gray died years ago, Morty Sklar and others moved away from Iowa City to future lives, and the young poets of the self-titled Actualist Movement seasoned to the accompaniment of the world's ongoing inspiration, here meant in the literal sense of breathing in and out, becoming new and growing old all at once, and for all time. The Actualist moment marked an era of social democratization when the breaking down of cultural shibboleths freed these young artists from institutional over-sight. Actualism belongs to a lineage that includes all movements arising out of a rejection of orthodoxy, and makes these poets literary and philosophical kin to Europe's Symbolists and Imagists, and here in America to the Beats, but also to hip hop artists who have ridden on the rhythms of the vernacular in their songs.

Movement? Restaurant? Song? And, almost fifty years after its sturdy blooming under an Iowa sun, is Actualism dead? Does that even matter, given the certainty that Actualism's brand of art, and song, continues? For, as Sklar cannily notes in The Spirit That Moves Us Press's 1980 book, *Cross-Fertilization: The Human Spirit as Place*:

> "Is Actualism, then, a movement? And what is the future of it? For most of us it's simple: Whatever we're doing, either as individuals or smaller or larger groups, in Iowa City or Berkeley or wherever, we're not trying to keep Actualism alive…we know where it came from and we know that if the label comes off the can of goods, the contents are the same."

Way Way West
The Actualist Dispersal to the San Francisco Bay Area
by Steven Lavoie

The Actualists ARE the Actualists. They aren't Actualists because they ascribe to something known as Actualism, the way a Surrealist practices Surrealism. They are Actualists the way John, Paul, George and Ringo are Beatles.

By the mid-1970s, they began a dispersal that would place Actualism at the center of cultural activities in distant cities across North America. In 1975, that dispersal brought George Mattingly and Darrell Gray to the vibrant and flourishing poetic community of Northern California. Mattingly was new to the West Coast. Gray was returning to his birthplace in Oakland.

They arrived to a region very familiar with groups of creative people who distinguished themselves by self-identification with certain colleagues. That tradition among poets and artists was introduced to the San Francisco Bay Area late in the previous century by The Bohemians, whose name, uttered in the lower-case, would come to stand for a particular lifestyle that would endure in this region. But unlike the Bohemians, the Actualists would not lend their name to a way-of-life. Instead they would find one that had much in common with the world they left in Iowa City.

And they did not come out of the blue. Ted Berrigan, resident poet at the Iowa Writers' Workshop (hereafter "IWW") in the tumultuous period 1967-1969, instilled his fervent advocacy of mimeograph publishing, encouraging all young, ambitious poets he encountered to start a magazine. The advice was well-taken in Iowa City. This strategy was well underway in the San Francisco Bay Area, where the underground press had helped to spur a youth uprising of historic proportions in protest of the Vietnam War and where Richard Brautigan used self-publication to penetrate the mass literary market.

Many of the Actualists launched their own journals, Mattingly and Gray among them. Copies of Mattingly's *Search for Tomorrow* and Gray's *Suction* had reached the Bay Area where friends of Brautigan and a larger circle of young poets were collecting around Cranium Press in San Francisco, where Clifford Burke shared use of his letterpress, with Keith Abbott, an old friend of Brautigan's from the Pacific Northwest and Pat Nolan, who had become allies in the Monterey Bay area, among others, weathering the height of the Flower Power insurgency of 1967 there.

Both had mimeograph magazines. Abbott's *Blue Suede Shoes* was launched in Bellingham, Washington while he attended Western Washington University and he continued its publication from an apartment in the rapidly crumbling hippie headquarters of San Francisco's Haight-Ashbury District. Nolan published *The End* from his residence in Oakland where the Black Panther Party was actualizing its grass-roots formula for social change. The Actualists began submitting to these and other little magazines underway at the time.

The work of other young poets of the San Francisco Bay Area, notably Andrei Codrescu, became known to the Actualists, too, who were sending their work for consideration in the Iowa City magazines. Codrescu would join Allen Ginsberg in an elite group whose work would find its way into *Matchbook*, Dave Morice's journal of one-word poems published as part of his Joyce Holland-hoax in the early 1970s. Morice was attracting particular attention among young poets for his theatrical and Dadaesque literary experiments, not to mention his appearance on NBC's late-night show, *Tomorrow* with Tom Snyder, which made him the envy of many fame-hungry young poets of his generation. This broadcast made Morice a peer of the rock stars and to the Actualists and to the Bay Area poets with whom they were finding affinity, rock stars had become cultural icons and poetic inspirations.

A mutual appreciation of rock 'n' roll distinguished these poets from generations before and from others of their contemporaries. It guaranteed, too, a certain amount of instant camaraderie, providing what jazz had provided for the Beats. The songwriting talents of the rock stars contributed to the poets' poetics while the interactive and multimedia components of the bands' live shows helped to inform the poets' public presentations.

By 1975, Keith Abbott had abandoned the crumbling infrastructure of the Haight-Ashbury for a house in North Berkeley where he lived with his wife and young daughter. A party there welcomed the Actualists (George Mattingly and Darrell Gray) shortly after their arrival to the Bay Area. Invitees include a vast array of local poets: defenders of Robert Duncan and the Black Mountain Poets, some young post-Beats from North Beach, acolytes of Philip K. Dick who was not long gone from Berkeley, and lots of rock 'n' rollers, most either too shy or too self-conscious to pose the burning question, or else already in the know and not wondering. The question was answered when, in gloaming's dimness, Darrell Gray marched assertively through the front room of Abbott's house, heading toward the stairwell to the second floor of the Abbotts' one-story bungalow. It had no stairwell to the second floor. Nevertheless, Gray headed on with Quixotic determination, smashing hard, head-on into a bare, white, plasterboard wall, angered by the sudden and unexcused disappearance of those stairs he was about to climb. Mattingly shrugged and carried on the warm and friendly conversation he brought to the Bay Area with him while Gray grappled, half-dazed from the impact, with this current disturbance of our physical realm.

The Actualists had arrived.

They each came accompanied by their prodigious talents. Talent was not a prerequisite to qualify a poet for recognition in the Bay Area literary community of this period. To an objective outsider, it may have seemed instead, that talent posed a primal threat to many of the young poets who relied so heavily on adherence to the poetics of one or the other local literary giant of an earlier generation. These Actualists had talent.

Mattingly arrived with an impressive body of poetry that he would collect into a monograph of the press, Blue Wind, that came with him from Iowa City. He had his poems to peddle, the books he published, along with instincts for design that allowed him to quickly establish a career for himself in the graphic arts and book-publishing trades. He joined a burgeoning community of small-press publishers operating under the roof of the West Coast Print Center, an institution founded by Don Cushman with funding from the National Endowment for the Arts, that would enable many of the challenging and boundary-stretching younger poets of the period to reach print in one or the other of a broad array of literary presses.

There he would join former classmates at IWW— Curtis Faville, Bob Perelman and Barrett Watten who had NOT become Actualists during their stays in Iowa City, to carry on publishing activities at the center. Faville founded his magazine L and its eponymous publishing imprint, Barrett Watten expanded This, the magazine he cofounded with Robert Grenier, into This Press, publishing, among others, Clark Coolidge, known to the Bay Area rock-and-rollers as the drummer in Serpent Power, the psychedelic-era rock band fronted by local poet David Meltzer & his wife, and Perelman continued publication of his journal, *Hills*, utilizing the printing equipment at the center.

Each of Darrell Gray's West Coast publishers had a presence at the center. Besides Mattingly, who published Gray's *Something Swims Out* back in Iowa City, Alastair Johnston of Poltroon Press (and Transitional Face) set much of the type at the center. Poltroon would publish *Halos of Debris* in 1984, Gray's final collection, showcasing the shimmering lyrical brilliance that came with his extraordinary gift. A third press with ties to the center, Sombre Reptiles, would publish Gray, too. (Its founders, Jerry Ratch and Mary Ann Hayden found obvious inspiration from rock music, naming their press after a song by Brian Eno, formerly of the band Roxy Music.)

While Gray's alcoholism progressed, Mattingly's career flourished. He fell in with a circle of young designers that included David Bullen, Johanna Drucker and others, carried on friendship with Keith Abbott and many other poets whom he'd met along the way.

Among poets and writers, Gray managed to develop and maintain a close friendship with Jim Nisbet, who has built a cult following for his often savage noir novels, but who began his literary coming-of-age as a poet. Nisbet has remained a loyal advocate of Gray's legacy and a champion of the prodigious talents Gray possessed. Gray would find companionship, too, with another group of University of Iowa alumni who had leased a space on Blake Street in Berkeley to engage in performance art.

G.P. Skratz writes more about the work of this group in his essay in this volume. Bob Ernst, who attended the IWW while Ted Berrigan was in residency, co-founded the Blake Street Hawkeyes at the space, out of which emerged George Coates Performance Works, presenting its ambitious, large-scale multimedia pieces incorporating new technologies in new ways or for the first time in theater. Coates openly acknowledged the role of the Actualists in the breakthroughs he would help bring to performance art and the exprience of art in general.

While veterans of the Blake Street Hawkeyes were expanding and institutionalizing a heritage of the Actualists, some poets seemed to be getting dismissed—even denigrated—here in the Bay Area. Out of nowhere in the 1980s, poets began being pegged with the designation "post-Actualist," a term used to lump various non-conforming, sometimes personally acquainted poets and writers together into some kind of literary "school," seemingly to exile them into some kind of anachronistic oblivion. Nisbet and the circle that has come to surround him seemed to be the ex-emplar of this amorphous so-called "post-Actualist" school.

The editors of *Life of Crime*, the notorious newsletter of the Black Bart Poetry Society, co-founded by Pat Nolan, an early compatriot of the Actualists, recognized this tactic early on and solicited Dave Morice to help debunk the strategy by inviting his collaboration in the "Post-Actualist Manifesto," later reprinted in an issue of *Semiotext(e)*.

The manifesto exposed the fundamental paradox embodied by the Actualists, a paradox that Coates and his contemporaries in performance were able to absorb into the kernel of their aesthetic. At the same time, the manifesto revealed the nonsensicality of the term "post-Actualist" used as a descriptor. To be an Actualist, you must declare yourself to be one. You cannot be an Actualist if you don't. The act does not require the em-brace of any aesthetics, any poetic principles, sets of stylistic approaches or techniques of expression. But you did have to self-designate. Further-more, by definition, an Actualist could not be designated as such by a third party. Thus the phrase "Actualist poem" is nonsense. That would demand that "actualism" somehow be illustrated in the poem, when "actualism" describes a particular point-of-view within metaphysics and is not appli-cable in poetics. Therefore, it can only be an "Actualist's poem," i.e., one written by one of the Actualists or in the case of a collaboration by a group of Actualists, an "Actualists' poem." Actualist as an adjective is empty of meaning. With that in mind, it is bewildering to try to get your mind around the meaning of "post-Actualist" as an adjective or as a designation for anyone or anyone's work, unless of course it contains a misplaced hy-phen and should be represented as two proper nouns, i. e., "Post Actualist," in the manner of "Post Toasties," however unlikely it might be that anyone at Post Foods would elect to assign its brand to any flavor of poet.

As for the Actualists in California, only George Mattingly survives in the Bay Area scene. Steve and Sheila Toth resettled in northern California.

What Is Actualism
by Michael Lyons

from his *The Punctual Actual Weekly*

Well of course that is one of those questions that if we could answer it, the answer would not be an actualism. We get into the problem of Tristram Shandy, that it takes longer to codify a realization than it does to actually have one. But basically we could say that actualist poetry is poetry about objects of the common world. Or we could say that it was a brief, lucky, happy-go-lightly time in poetry when readings and poetry were about connection at least on some level with someone. But there is a lot more to it than that, as we shall see. We could say that it was a cross-sorting of small talk and big talk (as O'Hara showed us how to do). Or we could say that it was the reaction to the deepening influences of ecology, relativity, quantum mechanics and uncertainty, and chaos, and an attempt to go beneath the real, beneath the existential to the forces forming reality. But let us not get ahead of ourselves.

Let us look at the concrete example of an Actualist poem by Darrell Gray, from his *Essays & Dissolutions*, Abraxas Press, 1977

The Syntax

How well we remember the accidents
like strands of hair
on the polished table,
and before what you said,
    wasted or devised.

I saw the top of your head (the neckline

33

and the branches,
branches imposed themselves against
your face
accidentally dark

the wet leaves
slanting
the window

This poem is a good example of an actualist work because it is both looking through and looking at. It presents the situation of using your optical
machinery: To see a thing we must adjust our visual apparatus in a certain
way. In this poem we are looking at the face. Looking at what the face is
looking at. Looking through the eyes in the face. Vision travels through the
pane AND it is detained at the window AND it looks at the garden outside.
The either-or opposites which exclude each other have been accommo-
dated into a both-and. This, penetrating beneath the surface of reality to
deeper forces shaping reality, and this, fusing logical opposites, are attri-
butes of an Actualist poem. Gray discusses how "The Syntax" emerged:

"Here, I was consciously working with 'e's, 'i's and 'o's, vowels with 'a's
generously interspersed. The consonants fell into place almost by themselves. I didn't calculate them, for what I wanted was the openness of
statement, statement becoming recognition in the act of its finding a term
for itself, in my attention. Hence the looseness of the poem. At the out-
set, I didn't know exactly what I wanted to say. I considered the occasion
an almost musical one, in which variables of sound and meaning would
seek a norm, and that norm turned out to be one of vowels. On retrospect,
the norm became too dominant, and the verb which should have been
most active, whatever its linguistic orientation, was 'imposed'…too weak
a word to carry the impact of the statement itself. I tried alternate words:
thrust, whirled, dilated, even the word 'honed.' But what I wanted to say
always intervened. I wanted to say simply that the branches, intimate as the
branching blood vessels of the eye, intervened between the larger reality
that I was, in the poem, trying to establish between myself and the person
addressed."

Gray's "Actualism—A Manifesto" opens with: "Actuality is never frustrated because it is always complete." I read it in a journal called *Gum*. It

34

was a series of short aphoristic precepts, 15 one-liners.

Another one went: "We write in words to disguise ourselves, as a protection from the fact that words are writing us." We can see in this the sense of modern post-uncertainty zeitgeist, the prolegomena of the poet's work: to enter into and engage more and more deeply the processes of semiosis at work in the world of which we are information in its circuit. It is semiosis that transforms sounds into words, and word sequences through transformational grammar into concept structures, through which we know and are known. I read that aphorism, as Actualism is a writing as a vaccine against any kind of literacy that was not self-aware, but only continued to purvey received ideas driven by marketing forces, that sought only to manipulate the user towards the ends of its convention and that did not lead to an opening of the field. We didn't have the concept or meme or episteme but knew being absorbed into the system was coercive; there was a transcendental reality that we had to be trying to get to. At the time I thought all art should aspire to the actualism of improvisational jazz. For me that sense of being in the moment that jazz gave you (no doubt heightened by moving the participant's sense of involvement through its basic time structure being syncopated) was such a bracing attention. You felt like you were on the edge, moving into the now. Actualism was like existentialism drained of its nihilism and infused with jubilance. By letting the reader feel himself adrift somewhere in uncertainty, he could participate more in the shared creative act. For me at the time, Actualism was from the Beats, that rollicking road quest, of being a stranger in a strange land.

I was not at the Iowa Writers' Workshop where Darrell studied with Ted Berrigan and Anselm Hollo as they brought the New York school to the midwest, where it got infused with a kind of cosmic cowboy / indegenous shaman psychedelic roots thing mixed with the west coast Buddhist beatniks bebop jazz sensibilities. l was into all this and the absurdist humor of Texas, mixed with the intellectual sci-fi of Pynchon, Borges, Burroughs, and blended with my own sense of *puer aeternus* in J.D. Salinger. Too, I was on a quest for the modern contemporary myth in science, and its laguage of forms, mathematics. I was after a literature that reflected the profound changes in our understanding of the world given us by quantum mechanics. As I look back on it, I see these aphorisms in the Manifesto were related to the philosophy Darrell Gray already understood and which would ultimately be the Vedanta verified in a full-on Kantian exposition. Another aphorism is the analogy: "Actualism is to Chemistry what Fatalism was to the Middle Ages." This shows, humorously the hubris of how Actualism was to fulfill Valery's prologomena for poetry to be a chemistry for as yet undiscovered elements. The manifesto ends with: "Why belabor the impossible?"

I read Darrell's "What is Actualism" essay in another journal, *The North Stone Review*, where I learned that the opening line in the Manifesto was from William Carlos Williams. We do not get a simple answer for our question, What is Actualism? But in this essay Gray introduces the concept of the Automorph which is a rich symbol to lead us into a perception of the Actual:

"Distinctions occur in the world, it is true: a beautiful young woman may be seen pushing a baby carriage into the park across the street from where you are walking, and you may think how odd it is that this is so."

The essay into aesthetics continues, while moving our mind around in a space, following a story about a woman pushing a baby carriage. This whole idea of the spatialization of mind is a central one in modern poetics and practiced rigorously in the amphictionic theatre. Stated as a metaphorical equation: "voyage in space = quest for being." In the essay the revolving wheels on the baby carriage bring us back to the field of movement that Gray wants to talk about:

"And the thought of sadness leads also like a reflection on the water's surface. But where? Where does it lead, you ask? And the answer comes to you that it leads into a waiting, a waiting stretched so thin that it shines. So shining waits and includes its waiting, and shining is actual, as poetry is actual and shining."

This image of poetry as a waiting depicts poetry as being on a path that has been changed, deflected; we are given an unexpected pause. We have the three concepts, waiting, shining and the actual convolved here. A shining waiting, would bespeak a mind that was self-aware enough to be involved with the processes of the moment, rather than an impatient waiting for what was next. It suggests rather than the ego grasping and planning, it is waiting neither bored nor pushing nor desperate, but simply present, ready.

It is an image of poetry as a reflection on the surface of water, a shining on time's surface. This visual metaphor—that REALITY IS A MIRROR, reflecting the world of the possible, a mirror in which the world of the actual is reflected—would become a central study in Gray's essays. It is the central metaphor of the Vedas, and also of Peirce's semiology.

"Surely if one goes back far enough, back to the first or 'Alpha Street,' the turning will cease. And the stillness will be beautiful again, and not the terror of stillness that is the deserted streets of the world."

Then he introduces his idea of the Automorph, a sensed presence in the stillness at the heart of the world where we have been brought by poetry.

"If one is a poet one goes back to the original stillness to find what it is he has lost. Whatever it is, he has lost it by being a man. He will not find it by being a man any longer. Which is to say he will not be a man when he gets there. He will be an Automorph...for an Automorph is to man what a man is to his dreams, desires and loves. And here is the strange part—strange only because it is so near we do not notice—the Automorph dwells within the being of every man, as well as every animal, tree, and flower."

We will see later when we explore Gray's commentary on the Vedanta in his essay "The Transcendental Critique of Knowledge," that the Automorph is Atman. In that essay he studied extensively the reaction to apprehending or trying to perceive, the emergence of this atomistic Atman into the world of the actual from the world of the possible through various coercive integrities and the process of noumenal ingression, phenomenology. This mode of being of itself, the Atman, is what Peirce calls Firstness. Secondness is the Actual. Let us explore the analogy. Automorph:man::man:dreams.

I read that to mean the automorphic self is an adjective for the Self of Jung, that organization of energies that we have inherited from evolution that emerges when we experience joy reflected in our art. The analogy goes: Dreams, loves, desires are created in man's mind to help him know himself, to guide him. Notice the progression of this essay from image to icon to indexical movement to symbol. It is the semiosis process of the universe emerging, becoming actual.

In "What is Actualism": "Man waits for feelings to come to him, but in the Automorph they are already there. Man dreams, but the Automorph has no need to, for what is a dream when everything is equally present and equally clear. Man's dreams are merely the shadows of the Automorph's joyous movements and sometimes when it is moving very rapidly man's dreams are thrashing into glowing images, fragments of desire hurled down from the physical world, and these images obsess and perturb the sleeper, making him forget who he is."

Gray talks about the artist's ego and how it makes him feel separate, and how art and poetry seek to make him feel ego-less. "Can it be that art makes us sad by trying to protect us from that which poses no threat? I think that is true, for there is something in man that wants to feel it is different. It wants to be the only man, when it is very much more. Some call this the 'ego' by which they mean a distinction between 'man' and 'Nature.'" He goes on to suggest the artist's ego "is the source of the Pathetic Fallacy of poems stuffed with symbols and metaphors, how they appear dredged up. To be actual is not to possess Actuality—it is to be possessed by it. William Carlos Williams, a great Actualist poet, once wrote: 'Actuality is never frustrated because it is always complete.'" Toward the end of the essay Darrell writes:

"I want to emphasize that Actualism is not an aesthetic "Movement" in the usual sense of the word. It owes nothing to literary history that it could not find elsewhere, least of all aesthetic theory or literary criticism. Actualism begins when the Automorph in man's being decides to wake him up. When this waking-up occurs in language, the result is an Actualist poem, novel, or play." Gray gives many sources for his thoughts on Actualism, and WCW was certainly one. The good doctor brought a lot of new life into poetry after Ezra Pound and T.S. Eliot.

Though I think very highly of Pound and Eliot, there is much more sweetness to be had from learning what other poets have taught us about seeing. The titles for most of Gray's books were phrases from WCW: *Scattered Brains, The Beauties of Travel, Something Swims Out, Halos of Debris*. He read the master well.

The poets are inspired by trying to understand some grand design. Walt Whitman really saw it. I was so touched by reading his poetry when I was a young hippie embarking on many long trans-continental hitchhiking voyages. I wanted to really exist. I did cast my fate to the open road and revel in just being and knowing I was part of something great.

II. BIOGRAPHIES, POEMS & PUBLICATIONS

The Iowa City Actualist Community

ANSELM HOLLO
(1934–2013)

Anselm was the author of more than forty books of poetry, including *Notes on the Possibilities and Attractions of Existence: New and Selected Poems, 1965–2000,* Coffee House Press 2001, which won the San Francisco Poetry Center Book Award.

His many honors and awards included a fellowship from the National Endowment for the Arts, grants from the Fund for Poetry, the Government of Finland's Distinguished Foreign Translator's Award, and the Gertrude Stein Award in Innovative American Poetry.

Anselm was one of the Writers' Workshop's teachers who was looked up to by counter-culture students. It was there and later in the Iowa City community that he influenced and befriended a number of students who were to found the Actualist poetry movement, and was included in *The Actualist Anthology,* The Spirit That Moves Us Press, 1977.

Eulogy for Anselm Hollo, by Allan Kornblum

Born in Helsinki, Finland, April 12, 1934. Died in Boulder, Colorado, January 29, 2013.

Dedication: A Toke for Li Po

born in pa-hsi province
of szechwan
lived muchos años
at the court of the emperor

ming huang, but was banished
as a result of falling
in disfavor? with the empress
kao li-shih, & wandered about china thereafter

only occasionally attached to a patron
leading a "dissolute" life, addicted? to drink
writing the poems about the joys of that life

notably wine, & woman, & all the rest
& agitation of the sensational universe

came to his death by falling
out of a boat & drowning
in an attempt to have intimate intercourse
with the moon
in the water

one of those of
whom it is said:

"he took the charge well"

That poem appeared in *Heavy Jars*, published in the fall of 1977 under the Toothpaste Press imprint, the first of many of Anselm's books we collaborated on over the many years we knew each other. I'll return to the poem shortly.

Anselm's father was a professor of philosophy at the University of

Helsinki, and an important translator of major works of fiction and

philosophy from many languages. In a way he was like a one-man Penguin Classics, introducing—in some cases for the first time—authors from Russia, England, Germany, and France to Finnish readers. But Anselm's mother wanted him to be a scientist, like her own father. His long, rich, literary career—regarded as a treasure by so many—was a disappointment to her. But his was not an unhappy childhood: in another poem from *Heavy Jars*, "Helsinki, 1940," Anselm charmingly revisits his six-year-old take on World War II—the excitement of the "big lights in the sky" and the intimacy of the bomb shelter, where he was "safe in the earth, surrounded by many / all of whom really felt like living."

The one part of his life I wish I knew better was his work at the British Broadcasting Corporation. In addition to reading the nightly news in his pleasant, rumbling baritone, Anselm collaborated with other staff writers on a number of radio dramas in the early 1960s. Released in printed form for staff use only, and presented under a variety of pseudonyms, those scripts are now lost forever. Don't those days sound like fun? It was during those United Kingdom years that he and Josephine Clare had their three children, Hannes, Kaarina, and Tamsin.

Anselm told me that Paul Blackburn was responsible for getting him his first job in the States, at SUNY Buffalo in 1965. He returned to Finland and the U.K. for visits from time to time, but after that first gig, he was able to find one teaching job after another—like Li Po finding his patrons—enabling him to make his home in America. Eventually he and Jane Dalrymple-Hollo settled permanently and very happily in Boulder, where he became a valued member of the core faculty at the Jack Kerouac School of Disembodied Poetics at Naropa University.

I first met Anselm in the summer of 1970 in the English/Philosophy Building (EPB) at the University of Iowa when I arrived in Iowa City from

New York's Lower East Side, determined to start school over as a poet. (I had previously attended N.Y.U. as a voice education major, but dropped out.) I went from one office to another at the EPB looking for submissions for the first issue of my soon-to-be published mimeo magazine, *Toothpaste*, and was starting to get discouraged. I was not yet aware of the hostility between most of the faculty at the Writers' Workshop and the St. Mark's Poetry Project. (They say academic feuds are so vicious because the stakes are so low. With even lower stakes, poetry feuds can make academic feuds seem like tea parties.)

But then I walked into Anselm's office—he was a welcoming revelation, as he has been all his life. With (as I later learned) his signature chuckle, which seemed to bubble up effortlessly from the depths of the earth, he told me he would be delighted to participate, gave me his address, and told me to visit him at his home, where he would give me some poems and we could get to know each other. Over the next few decades, we shared a protégé/mentor relationship that continues to reverberate in my life.

Between 1970 and 1972, Anselm invited me to join him on two trips to the University of Northern Iowa in Cedar Falls to hear Andrei Voznesensky and Gary Snyder read. The drive was about an hour long. We arrived late for the Voznesensky reading because of a flat tire. Never mechanically inclined, he suggested we tie a handkerchief to the radio antenna and wait for help. I had never changed a tire before, but for reasons that seem foolish now, I was confident that I could do so. Fortunately my wife Cinda was with me for that adventure, and together we got the job done, and somehow arrived just as a nice-but-colorless man from the Russian language department began to introduce the evening. In stunning black clothes and boots, Voznesensky looked and read like a rock star. Later, at the reception, the grateful guest poet told me that Anselm's City Lights chapbook, *Red Cats*, was the first book to introduce him and Yevgeny Yevtushenko to American readers. Anselm was later embarrassed by the translation, because his Russian was actually quite primitive compared to his knowledge of German, French, and the various Scandinavian languages. But in its day, that little booklet, which appeared in the midst of the Cold War, was truly groundbreaking.

On the next trip, we arrived early enough to join Gary Snyder for a pre-reading dinner, accompanied by someone from the English department who was responsible for getting their guest to the auditorium on time. Anselm was very close to many poets; with Snyder it was more of a "lots-of-friends-in-common" relationship. But they clearly enjoyed each other's company and conversation. Somehow the conversation that evening wound up straying into, and then focusing on, the migration of peoples from Central Asia into Europe between 400 and 800 CE; the two of them just dug into that obscure period of history as if they were chewing over last week's news. I was amused to learn from their discussion that there had once been a seminomadic tribe called the Alans. But I also remember feeling astonished by their extensive knowledge, and reminded of the serious reading that was yet ahead of me.

Of course the great adventure of that period was a week-long trek to a "National Poetry Festival" in Allendale, Michigan, with Anselm, Darrell Gray, and a fortunately sober (if at times stuffy) poet (name now forgotten) who did most of the driving (Anselm and Darrell were drinking, and I didn't know how to drive in those days). I spent a lot of memorable time with Ted Berrigan and Robert Creeley (with whom Anselm was very close), and some brief but valued time with Philip Whalen (whom Anselm idolized), Paul Blackburn (who was dying), and Joel Oppenheimer (whom

I remember as supremely sardonic). I cemented a lifelong friendship with Ken Mikolowski of the Alternative Press (I had met him earlier at a small press conference). And I also very briefly met and/or attended readings by Robert Bly, Armand Schwerner, Robert Kelly, Diane Wakoski, Sonia Sanchez, Tom Weatherly, John Logan, Gregory Corso, and many more. Oddly enough, the school hosting the event was in a dry county, and everyone was looking for twelve-packs. So on an afternoon I'll never forget, I sat in the backseat of Anselm's car listening to Robert Creeley brilliantly expound, zooming intently from topic to topic, while Anselm at the wheel and Ted Berrigan riding shotgun searched for a liquor store in the next county. I remember that we were eventually successful in our quest; I remember Creeley offering to put us up at a motel when we seemed hopelessly lost; and I remember Anselm and Ted assuring Creeley that they could find the way. But how we eventually did get back to that small-town campus is lost to the fog of time.

By the time *Heavy Jars* was published, Anselm had given me poems for each of the seven issues of Toothpaste, had stored the first printing press I bought in his garage until I had a home for it, and had attended my wedding. But most importantly, he encouraged me to believe that I could make a significant contribution to the literary community as a small press publisher. That encouragement gave me the confidence to get started, and today I'm so pleased that our first book together continues to hold up as one of my best printing efforts. It also includes the kinds of connections/ associations for me that e-books will forever, inevitably lack.

The Plantin type had been given to me and Cinda as a wedding present from Harry Duncan, our letterpress printing teacher, who sold us his house when he moved to Omaha. Under the Cummington Press imprint, Harry had printed first editions by William Carlos Williams, Wallace Stevens, Robert Penn Warren, Allen Tate, Yvor Winters, as well as Robert Lowell's very first book. He is now long gone, but Duncan's devotion to his craft continues to inspire me.

The type was named for Christopher Plantin, whose press began in 1555 and closed shortly before World War I, when surviving family members donated the shop to the city of Antwerp, which turned it into a museum that I hope to visit someday. Plantin's motto was Labore et Constancia—By Labor and Constancy, or as some might translate it today, hard work and tenacity—both needed to run a publishing house. I have absolutely no doubt that Duncan was sending me a message with his gift.

In the Tom-Sawyer-and-the-picket-fence spirit that has always been part of the survival of small literary publishing houses, Alan Frank, then owner of a delightfully dinky secondhand bookstore in Iowa City, volunteered to handset the type in return for learning how to do so.

And the cover art was donated by Patrick Dooley—who also designed the Toothpaste Press printer's mark, which appeared on all our title pages— in return for the honor of participating in a book by Anselm Hollo.

 he Toothpaste Press Cinda and I were married in August 1972. We somehow managed (with the help of many friends) to get the half-ton Challenge Gordon platen press into our new home that fall. We spent the next year accumulating the additional equipment needed for an active letterpress print shop: type cabinets with cases filled with a variety of fonts and sizes of type, galley cabinets and trays for storing work in progress, leads and slugs, a lead and slug cutter, a paper cutter, composing sticks, a proof press, an imposing surface, furniture for locking up type, quoins and quoin keys, and so on. By fall 1973 we were printing our first full-length book, and by the time *Heavy Jars* came out in 1977, the Toothpaste Press was starting to seem almost "established." But literary history is littered with stories of small presses that burned brightly, faded, and were snuffed out within a single decade. It still remained to be seen whether I had a life-long career as a literary publisher in me, whether I had the dedication.

Which brings me back to the poem at the beginning of this reminiscence, the poem I chose to represent Anselm, or perhaps to represent my feelings about him. Of course some might read the poem, roll their eyes, wag a finger, and lecture about what could seem like a justification for the excessive drinking that marred an early period of Anselm's life—if they wanted to merely gloss the surface, and be a bit of a prig. But to me, the poem turns on two meanings of dedication, and three meanings of charge.

Yes, the poem is dedicated to a heavy drinker, but remember that Anselm was a devoted teacher, and teachers only reveal enough to pique their students' interest, hoping they'll do some reading and learn more on their own. Li Po did write of the pleasures of wine, but was also fanatically devoted to the classics, studied traditional Chinese poetic forms while stretching their possibilities, and yet, like Anselm, wore his scholarship lightly. And like Anselm, many of Li Po's poems feel like an ongoing conversation with all the great writers of the past and present, whom they both regarded as part of their family of favorite drinking buddies. Anselm of course knew the story of Li Po drowning while embracing a reflection of the moon was the stuff of legend, but I believe he included the tall tale because it spoke to him of the all-out lifetime dedication to literature their work and lives embodied.

And then there is the charge, all toted up. A life of bills that cannot be paid on time; the moments of feeling ridiculous when introduced as a poet, of all things, at class and family reunions; and within the "field" itself, the awards others win, the reviews others get, the doubts in the dark of the night. It comes to quite a sum and can levy a heavy toll over the years.

The poem also speaks to me of the charge as in the responsibility of the poet for the language, for the fleeting ideas that seem to arrive like news from Alpha Centauri, the illusions that somehow reveal a truth, or what seems like truth but is ultimately a beautiful and perhaps tempting illusion. That charge doesn't suit all poets comfortably. Some wear it like badly fitted clothes that never were and never will be in style. But in the hearts of a rare few like Anselm Hollo, that responsibility glows softly and steadily with a casual grace, a light that forever gives students, readers, and dear friends indescribable pleasure, and at times, desperately needed hope.

Finally there is the charge, the attack, the poet diving headlong, with single-minded focus, into the work, never knowing how circuitous a route the poem may ultimately take, or how many obstacles may block the path.

And that reminds me of one of my fondest and most amusing moments with Anselm, which took place at the Qounty Quart House, a working man's bar in West Branch, Iowa, where Cinda and I lived in Harry Duncan's former house from 1972 until we moved to Minnesota in 1985. After downing a few beers, Anselm put a dollar down on the edge of the pool table, waited his turn, put a quarter in the slot, racked up the balls, and prepared to play the winner of the previous game. Suddenly, after gazing at the tight triangle at the far end of the green felt, he looked up at his opponent and asked, "Do the pool balls ever remind you of the Roman legions, lined up in formation, waiting for their orders?" After a puzzled "Huh?" Anselm said, "Ah, never mind, it was just a thought." Then he leaned over the table and positioned his cue for the break.

To soldiers, police, or firefighters, speaking of a poet on the attack might seem completely incongruous. But how many of them would be willing to stand stark naked before the world with only their words to clothe them, as do poets over and over, year after year? It is one thing to charge into a fight or a burning fire, but it takes another kind of courage to plunge into the hidden recesses of the mind and the heart, and to reveal both the marvels of the mundane and hidden secrets that range from the silly to the sublime.

As Shakespeare said, in a lifetime we all play many parts. Anselm Hollo was a loving son, brother, husband, and father; an omnivorous scholar; a meticulous yet graceful translator; a teacher to thousands of grateful students; a faithful and endlessly entertaining friend; a brilliant raconteur; and at his core, a simultaneously gentle and fearless poet. With his earth-shaking laugh that at once embraced and brushed off the absurdities of life, Anselm Hollo was definitely "one of those of whom it is said, he took the charge well."

(from *The Actualist Anthology*)

SONG OF THE TUSK

the elephant
    bogged down
thousands of years ago

no no those are untrue statements
it is I
    am in the glass case
        counting
            the stubs of museum tickets

it is the elephant
    walks the downs
        laughs at the sea
            growling

there is no such thing
    as thousands of years
I drop a stone on your head
    from the elephant's back

show me
    show me the thousands of years

I walk through the water
    throwing stones at the women
        on the beach
    the honeymoon women
        their eyes far apart

frightened
    they close the dark case
        over themselves
    for thousands of years

A WARRANT IS OUT FOR THE ARREST OF HENRY MILLER
    (November 2, 1962)

get that man!
    what rooftop
chases! zig-
    zag sprints in alleys
smelling of garlic
& good fucks

    get that man!
    he's alive…

skittering
      down fire escapes,
the women watching
       with big startled tits
    rock-drill roar
    & torch flash
    down into fall-
        out shelters—

but all the while he sits on a mountaintop
& smiles at sparrows hatching
at the foot of the ladder to man's heaven

& says yes now
they're chasing
everybody

THROUGH TWO LAYERS OF GLASS

through two layers of glass
the far end of this restaurant
a man
whose head is
a glob
of light
like anybody's
any body
he is formless form
by means of maya
& all her daughters, assumes
innumerable forms
of which I am one, eating out alone.

THE DISCOVERY OF LSD A TRUE STORY

the dose of a mere
fifty micrograms totally altered
the consciousness of professor Albert Hoffmann
motel hit geode intersection
swerve hit geode albert
inadvertently
inhaled it
blast core city ominous rock
spiraling rites of light
inhaled his consciousness
& exhaled
"phew! wow! pow! zat voss somsink!"

STRANGE ENCOUNTER

megalomaniac
midgets
exist
but
uneasily,
yes,
officer.
my name is
kid sky.
I live in
the elevator.
"you're under arrest."

LOS SEDENTARIOS

most of the time we sit down
to write "sitting down" down

Mark Twain made a contraption
enabled him to be funny in bed in writing

Goethe and Hemingway
risked varicose veins at the high desk

sitting down we get
fat round the ass

short poems
not too frequent
are the least fattening

if you're sitting down while reading this
now is the time to get up.

GOOD STUFF COOKIES

2 gods
2/3 cup hidden psychic activity
2 teasp. real world
3/4 cup sleep
2 cups sifted all-purpose iridescence
2 teasp. good stuff
1/2 teasp. pomp & pleasure

beat gods hidden psychic activity
real world and sleep together
sift together iridescence good stuff
pomp & pleasure
add to real world mixture
drop by teaspoon
2 inches apart on cookie sheet
press cookies flat
with bottom of glass dipped in sleep
bake at 400 F 8 to 10 minutes

2 dozen cookies good stuff

poetry

& It Is a Song. Migrant Press, 1965

Faces & Forms. Ambit Books, 1966

The Coherences. Trigram Press, 1968

Haiku. (with John Esam and Tom Raworth), Trigram Press, 1968

Tumbleweed. Weed/Flower Press, 1968

Doubletalk. (with Ted Berrigan), TG Miller, Nomad Press, 1969

Maya. Cape Golliard, Grossman, 1970

Sensation 27. Institute of Further Studies, 1972

Some Worlds. Elizabeth Press, 1974

Black Book. Jim Garmhousen, 1974

Notes & Paramecia. Self-published, 1976

Lingering Tangos. Tropos Press, 1977

Soujourner Microcosms. Blue Wind Press, 1977

Heavy Jars. Toothpaste Press, 1977

Lunch in Fur. Aquila Rose, 1978

With Ruth in Mind. Station Hill, 1979

Finite Continued. Blue Wind Press, 1980

No Complaints. Toothpaste Press, 1983

Pick Up the House. Coffee House Press, 1986

Outlying Districts. Coffee House Press, 1980

Space Baltic. Ocean View Books, 1991

Near Miss Haiku. Yellow Press, 1991

Blue Ceiling. Tansy Press, 1992

High Beam. Pyramid Atlantic, 1993

West Is Left on the Map. (with Jane Dalrymple-Hollo)
    Dead Metaphor Press, 1993

Survival Dancing. Rodent, 1995

Corvus. Coffee House Press, 1995

AHOE (1). Smokeproof Press, 1997

Hills Like Purple Pachyderms. Kavyayantra Press, 1997

AHOE (2). Writers Forum, 1998

rue Wilson Monday. La Alameda Press, 2000

Notes on the Possibilities and Attractions of Existence.

Coffee House Press, 2000 (*from which this list of publications was compiled*)

The Tortoise of History. Coffee House Press, 2016

poetry translations

Some Poems by Paul Klee
Red Cats
William Carlos Williams—Paterson (in German, with Josephine Clare)
Allen Ginsberg—Kaddish und andere Gedichte (with J.C.)
Gregory Corso—Gasoline und andere Gedichte (with J.C.)
Paavo Haavikko—Selected Poems
Pentti Saarikoski—Selected Poems
The Poems of Hipponax
Pentti Saarikoski—Trilogy
Mirkka Rekola—88 Poems
Kai Nieminen—Serious Poems

prose translations

Jean Genet—Querelle
Franz Innerhofer—Beautiful Days
Olof Lagercrantz—Strindberg
Peter Stephan Jungk—Werfel
Lennert Hagerfors—The Whales in Lake Tanganyika
Jaan Kross—The Czar's Madman
Rosa Liksom—One Night Stands
Lars Kleberg—Starfall: A Triptych

plays and screenplays

Bertolt Brecht—Jungle of Cities
Georg Buchner—Woyzeck
Francois Truffaut—Small Change
Louis Malle—Au revoir les enfants

Anselm also had poems published in a host of little magazines,
too numerous to mention.

DARRELL GRAY
(1945–1986)

*See "Darrell Gray: A Great Adventure," by Allan Kornblum above,
following "The Origins of Actualism," by Dave Morice*

(from *The Actualist Anthology*)

FOR GEORGE OPPEN

With the gaunt resolution
Of old age
Upon him, he moves—
And street-sweepers
       alike
A distinct utterance
Meant for no ear but
Overheard, succinct, allowed
As beasts are allowed
And particular slants of light
In the innermost
      gardens.
Naturally,
      that the leaves speak—

54

And no known form
Retract it—a populous
Of desire upon desire—
All centuries the same:

Sparrow's feet—
Sea's glitter—
That the faces of men should
Lie in the small rains, should lie
And give truth
To the flesh.

SONNET FOR ALL GREEKS LIVING NOW

The Gods live in a micro-world
where they go to work without even
getting out of bed. The Gods
eat macaroni soup and dance, dance

as the universe passes under them;
they're so great. The Gods never go
to the bathroom, nor do they drool
a particular macaroni particle onto

their Afghans. They sit in a room
of quadriphonic stereos, as Zeus once
sat on Olympus, bickering with Hera.
They lift their wine glasses slowly,

as if to see in the sudden surface,
worlds their imaginations might bless.

THE MUSICAL APE

I dream continually of a musical ape
Who writes poems in his sleep
And wakes to find them published in
The Paris Review.
              This does not

Startle him. He is a good poet, addicted
To long walks, admiring
The delicate twists and turns
History has made in
His life.
          Night by night, the poems
Grow   He becomes famous
Simply by doing nothing, by being
Himself.

Often a giant page
Seems inserted from above—
This makes the dream glow
Almost like the sky, just before he wakes.

THE ART OF POETRY

Write only
to young boys—they
are the best readers.
Women get wound up
in dreams, they see
in your images more
than you mean. But if
you mean more than
you say, write also
to women.

AN OLD SOUTHERN CRITIC TAKES A LOOK AT MY POEMS

grasshoppers, wheelchairs, rosebuds!
all those variably cloudy images

bundled up & flung at the reader as if
communication depended on an alien plug, a verbal

fire sale, syntax slashed to the bone
& what's more we haven't the slightest

buried symbol or submerged meaning
to hold on to—total mayhem—"with this kind

of aesthetic how does he tie
his shoelaces is what I want to know"

not to mention all those dim & unemphasized
figments that flash across the page

all those parking lots preposterous similes
"the stars like tiny lawnchairs in the sky"

where did the soul go
to drag these fugitive embers from its fire

and was there a first fire, a fire fashioned
after no other, a fire of the final mind

from which we emerge like schoolboys in a dream
to bone white rivers & the fear of owls...

Say something deep, like the fear of rivers, something
pure & lean we can teach our kids

the lyric is flexible form, I know:
birds, beasts and animals

in season sing their blunt reciprocal praises.
Mimeo machines murmur. Though that might be a

variable measure, all variance decrees
a cosmic tedium – "dialectic" we call it: nude idiom

of the thing reborn. The gentle researcher
tilts to the modular pinkness of the snow—

an erudite boy, addicted to spiral notebooks,
yoga, and the oblique "come on" of dark girls

...These old eyes grow older with each word,
& Ambiguity, like a pregnant queen, rules

the landscape where I sit. Ripe berries hang in tangles

57

over Samuel Johnson's grave—"like ornaments of indecision,"

you might say...And yet, there is an occasional
brilliant twist. I quote one poem, "Baffling Turns," in toto:

Asleep at 60 mph.

No doubt the poet here has in mind
how much eludes him. Or, as Allen Tate succinctly said:

"For where Time rears its muted head and all appalls
We know not where we stand nor where we fall."

poetry
The Excuses. Abraxas Press, 1970
The Beauties of Travel. Doones Press, 1970
Something Swims Out. Blue Wind Press, 1972
The Catastrophic Unrush of Beauty (broadside). Blue Wind Press, 1972
Time with Birds (broadside). Toothpaste Press
Scattered Brains. The Toothpaste Press, 1974
Good Morning: 14 Sonnets (with Allan Kornblum).
    J Stone Press Weekly, 1975
Ruby Port: The Food Poems of Philippe Mignon. Sombre Reptiles, 1979
Everything Else. G.P. Skratz & Darrell Gray, Poltroon Press, 2012
Wreck O' Lections. Darrell Gray & Alastair Johnston with guessed
    appearances by Anselm Hollo & Allan Kornblum. Poltroon P., 1987
Poem for Annabelle Patience Kornblum (broadside) Poltroon Press, 1977
Halos of Debris. Poltroon Press, 1984

prose
Essays & Dissolutions. Abraxas Press, 1977
The Plain That Became The Mountain. Tendon Press, 1977
The New Conventionalism: Observations on a Mode of
    Contemporary American Poetry. (S.R. Vandercook), 1979

Darrell's poems were published in numerous little magazines, including
Poetry Magazine. He co-authored the play, Bob, with Allan Kornblum
and Jim Mulac. It had its World Premiere at ACUTE ACTUALISM: A
Memorial Homage to Darrell Gray, performed in Berkeley at Blake Street

Hawkeyes Theater on December 7, 1986. It was originally published in *In The Light* #s 5 & 6: Actual Plays.

DAVE MORICE
(in his own words)

David Jennings Patrick Morice was the oldest of five children, born in Saint Louis, Missouri to Gilbert Morice, a Navy pilot, and Lillian Murray Morice, a ballet student. His siblings were Delaine, Craig, Michele, and Jeannie. When he was six years old he wrote and illustrated rhymed porquoi poems for his mother. In grade school he drew Billy the Hobo Bee, a comic strip about bugs. In high school, he wrote Frankenstein Versus the New York Yankees, a novel about monsters and baseball.

In 1969, Dave received a B.A. in English with a creative writing minor from Saint Louis University, where he'd studied under John Knoepfle and Al Montesi. Later that year he moved to Iowa City, Iowa to attend the University of Iowa Writers' Workshop, from which he received an M.F.A. in 1972 and an M.A. in Library Science in 1986.

While in the Workshop, he studied under Anselm Hollo, Marvin Bell, Donald Justice, Kathleen Frasier, and Jack Marshall. He was Beat critic Seymour Krim's research assistant. He took an optional art class, Life Drawing 2, at the end of which the instructor told him that he should've taken Life Drawing 1. During his workshop years, he experimented with writing poems of different lengths, styles, and forms, using different sizes, shapes, and colors of paper.

Although the thesis committee (Anselm Hollo, Jack Marshall, Seymour Krim, George Starbuck, and Kathleen Frazier) approved his mimeo book *Tilt*, university rules required a typed manuscript. His 81-word thesis, *Poems* contained nine small poems, averaging nine words apiece. It was the shortest thesis in Writers' Workshop history. The following year the Workshop made it a rule that a thesis had to be at least 35 pages long. It was his first published book, privately printed by Al Buck in a letterpress edition of sixty copies. The shortest poem in it is two lines long:

> at night
> the flies

Dave taught Introduction to Children's Literature, a graduate course in Elementary Education at the University of Iowa, for six years. He was married to Milagros Quijada, an architect from Caracas, Venezuela from 1985 to 1991. They had one son, Danny, who taught him more about children, language, art, wordplay, teaching, and life than words can express.

He lives in Iowa City with his partner Mary Jo Dane, whom he'd met when Danny was in the language arts class that she taught at Southeast Junior High.

From 1972 to 1975, Dave perpetrated a literary hoax: He invented "Joyce Holland," a minimalist poet and performance artist. "Joyce" wrote concrete and minimalist poems and sent them to literary magazines, twenty-nine of which published her work. (See section titled "The Joyce Holland Hoax" for more details of "Joyce" and her contributions to the Actualist movement.)

On March 3, 1973, on the 100th anniversary of the invention of the typewriter by Christopher Scholes, Dave wrote his first Poetry Marathon—1,002 poems in twelve hours—at the Grand Opening of Epstein's Bookstore, the literary Mecca in Iowa City in the early seventies. He typed the poems on three small sheets of paper at a time. The shortest was a one-word poem; the longest was a sonnet. The marathon, an Actualist event, took place a week before the first Actualist Convention.

In 1974, Muscatine, Iowa held its second annual Great River Days

Festival. Part of it was the Belle of the Bend Art Fair. Dave was invited to write a poetry marathon at the fair. Referring back to the 19th century traveling entertainers who went from town to town selling cure-alls and nostrums, he named his event "Dr. Alphabet's Medicine Show," and made a costume to wear for the occasion: a white top hat, shirt, pants, shoes, and cane all spangled with letters of the alphabet in different colors. During the festival he wrote a poem on adding machine tape while wrapping it around Joyce Holland (P.J. Casteel). He titled the woman-plus-paper public sculpture "The Muscatine Mummy." Shortly after completion, he unwound the poem from Joyce, tore it into small strips, and put them into amber glass medicine bottles labeled "Poetry Tonic." He and his assistants gave the souvenir bottles away to fair-goers.

One of the most theatrical Poetry Marathon productions took place in Lone Tree, Iowa in 1977, sponsored by the Iowa Arts Council and coordinated by music director Lynn Grulke. The Halftime Poem Across a Football Field involved two high school football teams, more than 300 people in the stands, sportscasters Paul Ingram and Eric Roalson, a band, student cheerleaders, Boy Scout assistants, Dr. Alphabet, and his sister Michele.

The Lone Tree Lions were playing their homecoming game against the Tigers of Morning Sun, Iowa. During the day Dave taught poetry to the students, comparing it to football, and the students wrote poetry cheers for the game. After school, the cheerleaders practiced their favorite freshly-written cheers, while Grulke's band rehearsed a rock version of "The Alphabet Song." That night at half-time, the band played their song as Dave began to spray paint a poem on a roll of paper that stretched from goal post to goal post. One of the sportscasters, Eric Roalson, announced the action over a microphone: "Is that a simile on the thirty-yard line? Yes, it is!" The cheerleaders shouted cheers: "Metaphor! Metaphor! Tell 'em what we're yelling for!" and "Hold that line! Make it rhyme!" and "Hey, hey, Dr. A, how many poems did you write today?"

It was also a windy night, and the work-in-progress started blowing across the football field. Boy Scouts and other attendees had to rush from the stands and stand on the edges of the paper so the writing could continue. When it was finished, the football players from both teams held up the 100-yard sheet of paper for the fans to see. Dave read the poem over a microphone. Then the game continued. Fortunately, Lone Tree won.

As Dr. Alphabet, Dave has written marathons in Iowa, Pennsylvania, New Jersey, New York, Connecticut, and London England. In addition to the four marathons described above, here is a list of ten more:

- 100-Foot Poem from Dawn to Dusk on the Longest Day of the Year (Centipede). Iowa City, IA: Epstein's Bookstore, June 21, 1973.
- Mile-wide Haiku (The Kohoutek Comet Poetry Marathon) Iowa City, Iowa: Epstein's Bookstore, January 15, 1974.
- Tomorrow Show Poetry Telethon: Poem Written on Joyce Holland's Dress (Hot Lights). Los Angeles, California: Tomorrow show with Tom Snyder, February 12, 1974.
- Poem Wrapping a City Block (Poetry City, U.S.A.). Iowa City, Iowa: Sculpture Festival, October 6, 1975.
- Poem on Stage (untitled). Iowa City, IA: Duck's Breath Mystery Theater Farewell Show, December 18, 1975.
- Blindfolded Poetry Marathon (The Dark Side). New Hope, Pennsylvania: New Hope Arts Festival, September 25, 1976.
- Poem Whitewashed on Dubuque St. (Alphabet Avenue). Iowa City, Iowa: Nonesuch Fair Art Festival, Blackhawk Minipark, April 23, 1977.
- Poem across the Delaware River (Interstate Poem). New Hope, Pennsylvania: New Hope Arts Festival, April 30, 1977.
- 100 Newspoems on a Computer. London, England: Books Etc., May 12, 1983.
- The World's Longest Comic Strip (untitled). Iowa City, Iowa: Iowa Memorial Union Bookstore, October 13, 1982.

In 2008, UNESCO designated Iowa City the third "City of Literature."
In 2010 the University of Iowa celebrated this event with exhibits of literary
magazines, books, and manuscripts. Tim Shipe, the University of Iowa's
Dada Librarian, invited Dave to exhibit his Dr. Alphabet costume and to
write an Actualist marathon poem. Working in the University of Iowa
Main Library and at local business establishments, Dave produced 10,119
pages of poetry over 100 days—from the Fourth of July to Halloween—and
titled the complete work the Poetry City Marathon, which he dedicated
to his sister Michele, who was his literary cheerleader for many years. She
passed away at the age of 52 on February 22, 2010 of a brain tumor. Dave's
son Danny wrote the introduction to the marathon.

Within the exhibit of the University of Iowa Libraries, Dave had a table
where he wrote a 100 pages most of the days. On some days, he wrote at
local businesses that had donated $100 to Sachter House Media, an organi-
zation run by handicapped people and student volunteers. The marathon
was shadowed by an in-live-time website set up by Joye Chizek. Joye has
published five books by Dave and one book attributed to Joyce Holland.
In her website, iowacitypoetrymarathon.com, Joye displayed information
about Dave, his marathons, the history of Actualism, and related literary

topics. Her imprint was JoMo Press. Her imagination was boundless.

As each 100-page volume was completed, a link to a graphic on the website took the reader to the complete document as written. The final day of the exhibit at the Main Hall of the University of Iowa Libraries, one of the glass cases featuring Dave's Actualist and Performance Poetry history was opened, and he put on his original Dr. Alphabet outfit one more time. In costume, he proceeded to write a five-page epilogue on transparent plastic sheets placed on six easels. A reading of the first portion of the 10,000 page marathon was followed by a reading of the epilogue.

After the 2010 display was removed, the University Libraries took-on the task of binding the massive volume for their permanent collection. The final text of 10,119 pages measured 8.5 x 11 inches by 2 feet. Bu Wilson printed them, and conservator Bill Voss bound them in the U.I. Conservation Department. It took over 24 hours over several days to bind, and required a special press built to enable all the pages to be bound together. It weighed fifty-four pounds.

Dave has the smallest thesis (81 words) and the largest book (10,119 pages) as bookends to all the other volumes in the University Libraries. The thesis appeared in 1972, and the big book came in 2010—thirty years separating the creation of the two.

*   *   *

In 1975, Dave began teaching a Poetry Class for People Over 60, funded by the Iowa Arts Council. The hour-long classes, which met twice a week, continued for ten years. The students exhibited three-dimensional poems, including Technicolor Pages and Poetry Mobiles—at the Iowa City Public Library, and they published their own magazine, *Speakeasy*, in four issues.

The Arts Council also hired Dave to teach week-long workshops in grade schools and high schools throughout Iowa. Many of his methods involved writing on objects: Poetry Lampshade, Poetry Robot, Cardboard Castle, Junkosaurus, Mirror Writing, and many other objects. Some of the methods took other approaches: Poetry Poker used playing cards with phrases on them to include in the poem. When the Arts Council heard about this method, they sent an observer to check the validity of the writing. The observer joined in on the writing and afterwards gave a thumbs up to the Arts Council. While Poetry Poker began the five-day workshop, the Poem Wrapping the School concluded Dave's visit. It gave students a chance to write and draw on a long sheet of paper taped around the outside of their school building. The festive atmosphere allowed students to talk between the lines.

Teachers & Writers Collaborative published his methods in *The Adventures of Dr. Alphabet: 104 Unusual Ways to Write Poetry in the Classroom and the Community*. Ron Padgett and Chris Edgar edited it, and Padgett named it. Andrei Codrescu discussed the book on National Public Radio's All Things Considered: "…It is my belief that if Dr. Alphabet's recipes are followed, many of our nation's problems would be solved. Take for instance, 'The Blindfold Poem.' In 1977, Dr. Alphabet wrote blindfolded for 10 hours at an art festival in New Hope, Pennsylvania. He became, he tells us, more aware of sounds, smells, and conversations. Wouldn't it be wonderful if we had a National Writing Blindfolded Day? The best part is, you don't have to be a kid to play."

In 1978, a Workshop poet told Dave that "Great poems should paint pictures in the mind." He jokingly replied, "Great poems would make great cartoons." She responded, "Hey, you know you're right." And Dave wondered how T.S. Eliot's "Love Song of J. Alfred Prufrock" and Sylvia Plath's "Daddy" would look as comics, so he drew them. The following year, at David Hilton's urging, he published them as *Poetry Comics* No. 1, which he mailed to poets around the country. The words of the poems were usually placed in cartoon balloons and panels in traditional comic book format.

From 1979 to 1982, Dave published seventeen issues of *Poetry Comics*. Most issues were 22 pages long. After the sixteenth issue, journalist Jeff Weinstein called him and said, "My roommate Peter Schjeldahl has been getting copies of Poetry Comics, and they've been piling up in the bathroom. I'd like to interview you about them for *Tthe Village Voice*." A month later, the *Voice* published a six-page article that included examples of the cartoons. Weinstein wrote: "Morice's inspiration is poetry itself. Poetry makes him want to draw comics."

The article led to a 200-page anthology, *Poetry Comics: A Catooniverse of Poems* (Simon & Schuster, 1980). Two more anthologies followed: *More Poetry Comics: Abuse the Muse* (A Cappella/Chicago Review Press, 1994); and *Poetry Comics: An Animated Anthology* (Teachers & Writers, 2002). A fourth anthology, *Poetry Comics Around the World*, is in the works. With the advent of desktop publishing, Joye Chizek brought *Poetry Comics* back

65

into the light of day. She published twenty-five new issues of the magazine, titling the computer version *Poetry Comics Online.*

Dave sent copies of the original magazine to poets and other celebrities, and dozens of people replied. *Poetry Comics* may have generated the largest letters column in a literary periodical. Most of the responses appeared in The Muse's Mailbag, the *Poetry Comics* letters column. The six responses below first appeared in there, and they were reprinted on the back cover of the first anthlogy:

"Bravo Bravo Bravo" Dick Higgins, writer

"The best buy in the universe." Robert Creeley, poet

"I'll take a lifetime subscription." James Dickey, writer

"You are the master of a thousand styles." Johnny Hart, cartoonist

"Excellent." Elizabeth Taylor, actress

"Very funny" George Burns, comedian/actor

(from *The Actualist Anthology*)

THIS IS TO SIGNIFY

that you, the reader, are aware
that everything
going on around you is made possible through the cooperation
of everybody, mind you, everybody,
who is involved, including
me and you, both of us.
Even though we might not be together,
we are here at the same moment
of time and space
on this very page, at this very point
in the power of language.
And you, the reader, are in control
of when and where we go
in your mind and the poem's.
You are the leader in this world.
I can only follow,
pushing for what it's worth.

IN THE MIDDLE OF A WIND TUNNEL

And here we are in the middle of a wind tunnel
    in which the wind has been turned off
        for us to see exactly where the wind
            goes in and where it goes out

And here's the ON OFF button that turns the wind
    on and off, of course, and we don't turn it ON
        until we're OUT, and we watch the fans
            and bellows generate enough energy

And here's the middle of the generator
    where the power for the wind is stored
        when the wind isn't being used.
            Sir, don't press that ON button.

And now we'll leave the tunnel because very soon
    the owners will want to turn the wind on
        and watch things blow from one end of the tunnel
            to the other and back again.

(the following from *Quicksand through the Hourglass*, Toothpaste Press)

I AM

a letter in a syllable in a word in a phrase in a clause
in a sentence in a paragraph on a page in a chapter in
a story in a collection in a dialect in a language in a
society in a culture in a civilization in a period in an
epoch in a tradition in an era in an age in a history in
a book in a set on a shelf in a section in a bookcase
on a wall in a room in an apartment on a floor in a
building on a street in a block in a neighborhood in a
city in a county in a state in a region in a country on
a continent in a hemisphere in an ocean on a planet
in a solar system in a constellation in a galaxy in a
supergalaxy in a megagalaxy in a universe in an infinity
in an eternity in a reality in a dimension in an existence

(the following from *Tilt*, Toothpaste Press)

LITTLE PINBALL MACHINE

me and Kornblum
   playing Crescendo
      at the Mill Restaurant

balling her?

      a lost quarter

falls out of the slot
      my
        enough for 3

tilting
bazooka bubble gum

      on Shoe,

    Shoe scuffs it up

soft   explosions

1	1	1	3	8

      —high

   moving

 flip it

    ah, a persona comes in

   grabs me around my stomach

     from bright lights

   "Guess who?"

 but Pinball Goddess,

   don't say those bad words

     just snap your fingers

each snap a free game

a "gift of the odds"

like a city of lights
on an electronic table
i want to hold you in my arms
and then, who knows?

Points clicks listening

              to the music

    snapping away

          the machine

   crescendos

       off the walls

*(the following is an unpublished collaboration with Darrell Gray
and John Sjoberg, December 1971)*

WORKSHOP COURSE LIST FOR NEXT YEAR

8:282   Rhyme Workshop
8:283   Rhythm Workshop
8:285   Onomatopoeia: When to Use It (Seminar)
8:286   Beginning Linebreaks
8:286   Advanced Linebreaks
8:287   Iambs, Anapests, and Dactyls: Comparative Study
8:289   Caesuras: Now and Then (Historical Study)
8:290   The Literary Origins of Variable Feet Traced to Their Roots
8:291   Poetic Anatomy
8:292   The Economic Implications of Free Verse
8:293   The Psychology of the Caesura and the Collective Unconscious
8:294   Stability Theory in Fluid Rhyme Schemes
8:295   Applied Imagery
8:296   Literary Genes and Chromosomes
8:297   Introduction to Doggerel

8:300   Natural Hazards of Poetry & Doggerel
8:301b Field Trips with Pencils
8:301c How to Correct Incorrections
8:301d How to Write Right
8:301e The Poet in Action
8:301g Poetaster Laboratory
8:301h The Alphabet and Its Purpose in Reality
8:312   Successful and Unsuccessful Metaphors
8:313   The Disappearing End Rhyme

(the following from *Universitas* newspaper)

SKELETAL

The grass-lipped skull
Kisses only the wind,
And Time worships
At the breast-bone's tangent.
He has love
For the souls of rocks.

Dave has published extensively in periodicals and books. For a complete list of his published works we refer you to a nine-page listing in his biography, Dr. Alphabet Unmasked *by Joye Chizek and Tom Walz. The list includes novels, poetry books, children's books, poetry comics, teaching manuals, wordplay books, pseudonymous writings, stage plays, and more. All but the last of the following is confined to his poetry publications*:

Tilt. Toothpaste Press, 1971
Poems. Al Buck Press, 1971
Paper Comet. Happy Press, 1974
Snapshots from Europe. Toothpaste Press, 1974
Jnd-Song of the Golden Gradrti. Happy Press, 1977
Children Learn What They Live. Happy Press, 1979
The Cutist Anthology. Happy Press, 1979
Quicksand Through the Hourglass. Toothpaste Press, 1979
Birth of a Brain. With Steve Lavoie. Happy Press and Black Bart Press, 1985
Sacred Clowns, Holy Fools. With Steve Toth. Vortex Publishing, 2009.
Voyage of the Money. Broadside privately printed by Al Buck.

A Cigarette is a Glass of Milk Broadside. Toothpaste Press

"Lucy in the Sky With Darrell: Actualism." Exquisite Corpse online:
http://corpse.org/index.php?option=com_content&task=category&sectionid=4&id=17

STEVE TOTH

Born 1950 in Bemidji, Minnesota, grew-up in a Chicago south side suburb and later in Green Acres. He started writing very early, "just after he discovered crayons." Graduated West High School in Davenport, Iowa and matriculated at the University of Iowa in 1968, planning to study computer science, but then he discovered the Writers' Workshop and worked on his writing skills as an undergraduate in the Workshop.

Workshop teachers who stand out in his memory are Jack Marshall, Phil Dacey, Richard Harris, Norman Dubie, and Donald Justice. There he met kindred spirits who were to make up the group of Actualist poets of much local and some national notoriety, among them George Mattingly and Allan Kornblum. By 1972 Steve had earned his B.A. Only one person in each graduating class was allowed to claim a degree in Creative Writing, Poetry. Norman Dubie made sure Steve received this honor.

At first, Steve found in the Workshop a culture of literary exploration that was not bounded by the classroom walls. The students critiqued each other's writings, both on and off campus, inspiring one another. Soon the work of those who were to become the Actualists was being published in the ubiquitous little magazines of the time, as well as in underground newspapers. Unfortunately the Workshop would not accept their little magazine publications as homework assignments. Their work generated both local and national interest. The Actualists became for a time a phenomenon on the American poetry scene. Steve remembers that "We were like rock stars for a while, and there was a time when even our throw-away poems got published."

While at Iowa Steve met and married Sheila Heldenbrand. Together they edited *P.F. Flyer*, a single sheet of paper printed on both sides consisting of drawings, cartoons and poetry and printed offset. It was offered at no cost. Copies were left in local bookstores and in waiting rooms on campus and at the University Hospital. In spite of the modest scale of their efforts, the sheets found their way around the country and as far away as England.

Steve recalls the big split that took place within the Workshop between conservative and liberal teachers and students. The time came when quality instructors such as Anselm Hollo and Ted Berrigan were no longer approved of by the powers that were, and were no longer employed. According to Steve, the Workshop also appeared to be shifting the times of their sponsored readings to conflict with local Actualist readings. Since the Workshop had the clout and the money, just what kind of a threat did the Actualists pose to them, he wondered. But not everything went against them. Steve remembers an occasion when people from the Everson Museum in Syracuse came to town specifically to videotape the Actualists. Back home in Syracuse these people maintained an ongoing video display about the Actualists and even paid some Actualist poets to travel to Syracuse to read their poetry before live audiences and on television. Actualist poets were invited by Warren Woessner to read on WORT Radio in Madison, Wisconsin, and to Chicago at a theater called the Body Politic.

As the times changed, some Actualists stopped writing, and both Darrell Gray and Ted Berrigan, who suffered from depression and addiction, died early deaths. In the late 1990s after years of ill health, Steve again took up writing. He began to review his life through memories and by reading his old journals, and was able to be creative again. He found his new audience on the internet. There he didn't have to contend with faint-hearted editors or publishers.

Steve began to write about environmental issues, which made him popular with protestors at the San Diego Harbor Seal Rookery. He was published in *Earth First Journal* and *Voices of Israel*. He helped edit Israeli Yosy Flug's book for his sister Joye Chizek, herself a publisher and poet.

In 2003 Sheila and Steve moved to Crescent City, California to retire. He has no specific plans for the future other than to keep writing.

(from *The Actualist Anthology*)

THE TURQUOISE MECHANIC'S SON

i am the turquoise mechanic's son
sitting in the drive eating doughnuts.
beautiful cars – light as quick silver
my car has an agate gear shift knob
my car has a roof of broccoli
its tires strong as root beer
its interior a flour bag
blowing away in the wind

its headlights of mahogany
its dash made of water
it holds the road with loving tread
its steering wheel encompassing small talk of crickets
    and with it i hang a louie

    before me joyful
    after me joyful
    above me joyful
    below me joyful

73

all around me joyful
we are going for a joy ride
sound of joy when the engine turns over

SYMBOLS

Things are born out of ideas.
The mind of man gets an identity from each experience,
Consequently nothing touches our attentions
Which is left unexplained to some part of us.
Where the same things are not available
They are grown in the fertile human mind.
Thus the savage has an explanation
For every experience in his world of phenomena,
And the same things shape themselves in our minds.
But just how is this accomplished?
Men and women look out
Upon anything that rises spontaneously.
What they see is far closer to depicting
What they are thinking about
Than any other symbol which they could later devise
To mean the same thing.

MAGIC SAM

perculator
perculator
perculator
perculator
perculator
perculator
perculator
humpbackhumpback
perculator
perculator

THE GOLDEN GREATS

I take to this music
like a hound takes to the chase.
My head is a lion's head.
My shoulder running out the door.
Give my regards to the weather.
Relate my laundry
to the candle,
my eyes flying into it
like moths.
Later in the Super Value
I have to leave without my change.
Pushing my cart through the streets
while people with lassos

sing about home cooking

They impress me right out of my wits.

"Be more breathless"

I tell them.
"You're supposed to sound romantic
not hungry."
And then I'm gone.

POEM TO A POTTED PLANT

You think you have always lived
In this city,
But look
There is an ocean behind it.
The rest of you is a lamp
Made of driftwood;
But this lamp uses electricity,
And you want a lamp
That will shine because it likes you.

75

THE HANGED MAN

he boards the plane
but parachutes out
just after take-off

saying how could I think
of going anywhere
when I'm already here

the plane's shadow passes
as he falls & leans back
against the will of the wind

tumbling to upside down
now falling up
being in the sky comes easy

you know sometimes I think
I'm at the end of my rope
but really I'm just hanging around.

(*The following is provided by Steve*)

REMEMBERING DARRELL GRAY #1

No one could sum up a situation
like Darrell Gray could
Some of us were out walking one day
At the corner the light changed
Squealing tires
Two cars drag racing for real
Everyone was talking at once
Darrell said
Fun with matter

One night after a poetry reading
some of us got tricked
into crashing a party before it began
When we walked in the open door & saw all that food

laid out with nobody in sight
we concluded that it must be a decoy party
designed to keep unwanted guests occupied
while the real party was going on elsewhere
So we dug into our task
of eating everything in sight
& scrounging in the kitchen for more
Meanwhile the guy who'd invited us
was taking the most expensive bottle
of alcohol next door to wait
for the real fun to begin
Which it did the moment the real hosts came home
with horrified expressions
They thought our decoy party theory was incredible
& let us know we'd stayed long enough already
But for Darrell the night was always young
Once outside he wanted to go back in
Why leave now?
They were so congenial

Darrell trying to show me why nouns
are actually slow verbs
Even this chair is only a chair as long as it's chairing
Space is just the time it takes to move

Darrell heating cooking oil in a frying pan for popcorn
When it really got hot
he reached above the stove & opened
the cabinet door to find the bag
A panicked cockroach leaped out
Darrell said he was instantly overdone

magazines
Search For Tomorrow, Gum, Toothpaste, Suction, The Spirit That Moves
Us, Fervent Valley, Milk Quarterly, Out There, P F Flyer, Poetry Com-
ics, Animal Crackers, Me Too, New York Times, Mag City, Out of Sight,
Deronda Review, and Voices of Israel.

books

The Gathering. no publisher, 1970
Gold Rush. The Toothpaste Press, 1972
Morning Glories. (with Sheila Heldenbrand), Oyster Press, 1973
Rota Rooter. Frontward Books, 1977
Traveling Light. Blue Wind Press, 1977
Lost Angels. The Toothpaste Press, 1984
Love Whispers. (with Sajadi, Melartin & Ruiz),
    Poetry Vortex Publishing, 2005
The Queen of Crescent City. Poetry Vortex Publishing, 2005
Still Making Love Not War. Poetry Vortex Publishing, 2006
Redwood Dreams. Poetry Vortex Publishing, 2008
Sacred Clowns, Holy Fools. (with Dave Morice),
    Poetry Vortex Publishing, 2009

Steve has been published on a number of Internet sites including:
groups.yahoo.com/group/warriorpoets/
groups.yahoo.com/group/tothpoetry/
groups.yahoo.com/group/poetryvortex/
peace.wikia.com/wiki/PeacePoetset al

SHEILA (HELDENBRAND) TOTH

Born May 1951 in Winterset, Iowa, the oldest of four children, and raised on a farm. Played basketball after school. Sheila said she wanted to be a writer as soon as she'd learned to read.

She attended the University of Iowa from 1969 to 1973, expanded her field of reading at the university library, and "after falling in love, wrote more prolifically." In 1972 she married Steve Toth. She concentrated on writing poetry and fiction under the tutelage of Donald Justice and Tracy Kidder, as well as Patricia Hampl. Joe Haldeman of local and national science-fiction fame was also at the Workshop at this time.

Concurrently, Sheila was involved off-campus with the Actualists, and read at Wesley House and the Sanctuary Tavern, as well as doing some out-of-town readings sponsored by *Milk Quarterly* in Chicago and at the Syracuse Museum.

Her first contact with the Actualists was when George Mattingly asked her to submit some poetry for his magazine *Search For Tomorrow*. She didn't get to spend much time in the Kornblums' apartment, which was a central meeting place for the Actualists, since she had to work at the Herbert Hoover Presidential Library. It was Jim Mulac who asked her and Patricia O'Donnell to read poetry at The Sanctuary Tavern, where Jim hosted the readings.

Her dream prose poems received such an enthusiastic reception at an open-mic reading at Epstein's bookstore in Iowa City, that Morty Sklar forwarded her radical new work to Leonard Seastone of Tideline Press, who published it in a limited edition. Sheila was disappointed that these same dream prose poems had been rejected by Tracy Kidder for inclusion in a weekly worksheet at the Writers' Workshop.

Sheila worked on the *P.F. Flyer* with Steve Toth. "It had a lot of submissions, and poets such as fellow Hungarian from Bolinas, California, John Batki, who when traveling through Iowa City would pick up copies at the bus station. The Madison, Chicago, and Annapolis poets such as Dave Hilton, David and Maria Gitin, George and Suzette Swoboda and Neil Hackman would stay with us when in town for Actualist Conventions when we lived in married student housing at the Kennedy apartments on Dubuque Street and Hawkeye Court."

Dave Morice trained Sheila for his job of checking theses at the Graduate College. Then Mary Beyer recruited her to work in the communal daycare before she quit that job. Patrick Dooley also worked at that daycare for a while, teaching art. During this time, Sheila published a small book of the childrens' dreams for their parents.

While working at the Graduate College, Sheila met Jeannette Bryant with whom she began to work in the field of television scripts. They wrote the Carol Burnett skit where Carol snips off the tip of a cigarette with scissors from her purse in a restaurant. Their agent, Eve Montaign, was impressed with the Carol Burnett script and took them to meet Norman Lear.

In September 1976 the Toths left Iowa City for California, following fellow Actualists Darrell Gray, Tim Hildebrand, George Mattingly, and Liz Zima. Sheila taught in a nursery school there.

Just as her husband Steve was to stop writing for a time due to major health problems, Sheila too stopped dreaming and writing after a series of particularly frightening nightmares. She began dreaming again in 1997 and began again to record her dreams, which tended to be very lucid and reflected accurately people and events in her workplace. Her dream work continued as she became involved in a dream experiment with seventeen dream website owners in August 2001. Since she was subsequently invited to join a Great Dreams group that attempted to dream about earth changes, political trends and other dreams for the benefit of society, they all started dreaming some common symbols. For example: the group owner dreams about laundry as a symbol for group karma cleaning. Sheila dreams about animals that can be interpreted as Chinese and Zoroastrian astrological signs for dating predictions.

(from *The Actualist Anthology*)

GOD SAID TO THE ANGELS

God said to the angels,
should I make man?
The angels said, no,
what do you need with man
when you've got us?
so he burned them up.
Then he asked the next angels,
should I make man?
They said, sure.

THERE IS A LITTLE HOUSE

There is a little house.
Inside is an old woman.
Someone says:
The good eye projects,
the evil eye attracts light.
She has a good eye.
She has white hair.
My innermost fears
come popping out of her mouth.
She jumps onto the running board
of the red ford truck,
and whispers in the window
in my ear, "Don't worry
you're going to be happy now."

CONCENTRATION

fly flying away
wishes it could stay,
straight haired people
in curlers,
curly haired people
with little bricks hanging
on the end of each hair.
alms for the rich—
give me what I deserve.
oh, lord,
are you the same guy I saw
yesterday?
heads, toes
tits, ass
I hear it's simple.
minds all about
delicately out of balance
like slices of pie
that don't quite come together,
like bums sleeping in a circle
their heads all pointed towards the fire
their feet all pointing towards the stars.

A WOMAN NEEDED SOME MILK

A woman needed some milk from the store.
She walked to her tree and said
"John, bring home a half-gallon of milk."
That night her husband came home carrying milk.
A man who had overheard
questioned her about this wondrous tree
and told her about the telephone.
"Oh yes, we are very poor, or we too would have a telephone."

SNOW IS FOR TRACKING THE INVISIBLE MAN

The barn was on fire.
The guards were no longer needed,
nor boots, nor cap for his head.
But people yelling out of cars
made him self-conscious anyway.
A Volkswagen topped by a red light drove by.
Red sparks like hairs on edge flew out.
First his bones appeared
then blood, nerves, finally skin, features
and a tattoo of a rose.
He built a house for himself,
a weird woman, and birds.
Why did you come back? they asked him.
For love, for love.

EARL THE PEARL

I join a group of women and children
working to break out of a large
building. They tell me they've started
a tunnel under the table. I look at it
and it is only a few inches deep. A
short guy on a white rabbit with red
eyes rides up. Some, he takes their
breaths away in baggies, some he saves
for later. Just when we think we are
going to escape, the man comes in and
asks us to deliver a bag of sugar.
Then he says, "and by the way, take
them to the ovens." We wait in the
basement for the ovens to arrive.
They are elevators. Janitors float
a few inches off the floor.
Their faces are dark and beautiful.
They just work there. It is my last sight.

THE PRESIDENT IS NOT FUNNY
—or "How I fought the law and the law won."—*Bobby Fuller*

Who in his right mind
would want to rule the world?
That's what's scary.

There are those who want to take us over—
who say democracy is a degeneration of the feudal system.
Some bestsellers say "they've got us by our money."
Think about what you wouldn't have if they called that in.
And all this time they've been giving us coupons:
"Save 10 cents on your next refrigerator."

I know that feeling from when I was a thief.
SOMETHING FOR NOTHING
something happens to you.
suddenly you can have anything in the store.
you start having dreams about stealing the display windows.
you begin to think you've broken the law of the universe
and no one can stop you.

The day two plainclothes women put the finger on me
I had $1.75 past felony. In other words $21.75
or one-to-five years,
but they were willing to make it
three years probation—
the same as Agnew got—because I was just a kid.

There's that tap on your shoulder
"excuse me, haven't you forgotten something?"
you and the evidence are taken away by two cops;
and you're cured of one form of materialism.

But, for Mr. International Banker,
who's to say, "excuse me,
haven't you forgotten something?"
and the cosmos doesn't have a statute of limitations.

84

books

Morning Glories. with Steve Toth; Oyster Press, 1973
The World Is God's TV. Toothpaste Press, 1975
Prose Poems. Tidewater Press, 1975
Storie di Ordinaria Poesia. (anthology), 1982
5 Dreams. (broadside), Tideline Press

Her writings have also appeared in *Black Maria*, *Out There*, *Gum*, *Candy*, and *The Spirit That Moves Us*.

CHUCK MILLER

Chuck Miller was born in Kenney, Illinois in 1939. He began writing while working toward a B.A. in Philosophy at the University of Illinois Champagne-Urbana. Before coming to Iowa City to attend the Writers' Workshop in 1967, he spent time in Carbondale, Illinois, Austria, California (where he met Ken Kesey and Neal Cassady), New York City, and Denmark.

Chuck's luck turned sour when he was arrested for possession and sale of marijuana and LSD and was sentenced to the federal penitentiary in Terre Haute, Indiana where he received books and support from George Starbuck (head of the Workshop at that time) and Robert Coover. He was released after one-and-a-half years for good behavior with a job offer from

George Starbuck. Chuck later took the FBI to court and his felony conviction was wiped from his record when the judge ruled that the drug bust had been a set-up.

Chuck returned to Iowa City, renting a room at 214 East Court Street where Dave Morice lived. In 1971 he received an M.F.A., but like many other non-conformist graduates at the time, was unable to get an academic position. In 1972 he moved to a commune in Brattleboro, Vermont with his girlfriend Judy Lawson, returning to Iowa City in 1973. In addition to many readings and events in Iowa City, he has given readings throughout the Midwest in Iowa, St. Louis, Champaign-Urbana, Chicago, Milwaukee, Madison, and Kansas City, as well as in New York and London, often selling copies of his books for food and gas money. He worked as a migrant laborer, farm worker, factory worker, coffee picker, construction worker, freight picker, tree planter, dish washer, but also as a math tutor at times and taught English in Shijiazhuang, China, Trinec, Czech Republic, and several locations in Poland.

Perhaps the best way to describe Chuck Miller and his poetry is to quote some of the reviews of his books:
"These poems are solidly conservative and scribe a traditional line through Celine and Vallejo and Kerouac to show us there is still 'some way out, some right choice' with courage and integrity, in this society of intellect factories and Mad (ison Avenue) Dogs. It doesn't always have to be flip or hear-no-see-no-say-no. These poems were created in and of the often necessary darkness and solitude of the Honest One around the corner, down the street—the poet getting by, and very quietly, unknown to most

of the students, arts administrators and promising young who occupy, however briefly, a circle of shifting approval."
—Walter Hall's review of *Oxides* in *The Actual Now & Then* #4, 1976

"One of the last living American writers strongly influenced by the tradition of American socialist writers from the 1930s, most notably his friend and champion, the late Meridel Le Seueur and Jack Conroy. Another influence is the Beats from the 1950s, most notably Kerouac. He's author of a dozen collections of what he (deliberately) calls "proletarian" poetry, dealing with barren, desolate places, the strangeness of human interaction and the small tragic destinies of down-and-out America, whose plight remains invisible and out of sight to the powers that be."
—*Boris Gregoric's blog* September 2014

One of the few recordings of Chuck's melodious voice can be found on YouTube: https://www.youtube.com/watch?v=ECxtVxplSCs

(from *The Actualist Anthology*)

HOW IN THE MORNING

why always in the morning?
because you must begin your life over again each morning
you fumble for your shoes
the leather thongs stiff and cold
fumble with your fly
make sure your prick doesn't get caught in the zipper
and by then the shadows are stealing up grey and clean
the sun a later gamble
that might make it through this hung over sky
then the long walk out from the private shack of our dreams
barely holding together
to the car slowly disintegrating
if you can get it going
drive toward the world
only just functioning on the grey edge of night
with its slouched coffee slurpers
and unconscious donut gobblers

its shoe factories stitching on soles
for the tender feet of our souls
its bellowing trucks, posts and positions
sinecures, backbreaking sweats
being fed the slimy exhausts
of the constant velvet farts of our metal skins
sewn onto us,
and it is all simple, grey, clear
if you don't think about it
there are those with their great life's works
and those who must do these very same great life's works
maybe Vallejo is riding with you this morning
looking for work the same as you
and he says "Understanding that he knows I love him,
that I hate him with affection
and to me he is in sum indifferent, I signal to him,
he comes, and I embrace him moved,
So What! Moved ... Moved"
and I say to him "that was damn good Cesar
should we try the employment office today
or the toilet paper factory should we try
the donut factory once more to make that
graveyard donut shift, or maybe the mental hospital
to see if they have an opening in the laundry
I used to do the laundry thing folded sheets
off the mangel"
Cesar is saying
"go for the pop bottles, fuck all this other stuff
these wood bees, let's just collect pop bottles
that's the surest way"
and so the morning comes grey over the hills
you drop the washcloth on your cold feet
and fumble with the delicate
birds of morning
opening their cages

THE DUKE OF YORK (COURAGE)

death departs and I am drunk
on wine, on talk
we set sail again
through the needle's eye of the horizon
past the mists
stand at the bar and the yellow foam churns past our prows
mariners bound east
for the hanging gardens of Maya
"I have seen the white beaches in the sky"

bandy-legged boozers quaffing it down
with their mustachios and rakish dissolution
their sexes have travelled also extensively
now half stirring under tables
or shaping the jib of slacks
sad corporals in a defeated army
sallow lasses dressed like gay pirates
ships great busted figureheads
seeking a more myth-like, less found, port

then in the quiet wake of waves
the roar of talk and laughter abates
our animated gestures fall stuporous into dank lagoon
the primordial boozers stare of lost muddled helplessness
yet in back of that red eye still flash the lost continents
we might be a tavern full of old sea dogs
smuggled through the centuries
or any such bullshit half swashed dope runners story tellers
under the barmaid's beer rag of our washed up fates
we're simply children
thinking of beds for the evening
and warm sexed creatures for nestling

FOR JUDY

in the West day is drawn into the smelter of sunset
each grain of light and all that it illumined
we might be out on the plain
weeping, protesting, crying out
this loss so utterly absolute

instead there is the subdued silence of dusk
lights in windows burn stoically
with a sort of frail transcendence
as though an old woman
lifted unsteadily
her withered arm
for a last gesture at day

a lake of dark comes washing up
stars put forth pale blossoms

what I loved incinerated
in a smoldering weeping

a cry
so far
it is a wire scraping in the throat of childhood's distance
filament of innocence

there was a house
with a cheerful yellow light
a woman wet with luscious peace
with the dark of her meditating eyes
who waited in quiet half-lit rooms

who waits no longer
turns
and enters the smelter of night
the black factory

THINGS AS THEY ARE

going out half happy
or half angry or somewhat tired
nonetheless everything in this snow
looks back directly
with a stark clearness
as i walk through this nonessential winter day
beautiful in a way which is neither grandiose
nor too little
all the elements have announced themselves
now they break and reform
in ways that are almost recognizable

tonight stars creak
like leather harnesses
alone in the solitude
of winter rooms
feel the harness of night around your back
and belly
the icy bit in your teeth
and be pulling it
alone in the dark
know there is no way out
or through, except the long strange road ahead
in which you are the uncertain captain
of this tramp steamer your life
various companions changing through the years
like stars in the same constellation
burning intensely but too far
in their fixed orbits
and the special ones
that come terribly close
the tail of a comet passing over
your trembling body
causing strange atmospheric disturbances
pulling out great gravitational hunks

91

finally always coming back to the same worn self
a cave glowing darker with experience
and less comprehensible in its depths

but in summer's first fragrance
still to break off bits of the milky way
and see the evening star
rising over the dark blue drifting up from the sunset
and rejoice as though you were young once more
and saw the dawn of hope rising just beyond your reach

I WRITE FOR THOSE UNKNOWN

i write for those unknown who were born unknown
who sat up in bed years later born again
and died unknown even to themselves
who could not know what i say
i write for Verlaine still praying the pietas
in his cell in Belgium
i write because i cannot sleep for having visions
for Van Gogh who splashed my wall with joy
and who painted absolute reality
i understood this and was unalterably changed
i write because i return to my bed at night
like a convict to his cell
i write because i have given up all hope
and do not even know what i say
i write for no reason at all
because time is running out
and nothing ever changes
i write because there is a vast commune
spread over the earth
and we are all touching hands in the mist
laughing gently and with compassion
i write because nothing comes back
and i have lost treasures of the wildest imaginings
I write because i am chewing the last rag of solitude

and still find a kind of delirious nourishment there
i write because when i opened my pipes
out came a pineapple made of pain
i write to have my 2 cents worth of erratic song
and be part of the collective madness
i write because i am soon to sleep
and will rise tomorrow
to hawk my bones on the streets
just as you in your turn
will stumble half conscious
from your hovel
we will bump clumsily into each other
step back squinty eyed and suspicious
not recognizing nor understanding
go our blinded ways

REQUIEM: A SURREALIST GRAVEYARD

there was Nadja's glove flickering somewhere
under the Mazda bulb
which i think of now and then
an imaginary semi-transparent thing lost somehow
in what we could call a quantum of our love
a space-time geometry with its coordinate seam
unzipped onto the void
does the void collect our mad love
surely the only kind which could exist
like a soft blue grave yard
upside down in a telescope eye
clasping us with the love of its ether arms
poor Mickelson-Morley trying to prove ether love with mirrors,
mirrors we can only disappear into with Huertibus
their love too fathomless for our mortal dimensions
but the ether wind spills down sometimes
wetting our seared black cheeks
and we realize it must be the kindly blue grave yard,

or is someone basting the earth in silence?
a great baked apple stewing in space
the gigantic spoon up-lifted
i hear silence running over the curve of the sky
but there is something i have lost
which we all wore then, remember comrades?
the good luck glove
i have lost the good luck glove
it kept me going in this rain of sad asteroids
i have lost the good luck glove
my hand like a socket in space
wanders already on that journey to another star

books
A Thousand Smiling Cretins. Friend's Press, 1966
Cahoots. Seamark Press, 1971
Oxides. Seamark Press, 1976
Thin Wire of Myself. Friend's Press, 1980
Harvesters. Morning Coffee Chapbook, Coffee House Press, 1984
From Oslo—A Journey. Friend's Press, 1988
How in the Morning. The Spirit That Moves Us Press, 1988
Carnival Story (a Video). Todd Case, 1992
Northern Fields. Coffee House Press, 1994
Dead Dog (for Goo). Pearl City Press, 1997
Crossing the Kattegat. Mica Press, 2001
Dingleberry. Flipbooks, 2003
Parsecs to Go, Poems of Protest. Prairie Rose Press, 2013

DAVID HILTON
(1938–2005)

Partly in his own words (quotation marks)

"Born in Albany Hospital (California) in 1938. Grew up in San Lorenzo. Spent banal and depraved youth hanging around jukebox, pinballs, pool tables in an underground ten-lane bowling alley where I was a 'pin-boy' by trade and blew a teenage fortune on beer and white port.

Got a M.A. degree from California State College at Hayward between factory jobs and the Army. It was at Hayward that I met Darrell Gray in 1965 or 1966 and suddenly the past ten years of poetry lit up the sky. Through all-nighters of beer and the Stones, I discovered everyone from Bly to Wright to Merwin, Snyder to Creeley to Ginsberg, Neruda, Vallejo— first intuitions of Actualism. Later, O'Hara and his "school" became essential to me to go with my enduring love of Whitman and Roethke. As I turn forty the example of Dr. Williams [William Carlos Williams] grows ever more lucid and thrilling."

At the University of Wisconsin–Madison David became close friends with poet and editor Warren Woessner who also hosted a poetry and fiction reading program on WORT-FM. David became a Contributing Editor of Woessner's Abraxas Press. He and Warren frequently visited Allan and Cinda Kornblum in Iowa City and West Branch, Iowa until Warren

95

moved to New York City in 1981.

"After receiving an ABD degree (All But Dissertation) from Madison in 1971 I took a position teaching English at Anne Arundel Community College in Maryland."

David was a longtime member of the Maryland Writers Council. In 1984, the Maryland State Arts Council named him poet of the year.

(from *The Actualist Anthology*)

THE IMMIGRANT

Today, a bush is a bush to me
and a bird, a bird. They sit
in one-word rooms in my head.

Ashore, great garden genitals
rise and flow above the walls
of the serene empress's vast domain:

in broken Poetry the best I do
is point and mumble, "Flowers?"
I own precious few sounds for life.

Rootlets surviving stone, plunge of green-
tipped wings into lightning dusk,
moss-softened boulders strewn down

white talus—all are foreign photographs,
but of my promised land! Well, I'm fresh
off the boat, staring hard, clutching

my ragged satchel of sounds.
I figure I'll be cheated blind.
But that's all right—I'm here.

I TRY TO TURN IN MY JOCK

Going for the jump-shot,
Giving the kid the head-fakes and all

Till he's juked right out the door of the gym
And I'm free at the top with the ball and my touch,
Lofting the arc off my fingertips,
I feel my left calf turn to stone
And my ankle warp inward to form when I land
A neat right angle with my leg,
And I'm on the floor,
A pile of sweat and sick muscles,
Saying,
Hilton,
You're 29, getting fat,
Can't drive to your right anymore,
You can think of better things to do
On Saturday afternoons than be a chump
For a bunch of sophomore third-stringers—
Join the Y, steam and martinis and muscletone,
But, shit,
The shot goes in.

THE MAN UPSTAIRS

Against a yellow accordion
he loses the War always. His gray voice
sings each night the kamikaze
pasting his buddy to the bulkhead.

1944. He hides the year inside
his trousers like a treasure still
alarming him. It sirens him down
the stairway that stops at my door.

He says he knows the arms of the police
are really rubber hoses
and if you give a woman an inch
she'll cut it off. And since

the silent mailman commits
only the big time thefts (the letter

from his mother announcing her rebirth)
he knows I've stolen his dish towels

on order six years from Proctor & Gamble
in Kansas City. He holds nothing personal
against Kansas City—all his friends
have vanished everywhere,

the caves go under everywhere.
And all of them were cowards anyway,
flattening themselves into extra coats
of mole-colored paint stuck

to the turrets of their battle stations
as the zeros fell drunkenly
upon the decks. At age 18
to survive as a coat of mole-colored paint,

after the attack to be chipped off
slowly, daily by the rubber hoses of
cops, bartenders, mailmen, landlords –
is only what a coward deserves though it is hard.

For such philosophy the Government
thinks he is 100 percent and
rewards him accordingly. So he
has time for his music

that rises each night like the whine
of an ancient propeller,
keeps rising
until he throws his body against the floor.

APRIL 29, 1975

We are
at peace. It is
as if the War

were a hideously deformed

idiot child
who, despite our

best care,
finally died.
And now we grieve

over this shallow
grave
called Peace.

LATE NOVEMBER, MADISON

Across the lake the lights
of the rich people
signal a code warm money.
We stand in a room
where a dog is yawning, and a boy
is reading his poems
written, he murmurs, from the bottom
of a pit of acute paranoia.

A mile of late November
to those stars across the pit
of water. Farm income will fall
again this year. Massive layoffs
from the second biggest
payroll in town. And
the poetry is poor,
is terrible, and we applaud.

THE SECOND PART

When the old bitch barks at the bottom of my iron backstairs
a music brims the dark flowing back home
and I'm helpless thinking She's come!...
then the noise drains and leaves
a lapping at my kitchen window...

99

tiny tongues laving a stiff lover!...sometimes I even look,
she is never there.

I am trying to say that in the silence
of this city I dread
that dog's bark... ,

among the rotting garbage cans
that dumb old girl tethered on a ten-foot rope
waking in rain to howl her gray dreams...
what loneliness crazier than hers?
Drunken growls and whimpers rise
from her owners downstairs.

2

I confessed a year ago, "I've nothing for your birthday."
"Just write a poem for me," she said.
And I did
and (better than America) it was
fleshed with pride and wonder
that we did love each other...

oh the laughter
in that poem awoke
my terror
that is its mate...
things have ways of evening out.

And this poem I'm willing now
is but the second part
graceless as a grieving hound
to that poem, that paean, that mock
I was so dumb to think
would need no further work.

CHRISTMAS POEM

There is nothing to complain of now
but happiness. The ice is warming itself

against the belly of a black child.
For a few hours I know that I can save no one.

Men have gathered inside footballs to warm themselves.
They are driving to the tropics in powerful ashtrays.
They are locked in a deserted drugstore, each singing
carols to his mother's beauty.

But I am taxed
only with this happiness that rose up
in the middle of the day like a golden hobo
walking to a strange
street, asking
for his son.

POEM

I want to be one of those poets
who owns a farm in Vermont or Kentucky
whose address is just his name
above the name of a town New Charity or Halcyon.

I almost cry when I think of that poet
driven from bed by the green cries of birds
and by the clean sunlight pouring in through the window
dappled and cooled by the trees right outside.

That queer feeling hits my belly when I think
of him cracking the crust of ice on whatever the water is kept in
and bringing the water again and again in cupped hands to his face
then drying his face with a blue flannel shirt
and putting the damp shirt on over bare muscles.

Then he walks softly into the dawn-shadowed kitchen
God! and he sits down with pencil and paper at a rough wooden table
and rubs the pencil strongly all across and down the paper
until a poem appears, which doesn't take very long.

Ah now the woman comes in, her robe does not cover her breasts

101

so casual and lovely as sleepily she puts the water on to boil…
soon the hiss of hot water poured from a pot, then coffee smell.
The sudden barking of a hound outside silences the birds.

The poet embraces his wife in the still brightening kitchen.
He is passionately careful for she is greatly pregnant.
A breeze slips in the open back door and flutters the poem on
    the rough table.
It is a poem in celebration of the coming of their child.

books
The Shot Goes In. Quixote Press, 1969
Moving Day. Abraxas Press, 1969
Not Me and Other Poems. Modine Gunch Press, 1970
The Man Upstairs. Modine Gunch Press, 1971
Huladance. The Crossing Press, 1976
The Candleflame. The Toothpaste Press, 1976
Inspector Duval's Toughest Case (with Tim Hildebrand).
    New Erections Press, 1970
Return to the Rat Planet (with Warren Woessner). Abraxas Press, 1972
Mr. and Mrs. Big Money (with Woessner, Hildebrand, Stephens).
    Abraxas press, 1975
Wish You Were Here! (with Woessner). Abraxas Press, 1976
Penguins. Floating Island Publications, 1980
No Relation to the Hotel. Coffee House Press, 1989
Smoke of My Own Breath. (with Peter Genovese), Garlic Press, 2001
Living Will. Coffee House Press, 2007
Quickly Aging Here (anthology). Doubleday Anchor, 1969

David's poetry appeared in *The Yale Review, Poetry, Abraxas, The North Stone Review, Modine Gunch, Mandala, Drunken Boat, Roots Forming, South, Minnesota Review, Poet Lore, Poetry Northwest, The Northland Review, Beloit Poetry Journal, Exquisite Corpse, The Iowa Review, New American & Canadian Poetry, Washington Review of the Arts, The Spirit That Moves Us* and other literary magazines.

JOHN SJOBERG
(1944–2017)

John was born in Aurelia, Iowa, 1944, which he calls the real Iowa: surrounded by cultivated fields, the Little Sioux River valley, fishing, walking. His father was a banker; his mother died when John was born, and he was raised by his new mother, Beth.

In 1962 he moved to Iowa City to earn his B.A. degree, then went to San Francisco in 1967 to be part of "The Summer of Love." During that time and upon his return to Iowa City in 1967 where he entered the poetry program in the Writers' Workshop, he recalls partying with such literary lights as Allen Ginsberg, Robert Creeley, Anselm Hollo, Ted Berrigan, Gary Snyder, and Kurt Vonnegut, among others. In the Workshop he studied with Anselm Hollo, Ted Berrigan and Marvin Bell.

Much of John's writing occurred in his art journals, which he brought with him wherever he went. These works combined art, lyrics, and poetry on the page in a neat felt-tipped spacey-style unique to John. Many of these works were signed "jon ii" which seemed to represent his persona when he was "off his meds."

John is a gentle person who cares immensely about the world and the people in it. He loved his cat, Liz, and often spoke of his first love "Peggy

Pureheart." For a time he lived in a room above the Montessori School where he provided after-hours janitorial services. His room was full of drawings, poems, album covers and objects covering the walls, and poems and books scattered everywhere. When moved to a new location, he was turning in circles in the center of the room tugging at his hair wondering how he could possibly start packing.

Years later John moved to Cape Cod for a short time before returning to Iowa City. He worked as a janitor at J.C. Penney until developing multiple sclerosis, a disease he still struggles with.

John was a regular participant in the Actualist readings, gatherings, and collaborations written on the shared typewriter at our apartment at 214 E Court Street.

John's poetry book, *Hazel* was published by Toothpaste Press in 1976. This was one of only two books I (*Cinda*) designed after taking Harry Duncan's typography class (the other was my class project, Steve Toth's *Gold Rush*). Toothpaste Press also published *Some Poems On My Day Off* in 1984, illustrated with linocuts by Stuart Mead, and printed in a limited edition of 500 copies signed by both John and Stuart.

Some Poems on My Day Off
by John Sjoberg with Linoleum Blocks by Stuart Mead

George Mattingly had this to say:
"John Sjoberg is the Artaud of modern poetry, and *Hazel* is the unexpurgated chronicle of a compassionate mind in body in universe."

John was also published in *Luna Tack*, *Toothpaste Magazine*, and *Me Too*.

George Mattingly had this to say:
"John Sjoberg is the Artaud of modern poetry, and *Hazel* is the unexpurgated chronicle of a compassionate mind in body in universe."

John was also published in *Luna Tack*, *Toothpaste Magazine*, and *Me Too*.

(from *The Actualist Anthology*)

WE TRY NOT TO TOUCH SO CLOSE

We try not to touch so close to our hearts,
But the night's unavoidable mind has made u
Try to bind our lives with
Strings we cannot find.
Its deep placed calls of softness
Draw our threadful thoughts
To hearts that are not there.

This compelling conversation avoids
The definition of our indispensable sighs.
This silence is all we need. We hear
The heart of love, and wait to see
Its daylight dawning, and stay the day into eternity.

OVERALLS

mary wears them
light blue

    she even wears a gold
sweater underneath
     & no one can define how
she walks, when she is
wearing them.

    O, she carries it over
when she's in other clothes,
yet have you ever seen a farmer
in a suit?

  well, mary can play a flute,
either-way, but is most lovely

   in her overalls.

AN ANSWER

why did george washington
try to kill himself?

it was morning and so george
had a cup of coffee. this
wasn't unusual. the ritual
of drinking a carefully poured
cup of coffee was
             the beginning
of the day. he had red sox
on. this was a rarity for

revolutionary times. (red
dye for sox was not invented
until 1833)
                    george's cat
was playing in the bed-
room. martha had gone
for the day. she'd been
leaving the house rather
early these last few days.
she usually left with jerry,
the indian cook for the
washington family.
            (jerry was a bright young
brave, since he'd had an
education back in the early days
days when he worked for the
measurement research corporation.)

                    the beginning
of the day. george looked out
of the house at the river and
all the maples that had
grown on this, his famous
plantation. george was re-
calling all the red-orange
maple leaves he'd picked
yesterday. it had been sunset then. their pet
peacocks had been strutting
all over the closely cropped lawn.
George felt good remembering
the peacocks. they always
reminded him of how terribly
immortal
            the washington
name would become. "ancestors
and descendents," said george

to himself in his

dove white kitchen.

THOUGHTS

You have a headache Rimbaud.
You have an ashtray on your head.
You have a headache and you're sick.
The ward has gotten your nerves
To get up to get a glass of water.
You are really tired out, tonight,
And you're awake and thirsty.

There's a pipe and tobacco
on the mahogany table.

THE DEATH OF DEMOCRACY

So, i finished another bottle of coke. while sadly
I have finished a 2nd article on the murders that
            went on in Santiago, Chile, of Allende
& his friends.

Those who committed these crimes did not come to
their Presidente's Palace like men with their guns,
or meet him face to face. Oh no! Unhuman monsters,
they stayed a very great distance away, saying, "You
have three minutes in which to surrender." Only then,
from some military base, some base hidden from all
human eyes did they send jet fighter-bombers

            to bomb the Presidential Palace.

For, all this time these monsters knew that the
people, the people of Chile, the workers gathered
together in the factories, only had handguns with
which to fight
            for Freedom won by election.

CINDA (WORMLEY) KORNBLUM

I grew up on a farm in Newton, Iowa and with the aid of a Maytag Scholarship attended the University of Northern Iowa in Cedar Falls for one year, then transferred to the University of Iowa. Actualist ties go back to Newton High School where I met and dated George Mattingly and later took a few bus rides from Cedar Falls to Iowa City to visit him where he lived in Ted and Sandy Berrigan's basement. I met Allan when he stopped by my workplace in 1970 to sell me a copy of Toothpaste Magazine. He asked me to help carry a 2' x 6' EAT sign he'd bought from Robert Harris to his apartment. One thing led to another and I found myself a part of the Iowa City poetry scene.

Friends congregated regularly in the apartment we shared with Dave Morice at 214 East Court Street until Urban Renewal replaced the house we lived in with forty-four living units. The Actualists thrived on the energy that flowed through the streets of Iowa City. In the early years Allan would sell a couple copies of *Toothpaste Magazine* on the street and we would have enough for a meal at Leo's or Hamburg Inn #1. We would stop at The Mill to see if Dave Morice was playing pinball, chat with one of the book-sellers or check to see who might be hanging-out at Donnelly's Pub. People even visited us when we weren't home. It was a lively scene with frequent poetry readings, parties, and visiting writers from nearby states and others who stopped on their way from one coast to the other via Interstate 80.

Allan and I got married in August 1972 and bought a house in West Branch "on contract" from Allan's printing mentor, Harry Duncan. Toothpaste Press operated out of our home in West Branch with the center of operations on the dining room table. We shared the house with apprentices and renters for a few years (Liz Zima, Jim Hanson, Steve Levine, Jim Mulac), and others came from Iowa City to work on the books (Ellen Weiss, Alan Frank, Al Buck, David Duer, and more). Allan hitch-hiked to and from Iowa City, lining up occasional printing jobs en route until he learned to drive.

My 1975-77 diary is an endless list of people, parties, restaurants, movies, plays, art events, and readings. It was a wonderful time, and I'm so happy there are others who are taking the time to catalog and describe the events that occurred. The Toothpaste Press and Coffee House Press archives are available at the University of Iowa Library in Special Collections. If you can find a copy of the 1972 *Hawkeye* (University of Iowa yearbook), you'll see what an influence the Iowa City magazines had. I graduated and Allan didn't, but pages 54–57 are devoted to *Toothpaste, Gum, Suction, Search for Tomorrow, typewriter* and other local magazines, and you'll find a photo of Glen and Harry Epstein at their book store on pages 110–11. We knew we were living in Poetry City, U.S.A.

(from *The Actualist Anthology*)

HEY ANIMAL—EAT THIS POPCORN

If you want to lead a calf
you have to know everything about yourself—

111

A full skirt flapping in the wind may threaten him
Every movement calculated, slow
as though you are part of the earth
growing imperceptibly
toward the animal.

It is my hand that is feeding you daily
It is my hand you can trust.

Then WHAMMO!
You and the calf are at the fair
You have taught him to trust you
so he won't jump at the applause
won't kick the kids who offer him popcorn
so he'll stand tall & square
when the bidding begins

SUNDAY

Yesterday I went to pick up the sack
of groceries
    & hit myself in the jaw.
Today I dropped the whole salt shaker
in the applesauce.
If that's love then I feel it strongly.

THE HONEYMOONERS

When a youngster
I thought they were saying "celery"
not salary.
The green crisp stuff
somehow a focus of the grown-up world.
My father didn't have a
salary: he had a farm.
And just as I wondered what city folks
did with their garbage if they had no pigs
I wondered why wives nagged their husbands
to ask the boss for more celery.

College years solved the celery question.
Along with the mayonnaise & ketchup
celery was the only food still in the refrigerator
at the end of the month.

WHILE THE GARDEN GROWS
    for Allan

Morty calls from the halfway house
either he's got car trouble
or a new girl. Our friends are so
predictable and we are too.
You have tried to draw a picture
of society's pliers—
I have tried to write a poem about Mason jars
We had to try it to know it wouldn't work
How else would we be here together now listening
to the rain while the garden outside (hopefully) grows.

ABC'S

Dog goes after cat
Cat goes after bird
Bird goes after air

113

SEQUITUR: A LOVE POEM
   for Allan

After ice-ages   come heaven & hell
After oceans   come plains & plants
After Eisenhower   comes you, my dear

After 'old man'   comes the undertaker
After temptation   comes 'overdrawn'
After forgetfulness   comes the foam

After illusion   comes sadness
After profit   comes the ordinary
After employability   comes the mobile home

A FLOWERPOT IS AN ASHTRAY

A flowerpot	is an ashtray.
A can of beer	is an ashtray.
A shoe	is an ashtray.
A litterbox	is an ashtray.
A toilet	is an ashtray.
A shirt pocket	is an ashtray.
The sidewalk	is an ashtray.
An aspirin box	is an ashtray.
Mashed potatoes	are an ashtray.
A bed is	not an ashtray.

(the following provided by the author)

WARM WINTER GOOD-BYE POEM

On this fine
spring day of snow

the neighbor's heart goes out
clearing the drifts

and I watch him shoveled
into the ambulance

wailing to friends & relatives
down the street
Town of West Branch, Iowa

The snow
so white across the garden

I want some color!
like maybe plums on the tree—

supple drops of purple would be
the only color in the universe today—

or tomatoes!
juicy red on the feathered snow.

Young mother earth is out today!

Awakened by the first days of spring
it's time for a night on the town!

She dons a white dress
and feathered boa,

lips painted red like tomatoes
and her nails & nipples
purple as plums …

If our youth
could come back to us

again & again
like the spring,

time could collapse
into the geographical sphere

whirling our house suddenly
back to 214 E. Court Street, 1972,

and overhead
like shooting stars

115

our friends arrive
from scattered cities

the poems they carry in their hands
getting slightly wrinkled
by the fond embrace…

a loving kiss
to warm the winter nights of our ninety's

neatly mounted
on scrapbook pages:

the collected good-bye kiss;
the memory of those we love.

3/25/78

magazines
Alternative Press, Buffalo Gnats, Dental Floss, In The Light, Iowa Woman, Me Too, The Spirit that Moves Us, typewriter, and probably others.

anthologies & other
Pushcart Prize II
The Burg: A Writers' Diner, edited by Marybeth Slonneger, included her
    "Late Night at the Hamburg Inn"

book
Bandwagon. Toothpaste Press, 1976

Cinda edited a newsletter, *The Actual Now & Then* in the mid-1970s.

ALLAN KORNBLUM

(1949–2014)

Allan was born in Beth Israel Hospital in New York City and spent his first year in Stuyvesant Town. He lived in Everett and Chelsea, Massachusetts, and attended high school at Pierre S. Dupont High in Wilmington Delaware. He enrolled as a voice major at New York University, and after dropping out worked as an usher at Filmore East and as a postal clerk at the U.S. Postal Service, both in New York City, and took writing classes at The New School and Saint Marks Poetry Project.

After finding out that Ted Berrigan and Anselm Hollo were teaching in Iowa City, he hopped aboard a Greyhound and made the cross-country trek to Iowa. He attended undergraduate workshop classes and again dropped out. But one class got his attention—Introduction to Typography, taught by Harry Duncan, which began a long career of letterpress printing, founding Toothpaste Press and later Coffee House Press as described in "A History of Toothpaste and Coffee House Presses" elsewhere in this book. He was an enthusiastic participant in the Actualist movement. His marriage to Cinda Wormley, an Iowa farm girl, lasted until his death in November, 2015. He received numerous awards including the Kay Sexton Award in 2012 for long-standing dedication and outstanding work in fostering books, reading and literary activity in Minnesota; the American Book Award in 1997 for Special Achievement as Editor and Publisher;

Literary Market Place Award in 1994 for Adult Trade Books; The American Institute of Graphic Arts Book Show Citation for Excellence in 1991, 1992, and 1993, and eleven Chicago Book Clinic Design Awards.

(from *The Actualist Anthology*)

HER HAIR IS WET

> *And behold the bee of sleep*
> *At the umbrella's tip.*
> —Reverdy

The soft lips of the heat register
Open, breathe, and above it particles of air
Solidify into furniture.
For no reason, you feel as if you should
Know the young girl in the zebra striped coat
Sitting on the newly formed and hovering davenport
And you start to say…
But she interrupts. My hair is wet, I hope
the plush of this divan isn't being ruined
I'd best walk around
I came in to get out of the rain.
You take her hand and lead her into the yellow kitchen.
Taffeta curtains are stuffed in a vase on the table
violets and grapes frame the windows
With the beginning and end of summer
Il pleut, she turns from the window eating a grape
Il pleut, she says again
And takes the memory of coffee you offer.

THE TRUCKERS

Move objects we desire
Closer to us
Almost 'within' our grasp
Like love which we know can't
Be held or bought

Yet we can smell
Yet can the wheels
Support the weight of what's in back
Of our minds, a sandwich
Perked up by the crisp vegetables
Living dreams that wouldn't crunch
If they weren't fresh
The driver knows this
And cares about the miles.

ALL THAT GLITTERS

There are limits to how long we live.
We are here because our parents were here.
Spring, summer, fall, winter, spring.
Sure aren't all that many great themes.
Iron rusts and silver tarnishes, but
all that glitters IS gold.
The bible tells me so.
The bible and Hegel, struggling from the
gloom of his books towards the kitchen
to see what the possibilities look like
from that angle.
Opening the window, he holds out a beer stein,
and an angel pees into it.
Drinking later with gusto, he wonders
why philosophy seems so pallid compared
to soccer on an autumn afternoon,
or Henry Ford's new factory in Detroit, U.S.A.

AWKWARD SONG FOR MY SISTERS

Sometimes the flautist's hands
grasp the flute awkwardly.

Now and then the dancer's body moves
into, then out of a clumsy position.

119

Occasionally the poet stutters
lovers sit on the bed to a loud thump.

Often one corner of the coffin
slips while lowered into the grave,

and the lurch brings
another wave of tears.

Is there a more graceful
shape than a tear,

or a more unselfconsciously
awkward gesture than weeping?

Sometimes it rains for a week, then
surprise, the sun shines bright

and every object seems to have
hard edges...colors clash...

nothing seems to soften the awkward song.
But it continues like light,

like an arm around a shoulder,
the artist adds another shadow,

the flautist a trill,
the dancer a whirl,

and soon grass will grow
over our mother's grave.

3 DAYS AFTER FATHER'S DAY
for Seymour Kornblum and John Wormley

I'm sitting on the second floor of my house in West Branch
Iowa looking across the rolling fields at interstate 80.
To my left some 1,200 miles
My father is at his office, organizing the data for his
Ph.D. thesis, he is 53, living near Philadelphia,
Working in Philadelphia, proving

That happiness physically retards the aging process.
Much closer to my right, only about 100 miles west,
Cinda's father is doing whatever must be done
To make the corn and soybeans grow.
When we visit the Wormley farm we sleep in the corner
Of the room, the exact spot where he was born
"Watch Out!" he jokes he knows about that kind of energy
Every year the corn and beans come up, a few new calves
He is a good German farmer.
I have been reading H.G. Wells'
Outline Of History and Cinda and I are certainly part of
The Great Pattern—mixing racial stocks.
I am semitic mixed with…no doubt some Russian or
Central Asian, Wells says there was a Central Asian tribe, the
Alans and there must be some psychic link, well there might be.
And Cinda, Aryan plus probably in the past
A little from the Mongol tribes that swept through Europe
Her eyes are almost oriental sometimes.
The Des Moines Sunday Register quotes Rabbi Heschel,
'But I would say to young people that in spite of the
negative qualities they may discover in their fathers,
they should remember that the most important thing
is to ponder the mystery of their own existence.'
The Des Moines Sunday Register also ponders the existence
of interstate 80, we humans are so impressed by physical
Things and Wells says the springtime human sacrifice
Spread throughout the world because it was impressive
Below my window is my first vegetable garden
I close my eyes and imagine a human sacrifice – it is impressive.
I open my eyes and there is interstate 80
I can see that 'occurrence' is spatially perceived.
That idea did not occur to me but when Darrell pointed it out
I flashed I laughed and said this is part of what makes living in
Iowa City worthwhile! and Dave and Cinda who were there too, agreed,
I said all the wheels in my head are turning and the wheels
on the cars are turning as they move from one side of my window

121

To the other and pass out of sight, East or West as Darrell's
Incredible diagrams showed, consciousness is outside space and time, i.e.
Hello Dad, you here? have a beer
Hello John, you here? have a beer
We all want to be accepted, to be high,
Between these ideas and the world sometimes damn hard
To get up in the morning, sometimes so exciting
I never want to sleep, then I do sleep
In my house in West Branch Iowa with Cinda
With my father and mother with her father and mother
We all sleep together when we sleep

SOMETHING PASSIONATE FOR CINDA

we are not the ones who are afraid of science
but neither are we the ones whom it aids
for I am still bored.
I wish a cyclone of love would whirl us away.

like Pecos Bill, but not quite.
the structures of our lives might crush us
when the tornado tears trees and buildings
from their roots and foundations.

I wanted to write you a love poem
to tell you how beautiful were the leaves
in the trees outside, but I was too bored.
I wanted to do something physical

like chop the trees down, or like
delivering the mail, but not quite.
like listening to a recording of the breeze
in the yellow leaves of those trees.

no, a stereo recording of the sunset
accompanying a silent film of a pianist
playing his piano for an hour and a half.
science doesn't deliver our mail,

but at least we can talk about
the latest-developments-in-science
we can't talk about the mail for long
before we're bored. now that I think of it

I wouldn't want to talk forever of science
either, neither would you. I'm blue.
I'm bored is what's the matter and I feel
as if I ought not to be as I'm in love with you

(the following from *Gum #6*)

THE PINBALL MANIFESTO

Every poem should be like
A game of pinball.
Lights should flash,
Bells should ring,
Numbers should spin,
And in the back of the readers' minds
They should always be hoping
For that free game.

magazines
quite a few, including many from the Iowa City scene:
Abraxas, Asphalt, Candy, Caryatid, Clown War, Gum, In the Light, Mag City, Me Too, Milk Quarterly, North Stone Review, New York Times, P.F. Flyer, Search For Tomorrow, Stone Press Weekly, Stone Wind, Suction, Toothpaste, typewriter...

books
Famous Americans. self-published, 1970
Tight Pants. Toothpaste Press, 1972
Good Morning: 14 Sonnets (with Darrell Gray). J. Stone Press Weekly, 1975
The Salad Bushes. Seamark Press, 1975
Threshold. Toothpaste Press, 1976
Awkward Song. Coffee House Press, 1980

articles

A Case for Type. *Publishers Weekly*, April 27, 2009

Henry Knox: Founding Father (and Bookseller). *Publishers Weekly*, August 26, 2013

In The Beginning Was The Word. *Rain Taxi* 16:4 / Winter, 2011

The Word: Heard It Through the Grapevine. *Rain Taxi*, 17:1, Spring 2012

The Word: What the Hell is It? *Rain Taxi*, 17:2 / Summer 2012

The Word: Bird Tracks. *Rain Taxi*, 18:1 / Spring 2013

MORTY SKLAR

*Parts of the following that talk about my The Spirit That Moves Us Press
have not been elaborated upon in order to avoid repetition in what appears
in "History of The Spirit That Moves Us Press" later in this book.*

Originally from Sunnyside, Elmhurst, and Jackson Heights, Queens, New
York City, I was inspired by the natural-voice aesthetics of the Iowa City
Actualists (when I came to Iowa City in 1971), the Beats, and the New York
Poets. The prose of Jack Kerouac also inspired my poetry writing.

"Morty Sklar writes from an honesty and courage of the heart. For that
I salute him, and all his peers, his colleagues, who share this inexorable
dedication."—*Isabella Gardner*

At high school graduation, having no inclination toward any profession and not wishing to join my father in the family small hardware store
business, I volunteered for the draft into the Army in 1954. Upon seeing
in basic training, parachutes blossom in the sky in a promotional movie
about the 82nd Airborne, I volunteered for it. I completed jump school, got
my wings and was proud that jump boots were considered part of a class A
uniform when I went home on leave. I otherwise had little to be proud of.
After four courts-martial, the last consisting of disobedience and direspect
toward both an officer and non-commissioned officer, I was dishonorably
dischanged in 1956 after serving eighteen months of a five year sentence in
the disciplinary barracks, where at least I learned to type, and also trained

125

for a weightlifting competition that I won. Ten years later my discharge was changed to an honorable one through the efforts of my guardian angel older cousin Norma.

I attended Queens College in Flushing, New York, but still without an inclination toward any profession, I later took a fiction-writing course at The New School where I learned a basic lesson for my prose—something I also applied to my poetry writing: On a piece I'd written, my teacher said "Too general—be more concrete."

I rented a room in Manhattan and shaped-up at employment agencies for "extra" positions as a waiter or counterman, working many restaurants and coffee shops from Greenwich Village to Harlem. At a lunch counter in Greenwich Village around 1958, I dropped a coin in the jukebox and chose Horace Silver's "Señor Blues." A man I had served said to me, "You dig Horace, huh?" and we talked about jazz. The man invited me to a friend's apartment where I met two other guys, all of whom became my first adult friends at age twenty-three. The pot we smoked, as well as the "Symphony Sid" all-night jazz program, relaxed me enough to enjoy their company. One of my friends would read contemporary poetry aloud, poetry that appealed to me even though an anthology I had once purchased titled something like Fifty Great Poems left me feeling that maybe I needed to study poetry in order to appreciate it. Of course I had never felt that way about jazz.

We dabbled in speed and heroin, but I went beyond dabbling and became strung-out on heroin for six years, my only clean time being short incarcerations and trips to Creedmoor State mental hospital.

Serendipity brought me, on November 3rd, 1966 to the birth of a therapeutic community rehab program. I was one of the first residents in the establishment of the program, which was renamed Phoenix House after a newsletter another resident and I created titled *The Phoenix*.

In the Re-entry stage of the program before graduation from Phoenix House in 1969, I met my first true love, who not long after returned to her hometown in Denver. I had been attempting an autobiographical novel, but emotion and impatience had poetry pouring out of me.

With my first full-time job in a long time, I resumed saxophone lessons and continued to write poetry. I decided to not go to poetry readings or

126

mingle with other poets until I was fairly centered in myself as a poet. Then one day I went to an open reading where I planned to read a poem or two of my own. I started to chicken-out and was glad nobody knew I'd intended to read. But after hearing some others read, I took heart, feeling that my poems were at least as good as theirs. After the reading a man who called himself John Cabbage (real name, Giovanni Gabucci) came up to me and said he liked my poems, and invited me to his place where he perused my notebook. His first comment was, "Your lines here are short, unlike the way you read them, which is more natural." Afterwards, I wrote a poem, "Giovanni Gabucci," based on the strange and adventurous life of the man as he revealed himself to me that day.

My main inspiration for writing poetry were the novels of Jack Kerouac, but my poetic efforts were reinforced later on in Iowa City by John Schulze, head of the Photography Department at the University of Iowa in 1972, which he established in opposition to the then-head of the Art Department who didn't acknowledge photography as an art. When we students posted our photos on the wall for feedback, various grad students noted such things in my photos as "blacks not black enough," "whites not white enough" and so on. My mentor and inspiration said after a pause, "Morty, your photographs are like your poems, and your poems like your photographs. Wonderful images." Rest in peace, dear mentor and friend.

In 1970 I wished to join a poetry workshop at the 92nd Street Y and submitted several poems to its leader, Isabella Gardner. Isabella, who came from an upper-class Boston family whose security she shunned for her independence, revealed her street smarts by saying in her acceptance letter that the workshop would be held at her apartment in the Hotel Chelsea—which the Y wouldn't have approved of had she told them.

The ten poets in Isabella's workshop were all different—which at the time I had taken for granted. It wasn't until I got to Iowa City that in many instances I wasn't able to tell if some poems were written by the same person or different ones—until I came in contact with, and was welcomed into, the community of poets outside the purview of the University of Iowa Writers' Workshop who came to be known as the Actualists.

Between the end of Isabella's workshop and my leaving New York City the following year, I rented a $40 per month room on West 20th Street in

Manhattan and worked for my father a few days a week. One day I was out making deliveries when a wave of thoughts and emotions overcame me to the point where I had to pull the old station wagon over to a curb and begin writing what became a three-page poem for my father titled "Jarashow"—the name of an old hardware store in Jamaica, Queens that still had a pressed-tin ceiling and where, when I was ten years old my father took me on his rounds. From then on, unless it was impossible to do so, I would stop what I was doing when a poem stirred in me and start writing it, and that seemed to give the poems more life.

Having no everyday friends and no strong involvement in New York City, but with no desire to move to any particular place, I attended the First National Poetry Festival in Allendale, Michigan in July 1971.

Robert Bly, Sonia Sanchez, Gregory Corso, Ted Berrigan, Anselm Hollo, Donald Hall and a host of other established poets were there. Along with workshops and poetry readings by them, there was an open reading where I read my poems. When the Festival ended, I headed for Iowa City after Audrey Teeter told me it was a nice place to live. She introduced me to poet friends at The Mill restaurant, among them Allan Kornblum, who told me he'd been falling asleep at the open reading at the Poetry Festival and my poem, "Bed," woke him up. Eventually Allan and Cinda Kornblum published my first book, *The Night We Stood Up for Our Rights*, by letter-press at their Toothpaste Press.

THE NIGHT WE STOOD UP FOR OUR RIGHTS

POEMS BY MORTY SKLAR

Just as the Phoenix House therapeutic community saved my life, so the community of poets and little magazine publishers in Iowa City gave me a life.

In 1973 I received a B.A. in English, but my application to the Writers' Workshop was turned down. In spite of that I was to befriend many of the students involved in the Workshop and the International Writing Program. I had taken an undergrad Workshop class with Donald Justice, who liked my work, and so I asked him if I could a Special Project with him—my *The Night We Stood Up For Our Rights* manuscript before it was accepted for publication by Toothpaste Press. Mr. Justice said he wouldn't be able to do it, and told me to try Stanley Plumly. Where I hadn't had the poor experiences other Actualists had in the Writers' Workshop, mine relates to theirs because Plumly was a Workshop instructor.

When I placed my manuscript on his desk, the first thing he said was, "New York Poet, huh?" I told him I had never thought of myself that way, even if I was from the City. He asked me to leave my manuscript with him, and he made an appointment for us to meet at his office. When that day arrived, there was an envelope on his door addressed to me. Rather than quoting the note inside, I'll paste a copy of it here. (Why, too, I'm wondering, did he type his name instead of signing it?)

```
Morty Sklar:

I'm sorry I can't make it this morning, as I feel
I will not be able to grant your request.  Three reasons
really:

1) You are not a member of t he workshop

2) I don't find in your work enough of the possibilities
necessary for a poet

3) I have never published a short story


                              Stan Plumly
```

A young student seeing a note like this addressed to him may have been crushed by the second statement, or at least disappointed or/and discouraged, but I was no kid at 38, and I was pissed that he would not at least have said this to my face. And if you're wondering what his third statement was about, don't take this as a sexist remark but it was about his being bitchy: When we had met I told him his name sounded familiar, and asked if he also wrote short stories.

How I came to publish my own magazine and press, including *The Actualist Anthology* is told in "The History of The Spirit That Moves Us Press" in this book.

In 1977, Ana Mendieta—a friend of my artist girlfriend, heard I was going to shave my facial hair and asked if I could give it to her little by little to apply to her face for a class project toward her M.F.A. in Intermedia. I generally don't care for conceptual art, but what she did afterwards was very interesting: she and a bunch of us went to Donnelly's Pub where she sat at the bar dressed in black pants, vest and sobrero, looking just like a vaquero.

In 1979, at forty-four, I met an Iowa gal, we married, and were divorced two years later. Perhaps our age difference of twenty-five years hurt us.

On October 21st, 1989 I gave my third annual leaving-Iowa-City reading at Prairie Lights Books, after which I drove a rented truck with all The Spirit That Moves Us books along with other belongings to Jackson Heights, Queens, New York City where I soon understood what my mother meant by "I feel like I'm living in a foreign country," and in 1996 published *Patchwork Of Dreams: Voices from the Heart of the New America,* which I edited with local friend Joe Barbato and which reflects the ethnic diversity of northwest Queens that had developed during my eighteen years in Iowa City. Even having met my Peruvian wife of twenty-five years is tied-in with assembling *Patchwork Of Dreams.*

I gave readings of my own work and held poetry workshops around

131

Queens and at Phoenix House facilities.

In 2008 I received the first Phoenix House Alumnus of the Year Award, for having introduced poetry to Phoenix House.

msklar@mindspring.com

http://the.spirit.that.moves.us.press.home.mindspring.com

(from *The Smell Of Life*)

MY SELMER MARK VI ALTO SAXOPHONE

I don't recall if I'd played "All The Things You Are"
or just sang the beginning and hummed
and scatted the rest.

I can't say that Rick, Doug, Audrey, Dr. Dick, Carlos,
Dan, Chuck, Jim and I and whoever else might show up
had played songs when we jammed at the bungalow
that Rick bought for $5,000 in Iowa City
on Bowery Street between Gilbert and Linn

—or in the downtown Mini Park before the new
Godfather's Pizza boosted the economy but took from us
the park's ambience by removing the bushes
we'd played among

—or at Carlos's pad, so small for our congas and bongos,
the saxophone, guitars—both electrified and acoustic,
the Goodwill toy piano and kazoo, and we singing,
chanting, shouting stomping,
fueled by weed, espressos, friendship, youth, and freedom.

No, not whole songs did we play, even when Carlos and Jim
—real musicians—kicked us off with one.
But it was music, once we got-up a head of steam,
or call it "good enough for jazz," but whatever,
"They Can't Take That Away From Me."

I confess—I never played a song in its entirety.

I played scales in the back of my father's store after hours,
and in my first apartment at 81st and Columbus
in Manhattan. Then I played the pawn shop tune with my sax
and my parents' wedding silverware, to cop heroin,
and eventually gave them the ticket for their silverware,
and retrieved my sax.

And one day I was again practicing scales:
In my Prospect Park West Brooklyn basement apartment
after graduating from the Phoenix House drug rehab program,
and then in a $40 a month room on West 20th
before leaving New York—where my next-door Basque
neighbor tried to push my door in when he'd
lost his job and came home drunk in the afternoon
wanting to sleep it off.

    I practiced in Iowa City in some of the twelve places
I'd lived, the last of which was the home of Jack's and Shirley's,
who'd invited me to stay until I could load all my possessions
on a Ryder rental truck and move back to New York.
    I took music lessons from Jim Mulac until the day Jack said,
"Morty, are you *ever* going to New York?"

Now, for Marcela I sometimes play my sax to salsa or jazz
that's on the radio or a record, and I play the flute she brought me
from Perú, and the pan flute she bought me in Russia.
    I listen to a lot of radio programs—from alternative medicine
to politics, personal and financial counseling, religion…
    One day when all the words began to sound like noise,
I hit the Newark jazz station and took out my sax to join in.

    "My musician,"
Marcela said.

(the following from *The Actualist Anthology*)

JARASHOW'S

    ancient store on Jamaica Avenue…

Handtruck up-
    on which I throw cartons of tools and hardware
    destined for that place, high ceilinged of pressed tin,
    with steel drawers of dozens and grosses of nuts,
    bolts, screws, pipes, fittings, nails…

At 160th Street and 91st Avenue,
    a block from the old Jamaica elevated train,
    I unload our '70 Chevy station wagon
    quickly, like my father, but not because the cartons
    —pieces of my life—are my future.

Old woman in black shawl, zinc grey hair
    and grey face, tells me:
        "I remember you, you were six
        when you came around with your father."

Driving back thru Union Turnpike towns
    past Utopia Parkway homes, I speak to Dad
    in my head: Mrs. Jarashow said she remembers me.
    —I told her, you mean my brother, and she said
    "No, you were six when you came with your father."
        He'll be pleased, for what came between us
        is gone, there's time to talk with my father
        who at thirteen headed a fatherless brood,
            rushing
                till now.
I having been well fed
    went another way blessed it comes to this
    as in old times when sons came home.

When Jarashow's was new
    with maple counters and zinc storage bins,

my father was selling hardware and tools from job lots
stored in my grandparents' basement.
    At thirty-five he'd failed, was starting out again
    hustling in the streets of Jersey City,
    lower Manhattan, Jackson Heights…
    —my father who (he never told me until I too
    did it) took chances, made a bundle in woolens
    on daring, lost, bought a barrel of peanuts
    and peddled them from a furnished room.

Father, see,
    I too have aimed for what I want
    —a little late and unsure, but now
    that doesn't matter.
        We have time before kaddish;
        everything's okay
        between you and me.

November 1970

CHARLIE "BIRD" PARKER

Exploiting the medium
for all it's got

    Bird flying forever

wait a minute
I'll get my saxophone

    Lady Be Good
    in four-four
    play a warped piano till it straightens out

I'm not always lonely
are you?

    bablee *doo* dah
    bablee *doo* dah

135

ODE TO GOOFY

Oh Goofy,
tap-dancing in the kitchen
in the moonlight of streetlight,
to the dripping faucet, a song
of environmental unconcern,
beauty of waste

Oh Coney Island
25¢ laughing entrance to Fear
thrill of dying

a dozen clams on the half-shell
salt air, hot sauce

Daffy Duck saltwater taffy
3 shots for a quarter,
rag doll reward

Midnight of the eternally open steeplechase,
trashed windy blacktop
of the sauerkraut mustard cotton candy night

    Oh, Light

Star travellers of Brooklyn
taking the subway home

Moonlight on the oil slick,
Mark Twain of the green condoms river,
Ellis Island ghosts
      Liberty

      Oh say
      can you see

MA

Ma
here I am,
your boy.

I have a degree now
and friends.
I'm sitting where
20-year-olds begin their lives,
listening to Chicago's
"you are my love and my life,
 you are my inspiration."

My elevator is ascending, Ma,
it won't ever come down again;
rising, but not above;
I look around: whatever's there
I want, whatever's there
is mine.

Mom om so high
I've one foot in Harlem
the other in the sky.
Come with me
come on, sit on my shoulders and see
the world you gave me.

THE SMELL OF LIFE

Rubbing alcohol
and a breeze at an open window,
warm February day.

Rubbing alcohol
and infrared-heated beef mashed potatoes and string beans
much the same as rubbing alcohol
ham French fries and broccoli.

Later, on the way to the tv room or the gymnasium
in striped cotton robe
my breath tastes like dinner
like all the dinners.

The alcohol touches at once
tonsillectomy, Mother's hemorrhage,
my electroshock therapy, heroin, hepatitis,
and awakens fear
but is inexplicably reassuring
like the odor of gasoline and sewage
near lower west side service stations and piers
where our family car sometimes took us
to relatives across the river,
furry arm of my mother,
aftershave of my father,
standing mainstream at the prow of the ferry
a breeze across our faces.

1976, ten years after my final trip
to Manhattan General detox

(*the following is unpublished*)

SHAVING TO DJANGO REINHARDT'S GUITAR

I sit to write this after hurrying to finish shaving
but instead I read the liner notes of *The Best Of Django Reinhardt*
then lean on my elbow at the table, pen in hand, an infusion of melody,
harmony, energy, Gypsy freedom, exquisite delight from Django's guitar
and Stephane Grappelli's violin permeating my being.

And so—as I've suspected in recent years, for whatever reason or reasons,
my poetry-writing days are over.

I'm more inclined to delight in the delightful and to ponder
the unfathomable of how a six-story-to-be building a hundred yards
from our eighth-floor window is being built from a hole in the ground,
concrete block by concrete block, brick by brick, steel beam by steel beam

rivet by rivet, riveter by riveter—so different from the way
jazz is built,

yet also an outpouring—if not improvised instant to instant—
by creatures who somehow came to exist, blood flowing through our veins,
hearts beating billions of times, building cities and civilizations,
cultivating food, evolving to the likes of Beethoven, Django, and those
who can dig them.

Well, maybe I will write poems again.

books
Riverside. Emmess Press, 1974
The First Poem. Snapper Press, 1977
The Night We Stood Up For Our Rights: Poems 1969–1975.
    The Toothpaste Press, 1977
The Smell of Life: Poems 1969 to 2005.
    The Spirit That Moves Us Press, 2008

magazines
*New York Quarterly, Gargoyle, Toothpaste, Gum, Me Too, World Letter,
Small Press Review, El Nahuatzen, Dental Floss, New Letters, Bicycle, Nitty
Gritty, Northeast Rising Sun, US 1 Worksheets, Telephone, Iowa City Creative
Writing Series, Lips, MidAtlantic Review, Alzheimer's Association Newsletter,
The New Pioneer, Abraxas, Yellow Brick Road, Legionnaire, City Scriptum,
Pangloss Papers, P.F. Flyer, Remark, Alive & Kicking, Phoenix House News,
Pearl, Free Flowing, Empty Window Review…*

anthologies
A to Z: 200 Contemporary American Poets, edited by David Ray;
    Swallow Press / Ohio University Press, 1981
Knock Knock: A Funny Anthology by Serious Poets. Bench Press, 1981
Humor In America. Open Places / Stephens College, 1985
Editors On Fiction. The Literary Review, 1992
A Poetry Anthology. edited by Robert Creeley;
    Des Moines Arts Center, 1992
Brother Songs: A Male Anthology of Poetry. edited by Jim Perlman;
    Holy Cow! Press, 1992
Cattle Bones & Coke Machines: An Anthology of Poems Examining the

Impact of Humanity on the Earth's Systems. Smiling Dog Press, 1995
Off The Cuffs: Poetry By & About the Police. Soft Skull Press, 2003
Words That Free Us: Voices of Recovery. Phoenix House, 2008
The Burg: A Writers' Diner. edited by Marybeth Slonneger;
    By Hand Press, 2011

JIM MULAC
(1943 to 2012)

(Jim's words are in quotation marks.)

"Jim was born 1943 in a suburb of Chicago. At eight his family moved to a small farm in Iowa, where he attended a one-room grade school and enjoyed a pastoral childhood during the early 1950s. His heroes were Roy Rogers and Ernie Kovacs. In high school he was deeply impressed by James Dean, William Blake, Robert Browning and Ray Charles."

Jim was in the Writers' Workshop as an undergraduate in the early 1960s, with a year away at San Francisco State College where he took writing classes and worked as a copyboy at the *San Francisco Chronicle*.

"Many things affected him in those years, especially Miles Davis, Eric Dolphy, Nathanael West, Jack Kerouac, Allen Ginsberg, and his college friend, Dave Margoshes who lived and breathed Faulkner and Ornette Coleman."

In 1965 Jim moved to Boston, where he was involved in the local poetry scene. In 1966 he returned to the Midwest taking a position as a news reporter for the *Rock Island Argus*. He and a friend were fired from this job as a result of publishing a literary magazine of political and social protest against the Vietnam War. He later worked as a city reporter for the *Moline Daily Dispatch*.

In the late 1960s Jim lived in the hills north of San Francisco, followed by two-and-a-half years as a city reporter in the Mississippi Valley. He returned to the University of Iowa in 1972 to finish a B.A. degree in English with an emphasis in Creative Writing, and remained in Iowa City except for a couple of months in New Orleans and a year in Chicago, both places in which he played solo piano hoping to gain steady employment doing so.

"He had been fortunate to eke-out a meager living by playing solo piano, then he compromised some of that time to operate a used book and record shop [Jim's Used Books & Records], where he wished the spirit of Actualism would prevail."

Jim enjoyed his time at the Workshop but felt that the atmosphere there was too academic and form oriented, essentially conservative. Its writing models were older, established, often academic poets such as Robert Lowell, Robert Frost, Donald Justice, and Elizabeth Bishop, and it was influenced mainly by poetry appearing in *Poetry Magazine*, the *Chicago Review*, and other journals with an academic slant. On the other hand, Jim and his contemporaries were interested in and had been influenced by Beat poets and novelists like Ginsberg, Corso, Ferlinghetti, and Kerouac, and more recently, by the contemporary New York and San Francisco poetry scenes.

In 1972 Jim became involved in a number of collaborative writing projects with Allan Kornblum, from whom he rented when the Kornblums moved to West Branch, Iowa, and later with Darrell Gray. Collaborations were a popular form of writing with the Actualists in general. One would write a few lines or a few pages, then others would follow. "Although many of the poems written in this manner ended in surrealistic chaos, many others contained great passages and many were completed with great originality and success." Some plays were written in this manner, two of them performed in 1973: *The Brick Apartment* by Kornblum and Mulac was performed in April with the Poets Theater and again as part of the Iowa Public Theatre Spring Festival, along with *Backyard* by Gray and Mulac at the Wesley House to an audience of about a hundred people. Jim and Allan also collaborated on a play in two acts called *Herbert Hoover*, performed at the Fall Actualization in the same year.

In the summer of 1972, Jim was performing as a solo pianist at the Sanctuary on South Gilbert Street, and felt it would be a better venue for the group's readings than the Wesley House because it was more public and the atmosphere was "less sober," and he organized weekly readings for three years, some of which were "open mic." Readers included people from the Workshop, local writers and invited poets from out of town. In one year Jim organized forty-eight weekly readings!

From 1975 through 1976 Jim resided in Chicago where he played piano and studied jazz theory. He returned to Iowa City in 1977 to open Jim's Used Books and Records at 610 South Dubuque Street. Jim continued hosting the readings at his store where they continued even after he sold his business to a woman who renamed it Selected Works in 1981. When Selected Works closed the readings migrated to the Haunted Bookshop.

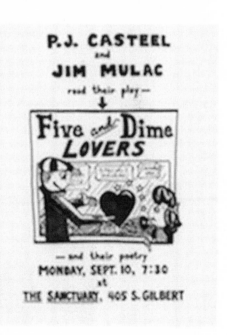

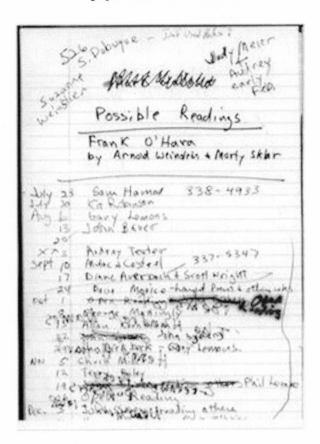

After selling his bookshop, Jim worked as a civilian instructor at sea with the U.S. Navy. In 1984, he returned to Iowa City, married Heidi, and resumed his career as a pianist and began offering private lessons.

From Jeff Charis-Carlson, who took piano lessons from Jim: "As a teacher, Jim specialized in working with adult pianists—often ones returning to the piano after decades away. His patient approach gave students a solid foundation in chords that allowed them to improvise and compose their own arrangements of jazz standards. Jim liked to joke that he didn't know whether music was distracting him from poetry or poetry was distracting him from music. 'That's the story of my life,' Jim said a few weeks before his death in June 2012. 'I knew I should focus on one or the other, but I had such a passion for both that I just couldn't decide.' "

He released a solo album, *Stay Here Awhile*, in 2000, and in the same year moved his family to Cedar Rapids where he continued to teach piano.

144

(from *The Actualist Anthology*)

AFTERNOON AT THE MOVIES

You are the star
& I'm watching your final picture.
Barely 20, it's clear you are a genius.
I admire everything, especially
your refusal to smoke out of doors
and the buttonless clothes you wear.
The film is about your reaction to the books that you've read
and begins with Irving Stone's Lust For Life
running through Ford Maddox Ford to
The Pictorial History Of Hollywood Stars.
There is the scene where you are on time for the bus
but decline to take it, or to refund your ticket
that I particularly thrill to, thinking as I watch
how your family and friends completely understood you
despite your passion for untenable individuality.
Outside the theater, inspired, though aware of the ticket
blotted against my windshield, I jam popcorn into the meter
and exclaim: "Beauty is ruthless, and so predictable!"

145

THE CALLER

Sitting in my car,
I talk to you on the telephone.
You are excited because someone has come
to the door, and you laugh
because you are naked.
This time I can actually hear
the knocking
but am unable to tell
who it is.

ELEGY FOR DUKE ELLINGTON

"The more you know, the more there is;
   the more music you get into, the more you want."
      —*Duke Ellington*

Like sweet brother Johnny Hodges dying alone
in a bathroom during the band's intermission,
the Duke became as cool as he ever wanted to be.
In the spring of 1973 I saw him in Iowa City:
74 years old, the loud snapping crack
of his finger & thumb, he was an old
man lanky as an iron tree, discreet when
he socked the machine of his hips, once
elegant and now with long, wavy grey hair
—loose and casual on his extended vacation.
Duke Ellington made a career of freedom,
"getting paid to do what you love to do."
More articulate than leaders of his world, he
could look at the keyboard & see again how easy
it would be to make a sound so beautiful anybody
everywhere would know how madly he loved us.

CARS

I've watched cars acting like gods
since my baptism in gravel, when I almost
shouted that their names weren't broken glass.
But even when Steve died I said nothing.
And if his wife had lived, I might not have
said: "Watch for reflections
along storefront windows."

Somewhere alone I muttered "Christ!"
the way I did Friday when Jerry Lee's car
stopped electrical power for twenty minutes.
Because I don't want to keep my mouth shut.
Not since the night those people climbed
up on the bumpers of a car
and bounced again and again.

FEELING YOU AGAIN

In a windowless room you hold a door open
showing us the snow falling, a street lamp,
old cars in a parking lot.
Soon it will be midnight in the Midwest.
I've been drinking here tonight watching
your shoulders, and thinking:
have three years touched all of you?
Quiet in your loins, like a principle,
I wait for your hand to throw a cigarette
out to the wind. I listen for the jukebox.

THE COFFEE DEN, CEDAR RAPIDS

In the window all the businessmen are
silver-haired, not wanting to look at the tall,
tattooed man at the cash register.
It is he then who picks up the change.

The waitresses between the wall & the
counter pass each other without looking.
They have amazing country voices,
too far gone for singing on the radio,
& their teeth and
sharp breasts on tv
would be too American for the world at large.
They are perfect for pie.

& I see the pie is gone,
though the lemon cream shines on
beneath the fork and the wadded napkin.
Putting this away beneath
the counter, she leans over to say:
"How are you?"
   "I'm okay."

GIRL CLINGS TO COMA

Elaine has been in a coma
for the past 25 years
the longest known
and listed in
the human unconsciousness
of world records.
She has set a human tragedy.

 "At first the doctors told us
Elaine wouldn't speak to me."
Mrs. Esposito
adjusted
her dark-eyed, dark-haired
coverlet.
"But she never did."
She receives from her mother a nasal tube.

The Espositos have been told
over and over

that there is no normal. "But,
I always hoped they were wrong."

In a pink-topped hospital gown
kept with blue bows
she is as immaculate
as a miracle.

1966

THING TO WORK FOR

Today, spading out thistles,
I remember Joanna Burden's name,
and how steady and quiet Joe Christmas
worked, walking home in thick legs.
Again they teach me how to breathe, while
a thousand times, turning in the pasture,
I brush your hair from behind my eyes,
till none is left to think about.
There are the blue flowered curtains
sunbleached in the Cinora Café, the face
of a farmer who "won't do that kind of work,"
a barefoot, fat woman in jeans, and yellow
tulips, plastic tulips in brown beer bottles
dustless to make each table nice.

SATURDAY NIGHT OUT

The entertainers are friendly
& there are more old songs now.
"The new ones don't have words yet,"
they tell us, "but the tunes
are from all over the place." Yes,
these two girls are crazy, & they can
sit with us, & later we can leave,
go to another place, visit with Scott Wright
about jobs we've quit, about D.H. Lawrence

149

getting Scott to write again.
    We switch
from coffee back to beer.
The lights come on.
We go home, where the drawing still looks good.
Sunday morning, Cinda's parents call & offer
an electric broom. Spring cleaning is beginning
in February, & the abstract works that were jokes
to begin with seem more & more naturally
part of the way things get straightened out.

magazines
The Destruction of Philadelphia, Me Too, Dental Floss, and
  The Spirit That Moves Us.

plays
Jim co-authored the play *Bob*, with Allan Kornblum and Darrell Gray,
World Premiere at ACUTE ACTUALISM: A Memorial Homage to Darrell
Gray, performed in Berkeley at Blake Street Hawkeyes Theater December 7,
1986, originally published in *In The Light Magazine*, #s 5 & 6: Actual Plays.

Jim coedited with Morty Sklar, *Editor's Choice: Literature & Graphics from
the U.S. Small Press, 1965-1977.* The Spirit That Moves Us Press, 1980

JOHN BATKI

My Life as an Actualist

Late summer 1969, arriving in Iowa City at age 26 with wife Beth and half-year-old son Joseph, I was a twelve-year old American. I had lived in New York State since coming over to this country as a "Hungarian refugee" from Budapest at age 14, and still had a major dose of old Europe in my veins and brains after the thousand mile drive west, further west than I had ever been. A weekend in Cleveland had been my previous westernmost penetration. For twelve years the Empire State constituted my America: Upstate, where my family lived, and Downstate, where I spent five proud years at Columbia University, getting ed-u-cat-ed.

The Midwest was my second America, where a quiet twang settled over my lingering Hungarian accent, an assurance that I was at last speaking real American. Paul Engle had invited me to assist in his International Writing Program on the strength of my brand-new Syracuse M.A. in "English and American Literature and Creative Writing" (a tall order!) that I had earned by handing in as my thesis a slim selection of translations from the poems of Attila Jozsef. Donald Justice, whose poetry and translation workshops I was taking at Syracuse, seeing my befuddlement had recommended I translate a Hungarian poet. So thank you, Don, for all your conscientious penciled comments filling the margins around my lumbering, doddering lines.

151

My other qualification in Paul Engle's eyes was the great publishing coup of having sold a story to *The New Yorker*—"Never Touch a Butterfly," the first story I ever wrote, spirited out of the air one late winter / early spring night in the glory days of new fatherhood soon after the birth of my first son, Joseph. Everything was new back then in 1969.

I arrived in Iowa City with a sketchy acquaintance with American letters (Nabokov, Salinger, Donald Barthelme and Bob Dylan my idols) and one October day I was unforgettably impressed seeing so many of the Iowa writers in deep mourning: Jack Kerouac was gone. I had only known *On the Road* until then, but over the next few years I read everything by Kerouac, and have been reading him ever since. Yes, meeting Anselm Hollo brought me into that picture, and from Anselm I received Pound, William Carlos Williams and Charles Olson, with Ted Berrigan thrown in, and a whole slew of local youth who soon called themselves the Actualists: Dave Morice, Allan Kornblum, George Mattingly, and above all Darrell Gray. Thank you for the intro, Don Anselmo!

My daughter Sara was born in Iowa City and so was my second story, "Strange-Dreaming Charlie, Cow-eyed Charlie," published in *The New Yorker* and then awarded the O. Henry Prize. I peaked early, I s'pose.

And in 1971 I stumbled upon, became a fringe member of, the Actualist Movement because that's what was happening in Iowa City and environs in 1971. Darrell Gray was so cool. His mild delivery masked a wicked streak of brilliance and sheer beatitude, and it was a delight to be in the know, to take part in the feast. Highlight for me of the Summer of 1971 was attending the National Poetry Festival at Allendale, Michigan. The resulting text, "At the National Festival"—the last of my quartet of stories Four Jays (uncollected to this day) appeared in the Fall 1972 issue of *Fiction*.

I am still not quite sure what Actualism (or for that matter Existential-ism, or ANY ism) really signifies, notwithstanding Darrell Gray's Actualist Manifesto. It certainly was Darrell's "brain child"—attractive, seductive, and habit-forming. The leading lights of the movement, for me, were Darrell Gray and Dave Morice. Darrell, our last great pure lyric and elegiac poeta doctus...and Dave Morice, genius creator of *Poetry Comics*, editor of *Gum* magazine, and of *Matchbook* the magazine of one-word poetry. I had the honor of my word poem "acetylcholinesterase" alongside Allen Ginsberg's "apocatastasis."

From Iowa City my road led back to Syracuse, New York, then Palo Alto, California where a one-year fellowship at Stanford was stretched into a three-year stay. During that time Darrell Gray moved to the Bay Area and we saw each other with some frequency. At one get-together in Menlo Park in the spring of 1975 we tape-recorded an evening of readings and called it Turkey Tail Review. I wonder if that old cassette still has traces of Darrell's faraway voice....

(from *The Actualist Anthology*)

SABINE

Last night in the rain I was frightened
but I clowned with you, Sabine.
You started the evening as a teenager,
youngest of the party, and by dawn you
aged 20 years, emerged as a woman
from a sea of looks and willpower.
Your scandic seaweed beauty, arching
little breasts (and oh the entire male-
female complex of emotions) played an
important part in my developing speech
acne in your direction. But you, I'll
never understand, accepting my invitation,
sighing "yes" "Yes" in an unthinkingly
volatile and filmic manner. These thrills
proved to be deceptive. What was it
that made you play the straight man
to my clown I still don't know.
Was it the blue horse of your loneliness
shying at the thunder claps of desperation?
Beyond those plosive "Yes's" and the sarcastic
change of personae you underwent from night
to morning (watched by both of us)
I have no clue to the motivation

behind your steadfast valor.
After breakfast at the Grand Hotel,
we walked arm in arm in the park,
I loved your black tulips then, Sabine.

TOURISTICISM

In the eye of the volute, we are
all the same. There, where
the palmetto cleverly masks
the intersection of echinoderm
and catharsis, lies the ancient
prodigy of dreams. Typically
pulvinar, it represents no ethnic
voice, and sounds the susurrant berry
for the famished hemlines.
"Appear in togas!" the command
was given, yet no one obeyed,
for the architecture of authority
had crumbled, it was the 3rd
century B.C. By now people
came to stare at the eye, bored
of balteus and echinus, toting
Kodaks of terminalism.

DOWN THE BLOCK

Herbert, the corner philatelist, tells me
        that sales are up. The snow quietly
        lies in the air.

Molly, the downstairs pragmatist, is out
        with her dog for a walk. Her plump
        dark thighs are bare.

What should we do? The wind does not answer,
        the trees stretch their arms, the snow
        does not care.

154

Let's have some music! The dog turns around,
    shakes his head, and says, "Melodies
    are rare."

NIGHT AND DAY

Hotbeds of colors and an entire language of old
steamer trunks wrapped in lace and leather of Persia,
feather & foam of distant seas,
if I could have seen your eyes.

Walking the city streets the grease of short fries
and kitchen smells bow down on your path
of swimming pool détentes and ancient Texan parties,
breakfast eggs cooking to your taste,
spongy, cavernous corporations unafraid of your mouth.

Delight in eights and foursomes, reptilian disasters
in the park, dualism gathered by your side solitary,
unbuckled and confidant that no evil is unknown
or unforgiven though unforgettable, you the three
of hearts draw a hand over your broken nose.

Day comes stealthily in Riviera sneakers
from its vacation in the Occident, your favorite
jewel thief who robs the night of its stars, careless,
in a white shirt, as you close your eyes.

MALLARME ON JULY 14, 1889

Mallarme liked his wine. Some of his favorites were Chateau
Haut-Brion, Chassagne-Montrachet, and the ever-mellow red
"Paisano." He also liked the color orange, and the long walks
under the plantains on the boulevards. "Publishers, publishers,"
Mallarme murmured on the afternoon of July 14,
after a pleasant stroll in the course of which he observed
the people of Paris dancing on the streets. His fingers
leafed through the heavy dictionary lying in his lap.

He picked out a verdant bouquet of verbs, adjectives, nouns, and other lesser parts of speech to present to his publisher. Mallarme was wearing a dark flowery tie, flowery not in the sense of the imprinted pattern, but in the configuration of the tie around his neck. Perhaps "butterfly" is a better description of the tie's lavish folds, a fluttering of dark wings under the poet's chin. Mallarme thought of himself in a perambulator as an infant, the 1843 edition of Mallarme, was that the same Mallarme as the young man who walked with a long loaf of French bread under his arm twenty years later, or the Mallarme now sitting in his comfortable fauteuil, reading the evening paper? "Here, Fido!" he called to his dog, an overweight Saint Bernard. Mallarme despised the papers; Mercure de Paris or Sentinel de France, it was all yellow journalism. He threw down the paper and picked up a copy of the Revue des Deux Mondes, fresh from that day's mail. Ah, another article by the Freres Goncourt! Biting into a still warm croissant, Mallarme perused the sheet, pensively stroking the back of his chocolate seal-point Siamese, Cleo. The entrance of the maid disturbs his ruminations: "M'sieur…the asparagus man is here. Will there be anything today?"

LOVE POEM

I am a traveler
for life
tourist on earth
alone, in company
and now it's you
    and me
  in Marin County,
home of the electric guitar.

poems
Falling Upward. Dolphin Editions, 1976

The Mad Shoemaker. Toothpaste Press, 1973

translations

Attila Jozsef—Selected Poems and Texts. Carcanet Press, 1973

Erno Szep—The Smell of Humans: a memoir of the Holocaust
in Hungary. unpublished, 1994,

Peter Lengyel—Cobblestone. Readers International, 1993

Attila Jozsef—Winter Night: Selected Poems. Oberlin College Press, 1997

Ivan Mandy—Fabulya's Wives and Other Stories. Corvina, 1999

Ivan Mandy—What Was Left. Noran Books, 1999

Gyula Krudy—Krudy's Chronicles: turn-of-the-century Hungary in
Gyula Krudy's journalism. Central European University Press, 2000

Geza Ottlik—Buda. Corvina, 2004

Gyula Krudy—Sunflower. New York Review of Books, 2007

Gyula Krudy—Ladies Day. Corvina, 2007

Gyula Krudy—Life Is a Dream. Penguin Books, 2010

GEORGE MATTINGLY
(in his words)

Born 1950 in Cape Girardeau, Missouri to a public school band-and-orchestra teacher and a farm girl from the Ozarks. In his first thirteen years his family lived in eleven different towns in Missouri, Illinois, and Iowa.

In 1964 George entered Phillips Exeter Academy, a boys boarding school in New Hampshire, where he began his career as a writer. While a student there, he found a summer job working on a cattle ranch in northeastern Nevada (mainly in the hay harvest, driving mowers, rakes, and swathers), and earning extra money at night beating Airstream tourists at bridge by kerosene lamps in nearby campgrounds. It was here that he fell under the spell of the Big Sky which would eventually attract him to the West Coast where he has spent most of his life.

After he was expelled from Exeter just before Christmas in his senior year for selling marijuana, college acceptances from Stanford, Harvard, and Columbia were withdrawn. He finished high school in his parents' town of Newton, Iowa.

A student teacher who had taken classes at the University of Iowa's Writers' Workshop (and was a huge fan of poet James Tate) convinced George to enroll at the University of Iowa. He lived in Iowa City from 1968 to 1973. In addition to required coures, he took all the Writers' Workshop courses open to undergrads.

Desperate to escape the frat boy atmosphere of dorm life, he responded to a note on the bulletin board of the Workshop offering room and board in return for child care for Ted and Sandy Berrigan's 5- and 3-year-olds, David and Kate. Ted Berrigan was one of several exciting young writers (including Anselm Hollo, Jack Marshall, Steve Katz, Kathleen Fraser and others) invited to join the Workshop faculty by then–Director George Starbuck (who was wonderfully open-minded to a wide range of writing quite different from his own essentially formalist work).

George lived with the Berrigans for a year. He was introduced to many of their friends, including New York artists, writers, and musicians (among them Lee Crabtree, pianist for The Fugs, who became a fast friend). He was invited to all the Writers' Workshop parties and readings (official and otherwise). In George's words: "My real education took place mostly off campus, after dark, mostly in thick clouds of smoke."

The atmosphere on campus was at first collegial and open and he even credits teachers whose work was very unlike his own, including Marvin Bell, at that time considered strictly an academic poet.

He also studied typography with Harry Duncan of the Cummington

Press, and it was in Duncan's class that he fell in love with typography, letterpress printing, and book design, which was to be his life's work.

George carried a notebook with him and wrote whenever the spirit moved him (which was often). Tim Hildebrand introduced him to the cheaper, innovative printing technologies (including xerography and the small offset presses new at the time). George and his artist girlfriend Deborah Owen decided to start a magazine, *Search for Tomorrow* (a tongue-in-cheek reference to the long-running tv soap opera) which published surrealist, Actualist, and New York School poetry, fiction, and visual art.

Search for Tomorrow achieved brief notoriety when the network television show's producer sent a cease-and-desist order, which George framed but otherwise ignored. Six issues were published, all varying in size, color, shape and content (a headache to acquisitions librarians, who universally referred to independent literary magazines as "fugitive publications").

In 1972 he published two books, the first a thin stapled book of collaborative works he called *Darling-Bender*, the name of a real estate company up
the street from the Berrigans' house on South Capitol Street. The other was
the first book-length collection of poetry by his best friend Darrell Gray
titled *Something Swims Out.*

other books from his press
Keith Abbott—Rhino Ritz; Gush: A Comic Novel About Unemployment
    in California; Erase Words; Putty
Ted Berrigan—So Going Around Cities
William S. Burroughs—Port Of Saints; Blade Runner: A Movie
Tom Clark—Who Is Sylvia?
Merrill Gilfillan—Light Years; To Creature
David Gitin—The Journey Home; This Once; Fire Dance
Maria Gitin—Night Shift
Anselm Hollo—Finite Continued; Sojourner Microcosms
George Mattingly—Breathing Space
Lorenzo Thomas—Chances Are Few
Steve Toth—Traveling Light

(from *The Actualist Anthology*)

GOODBYE SONNET

Outside cool July half an hour from morning
Charlie sends love from Salt Lake
Aretha Franklin fills the room
& distant truck sounds give life a constant disguise.
Smoke occurs to the plant by the clock.
It's a thought—smoke—to the plant—are my thoughts
that real? Orange drink for instance results from
the planter's affection for sharkskin, some oranges,
and chemicals with thoughts of their own.

Birds plant their wings in the sun.
Roberto Clemente goes to sleep in the sea.
I dream I am dreaming but everything's real:
the snow on tv and the pictures of you left in me,
though maybe the real you's got your thumb out by now
in the hamburger storms that drench America with identical details.

(*the following provided by George*)

HOMEWARD ANGEL

Up at 4   before my brain
in cold dark Berkeley brown shingle
not even hip-hop on the street   (that late)

Red Volvo   colorless blur on freeway

park   lock   hoist   hoof
to anxious fluorescent airport,
jumpy with smell of dreams deferred and after-shave,
pale people porting to map-points
to say hello to fellow people.

Beyond gravity or common sense, United heavy
powers over my family asleep in bed
over golf-course-ringed volcano (dead),

161

flooded islands (dead)   levee tops like fringing reefs
around sunken row-crop atolls (all dead).

Ridiculous flying box of humans in chairs (not yet dead)
cruises over gridded green of former inland sea
now inland demo of holy power of water
to grow life in crumbled anything on which it falls.

Free refills eight miles high
high power   high altitude   blues in space

Gliding over   ancient Tahoe   Mono   Sonny Bono
Playa Blanca   Playa Negro   Playa del Roy
Fossil politics   alluvial fans   Jokers Wild
highways straight as frontier talk
"The drone of flying engines
scrambles time and seasons"

over rocks on Trail Ridge Road (so old that they don't talk)

over 1046 Grant Street, Longmont   brightly lit
by Lani and Keith Abbott   formerly of Albany, Oakland,
Berkeley, Davis, Monterey, Church Stretton,
the Haight, Bellingham, Tacoma,

we all are every where
in this jet age.

In no time I'm in Iowa where
I've not lived in twenty-seven years

though when I land
I never left

am twenty-one

too young to think I'll ever suffer
any habit   good or bad

too young to see a future
or an end.

May 1999

DRIVEN

purple ceanothus
brilliant in a sea
   of fog
while on the air
   a voice advertising trust
dissolves in white noise
fish-tails round a curve
as life
takes a second
to straighten
and pass

   1985

BIRD SONG

leaf   to leaf   to roof   to sky
nodes of song roll round the fabric of space

white noise   the days wash over
bright muscle of speech

hear you say   you are here
as here moves   to hear you say you are

alight   the breeze

no work   no play,

just day

after day

BETWEEN THE BLINKS

(*A collaboration with Darrell Gray*)

As if sunlight were a form of memory remodeling the landscape
It occurs to the birds...and then to us

How we get through the day.
If all that matters were not moving,
How could birds focus their minute attention
at the tips of branches?

Their attachment to what we take from them
bends back to include their world
like the sensation of diving through miles of foam
at the end of which everything will seem

corrected. Not even the tops of buildings duplicate the eyes
in which they seem falling.

And if the next lips I kiss breathe the pliable sleep of trees
how much simpler airports are without planes.
And when it doesn't happen, the sound is simply carried
to a more real location.

inside a mule's head, for instance

or carried on the breeze
created by the disturbance we feel

emerging from history.

PHASE IN

Greek   insomnia   should the warm snow

gag like an oboe

proportioned and sad

from laughing

since money.

Angel   elastic   your bridges

     phase me

you feel like

    a perjurer's dream

Please

I don't know

I absorb

ELIZABETH ZIMA

  Elizabeth Zima was in High School when befriended by the Actualists, and worked at the Donut Wagon and Taco Vendor with Cinda Kornblum for a brief time. Cinda remembers a night when a group of Actualists "helped Liz write an essay for her class about the (totally made up) history of the plastic bag." Elizabeth moved to California where she also participated in Actualist Conventions in the Bay Area.

  She has in-depth knowledge of health care and has applied this in the fields of writing, editing, media relations, marketing and social networking. She has interpreted clinical and policy information for the media, consumers, scientists and doctors for print and the Internet.

165

(from *The Spirit That Moves Us*, Volume 1, #2, 1976)

Note from Morty: When this was published, women were not yet having an easy time getting published or being publishers (one exception was our Actualist community). Although this poem of 17 pages in an issue of 48 pages is by a woman, when I attempted to place it on consignment in a women's center bookstore (forgot the name) in Iowa City—where Elizabeth and I and my mag lived—they refused. Why? Because the mag was "by a male publisher."

PHOTO LIZ

I got motional problems
Quazars behind ma eyes
A transistor radio
Receiving a hump

Now he got spies all over
An he got fancy shoes
An he got chords
An he got shiny
An he poke me here

I ain't like no other woman I know
An neither are they
Neither are they
An you bunk-cat belchers
You affiliated stinkers
Your theories about me
Is as clean as your assholes
Which you are afraid to stretch out
Relax that Sphinx paw

A little hairy touch here
I put me heres
An every three months I been movin to LA
Lookin for that one jewel
That fawcet flash
Somethin that'll feel good on my muscles
I ain't found it
I don't ever expect to

I tell you I is frustrated
An I
Well I been mated like a dober bitch
Ever which way I could get it
I got
Tell I got so numb
Decided that I'd grown my own

Bein a male prostitute
Weren't easy
I got so stretched out
Ma own ma wouldn't recognize me
An the shits I takes
Jes slides out like a greased pickle

I tell you
I was married at the ten thousand foot level
A royal birth
An asp an teeth to prove
I was here and there

An it ain't worth shit to tell you
I never seen an eclipse in my life
But I seen everthing else
I seen God
I been enlightened for a few days
It weren't much
I even had Buddha standing on my nose
Dharma in my sinuses

A nostril fulla empty stink
I blew that out in my hand

You see I got no special facilities
I mostly wish I hadn't been carried and born
I sometimes tell momma
It's a waste you putting me here
Get somebody else

I got motional problems
It weren't easy bein queer
Sometimes I turn yellow
An the smells of my lovers
In bus stations
In the pizza joints
Why
I even got me whipped by a pig once
He come down so hard
Bust the shoelaces clean offa me

In the house of madness
I found my real friends
Debra
The one who married that fat Mexican
Jes waitin to be one of them pubescent Catholics
Suppin on free holes and bends
Somehow since the age of 13
She thought she was a girl
Ruined her mind
Poor thing
She talk just like one of them
But not me
Never me
I wouldn't trade in my swing
For that
Curly head baby doll momma handed me
I says momma, just you wait
I get me a real one

169

So's when I throw it up against the wall
We gets real liquids
Real smears
An momma looked at me funny
Said I got motional problems
And tried to tell me
I'm an inverted genius
But I know better
I'm just as stupid as the other
Sucked my thumb until I was sixteen
I knows better than that

An this is my love song
My love song

An them whiskers on my chin
Makes it hard to be a female impersonator
Gotta get up early to shave
So my lover don't know

Now he got spies alll over
An he got fancy shoes
And he got chords
An he got shiny
An he poke me here
He ain't like no other woman I know

Even I know who I am
But he
Whoa partner
He's still settling his bills
On the fix
That scalped his thighs clean
His only love machine gone
His maiden head split
He got problems too
Ain't we all
But I can settle them easy

I jest refuses to be
Here an now I refuses to be
Here an now

Rulers of the world
I Polish knocks you
An say I don't belong
Could never come to cause I's so numb

By the time I was 13
I knew that all men lied
I knew adventures smelled like cum
And nothing else
What man will offer up his soul for…
…for this female
This theng that's suppose to be so slippery
So damn learned in her ways of
Prattelin back porch claw
Who get up in the morning
And a walk with her butt out
Like she just got done washin her liver
An she's afraid it'll dry out
I say love yourself a wino
And your love turns to booze
An this is my love song
My love song
You punks

I got no time for the man in the moon
I ain't got time for Santa
I already know I's lost
It ain't comin if it ever was
An now I'm trying to figure out ma unbirth
Trying to leave the easy way
Back through the womb
Back to the womb
I get the giddy laughs
When I thinks of that

Warm slime
But not momma
Damn the female carrier
Like a disease that eats the knuckles
Off your nose
Back to the womb
No more

Now he got spies alll over
An he got fancy shoes
And he got chords
An he got shiny
An he poke me here
He ain't like no other pimp I know
An when he lies straight in my face
It crack
An he kiss it
An the gang green set in
A peelin and a burnin a hole
A tattoo on my face of words

I ain't original
Never have been
Never claimed to be
I stole what I could
When weren't nobody lookin
Took me years to steal this
An during those years
I grew lumps all up and down my throat
Fear lumps
Beetles in the hay of my digestive organs
A hootin and a hollerin to take me back
Take me back
To that dust bowl of a town
Those 500 resident truck drivers
An Ramona
With the huge lips

Like to smear my ass with her tongue
Red haired Ramona
From sea to shining sea
Ramona would lift up her dress for a nickel
I give her five bucks
Got a fist full more than I knew what to do with
Sweet Ramona
A street walker since the age of three
Even her eyeballs had stretch marks
She being a hilarious figure
Walkin the pavement
Her legs slappin together
Like a boat builder with spurs

Oh ship of the wilderness
A bottle tossed in the foam
You who could do no harm
Who had no art or craft
You winding up as a cheese spread
At the most expensive houses

It weren't easy havin a job to do
Makin the bucks
Keepin clean
Havin a swivel tongue in my head
An a smile on my face
When I'd like to eat the guts of those dead bosses
Corpse of my grandfather
As they played
Oh god of roses and cow manure
Oh benevolent doty
Who tells us we's all bad all the time
An most never perfect
Who needs it?
Who needs it needs a quality control smack on the head

He got spies alll over
An he got pointy shoes

173

An he got Chinese food
An the tightest ass I ever did see
Chin O'Charley
With them skinny arms and bleached out flesh
Stretched out over a pair of very feminine titties
Big suckey ones
He was my one and only
A huge mother
With a gravel eye
Ain't none a you ever had a breast like Charley's
Never felt your own
It's a shame too
Then you'd know it's just an exter piece of meat
A weight on your chest
Jest like to swell under a good excitement
An excitement maybe you never had
Oh you luckless beams of the good city lollipop
Where ever male's gooey
An not much more female than
A gull without sea spray
Eunuchs without color
That's what I'd like to call him
An this is my love song
My love song
You piece of chewable flesh
You piece of hermit crab
You slap on the ass
Bitch of an over heated hot dog

Ain't it something
Ain't it something when there's nothing left
For you to taste
Or all the drunks you ever had make one big hangover
Hanging over your spine
Like to break your back
An gut you with a spoon
An roast you over a grand burning fire

Ain't it something when there ain't a voice
You couldn't imagine
Or a come on you couldn't forget
Like a TV advertisement
All you boys with that masculine look give up
The lipstick gorilla has come unglued
An her lips ain't really purple no more
They's a ripe red and ready to be bitten
An I'm gonna bite them if you don't

It weren't easy being a bull dike
Had to carry my weight
Had to show them my stuff
An I weren't no pries in the morning closet
Like the other boys
I had to stand bull legged and bellow
Until some bitch fall down before my feet
These were lusty days
An momma used to remark that i
Sure stained my panties enough
An when were the slumber parties gonna quit
Cause I surely was old enough
Being thirty
That I could earn my own
An get married
To some nice professional money man
I jes say momma
I choose my own ass
And she stares and stares and whispers to daddy
I got motional problems.

Surely my being put here weren't part of the
Overall plan
I got too many complaints
To fit into this puzzle of wiped out looks
An kids with TV dinner glare in their eyes

I missed out on the colors

An my being white surely can't please no nigger
Black like he is
Oh my lover of cow slips
And exotic fruits that burst in your mouth
A monumental Monday for me
And you daddy O daddy of the night crawler
I squished on my way to the liquor store last night
Big slug her was
Her slime stuck to my boots
An I wished the reversal would come right then
I did there, in the street, holler
Back to the Womb!
You ax

Bein the executioner's daughter weren't easy
The heads filled the house
It were hard to sit on the porch with all them flies
Buzzin
And they did buzz
An daddy
Well he was silent mostly
Jest beats on momma occasionally
And hack off heads of men
He drew pictures with his ax
His legal words
His bread and board
Meat and bones being his grit
He carved fairy tales in the flesh
Bilingual sonnets
In his swing was poetry

Now he got spies alll over
An he got fancy shoes
And he got chords
An he got shiny
An he poke me here
He ain't like no other criminal I know

It were hard to unbreath me
To find the route back
To my closet
My womb
Giddy and gulping beers
On my way
Home to moon shot
Ground control

It were hard to unbreath me
It were hard to steer a coarse
Brand a battle on the ass of my grand old meer
A sailin ship
Axis the universe
And on and on

His hardon blocked my path
Her real flesh tit pins me to the wall
I runs
I runs real well
An prism of all color blinds me
I no fool or friend
I no sex
Of blood
Bound
There was no place
For the sexual misfits
Most were caught and sucked out of existence
There was no place for me

Now he got spies alll over
An he got fancy shoes
And he got chords
An he got shiny
An he poke me here
He ain't like no other I know

ROBERT CALDWELL (a.k.a. Lloyd Quibble)
(in his words)

Robert received a B.S. in Chemistry and English from Iowa State University in 1969. Drifting from field to field, he found an uplifting joy in writing poetry. He studied prosody with Will C. Jumper and through that contact was admitted into the Writers' Round, an elite group of University writers. Caldwell published several poems in *Sketch*, the University's biannual literary magazine. Some of his prose was read on WHO radio in Des Moines. He was awarded second place in the Iowa Poetry Association Annual Lyrical Poetry Competition, for "Tijuana Nights," using the name Lloyd Quibble for the first time. In 1969, he was accepted into the Writers' Workshop at the University of Iowa. Although discouraged from attending by the Chair of the English Department at Iowa State, he enrolled conditionally at the University of Iowa.

George Starbuck, Director of the Writers' Workshop, met with all incoming writers. Caldwell confided to him that he felt out of place among such talented writers. Starbuck assured him that he had been selected not only for his poetry, but because of his diverse academic background.

Caldwell received a research assistantship from the Workshop his first year and shared a house with other artists in the Amana Colonies. He

178

studied under David Ray and Kathleen Frazier and published the poem "Birthmarked" in the *Greenfield Review*. He was introduced to more abstract forms of poetry by Ira Steingroot and started his second year studying with Anselm Hollo.

```
cannibalcannibal
cannibalannibal
cannibalnnibal
cannibalnibal
cannibalbal
cannibalal
canniball
cannibal
```

This poem created discussion about what poetry was. Was this poetry? If it was allowed as a poem, shouldn't this be renamed the "Do Whatever You Want Workshop?" Hollo consecrated it as poetry and Caldwell was allowed to stay, however he lost his assistantship and whether due to a clerical error or someone had simply "forgotten" he was coming back, his stipend was given to someone else. With Kathleen Frazier's help, he found a job working with pre-kindergarten children at Eades School in Iowa City. Though not as lucrative as the assistantship, it provided sustenance and he found it far more stimulating painting, drawing, and playing with children than mimeographing worksheets for the Workshop.

Because of his shift away from conventional verse to more experimental and abstract poetry, the Writers' Workshop offered less useful criticism for his work, which found more acceptance in multimedia classes with Hans Breder in the Art Department. His thesis "pi r" surrounded by a black square (the irony that pi r-squared is the formula for the area of a circle) was accepted by a committee made up of Anselm Hollo, Hans Breder, and Donald Justice, who happened to be around to provide a third signature. Justice did not look at the thesis, which was good because "English" was spelled "Enhglish." The irony was lost however, when dealing with the stringent requirements of the Graduate College. The reviewers had not seen anything like it coming from the English department. First it was rejected because there was no table of contents. Caldwell protested that the poems did not have titles, he was told to use the first line of the poem, and his protest that some of the poems had no lines was met coldly with, "Well, do what you want, but we won't pass it without a table of contents." After several more attempts, his thesis was accepted and he graduated with an M.F.A. in Creative Writing in 1972.

Over time, he began to feel more a multi-media artist than a poet, but his preoccupation with language kept his poetic instincts alive. Influenced by Breder he constructed poems out of plexiglass, mirrors and wood. One piece was the word "EYE" constructed of a 3 feet tall wooden letters. The second "E" was reversed, facing the inverted middle letter "Y." Shortly before leaving Iowa City in 1972, he tethered the letters with a red floating ball to the footbridge crossing the Iowa River, between the Memorial Union and the art campus. This event was written up and photographed for the *Iowa City Press Citizen*.

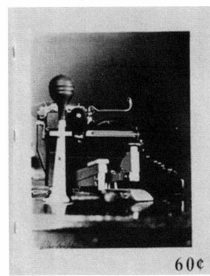

60¢

In 1971, Caldwell was influenced by Dave Morice's little mag *Gum* and Allan Kornblum's *Toothpaste*, and he began to publish *typewriter*, a small magazine featuring abstract poetry, much of it created with a typewriter, although other works incorporated stencils, rubber stamps, and an audio recording was included in the fourth issue. typewriter was published ten times in the seventies. Issues number one and two, as well as five to ten, in Iowa City, and three and four in Islip, New York. Caldwell travelled overseas and collected work from Czechoslovakia, Germany, Italy, United Kingdom and Yugoslavia. He published several of his own pieces but always used pseudonyms.

Caldwell returned to Iowa City in 1973 and continued bringing out *typewriter* magazine. Besides publishing some of the Actualists in it, he presented an animated film produced with Kent Zimmerman at the 2nd Actualist Convention (a.k.a. 2nd Actualization and 1973 Autumn Actualization), held at the Wesley House in November, using the pseudonym Lloyd Quibble. The piece, titled "wands," used refrigerator magnets projected overhead and recorded on 8mm film.

In 1974, during a citywide celebration of the Arts, he presented sticky city, an interactive piece in response to the destruction of Donnelly's Pub on South Dubuque Street, a haven for writers and artists since 1934. In 1974, it was razed to make way for urban renewal. The contractor erected a plywood barrier and walkway turning the corner at Dubuque and College streets. Caldwell called the piece kinetic because the sound of footsteps on the plywood walk and the repetitive two syllable word "city, city, city..." resonated when approaching the corner from the West or North. At the corner, letters gymnastically comingled with the word "sticky." It lasted several days before the contractor white-washed the barrier. Quibble responded by repainting the work. This version lasted approximately one week before being whitewashed again. Later someone else attempted to compose on the white wall and was arrested.

In 2006 he presented a five minute animation *The War Years*. The focus was a commentary on the neocons Cheney, Rumsfeld and Bush. The opening graphics were the words "BUSH" and "IT" animated back and forth under a red and white banner spelling "Amerrica."

Currently, Caldwell lives in West Branch, Iowa where he writes and paints. He continues to use a typewriter and computer for concrete operations.

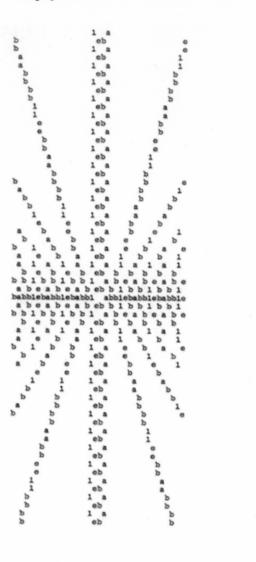

```
first
o     e
u     c
r     o
t     n
third
```

JOHN BIRKBECK
(1930–2016)
(*his words in quotation marks*)

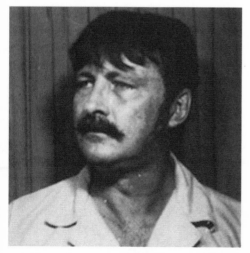

Born January 1930, "just as The Great Depression was getting under-way. Nevertheless, my childhood memories were as if from a Golden Age. When I was very young I was fascinated by maps, and Geography was my favorite subject in school. When I was eight years old I could draw free-

183

hand, a map of Europe and could also do North and South America. This love of Geography was a prelude to my early onset of wanderlust. I was always running away from home, not so much as an escape but as a running toward The Unknown. I was driven by curiosity about different places. I had always been puzzled and fascinated by boundary lines and frontiers. I'd marvel that a language could stop short of an imaginary line and another start up on the other side.

I became a compulsive traveler, and joined-up with the U.S. Air Force two times [*where he served until 1960*]. I was able to see most of the world. At last, I went to University, and took courses in varied and unrelated subjects, at last getting a degree in British Literature of the 19th Century. After my student days, I went to work as a scientific illustrator for James Van Allen, the famed discoverer of the radiation belts 'round the world which are named for him.

Late in life I became a poet, almost unexpectedly, and wrote poems in whatever spare moments that came my way. I hadn't published a poem until I was in my mid-forties and, after several years of rejection slips, I started to fly!

After retiring from my "day job" I accidentally fell into a new career in television. I have become the host and producer of a show on one of our local cable channels called *The Poets' Corner*. This is a whole new vista for me, and I'm absorbing more new knowledge and experience than I ever have before. I'm now convinced that this is where I should have started in life!"

John had enrolled at the University of Iowa's Writers' Workshop. Among the faculty at the time were Nelson Algren, Vance Bourjaily, George Starbuck and Kurt Vonnegut, but he felt he didn't know enough about writing, and was put-off by the process of criticism, so he eventually switched to majoring in nineteenth century British literature in the English Department.

John felt that in the Workshop were the east coast intellectuals with whom he did not feel comfortable, and the rebellious—who later became known as the "Actualists" and with whom he soon felt at home. He remembers feeling intimidated and looked-down-upon by some of the teachers and more successful writers. Since one cannot lay down objective, unchallengeable guidelines as to what represents true art and literature, the judgement on a student's work often came down to what the teacher or the fellow student liked. It was felt by a number of students that there was a prejudice against working-class subject matter and the presentation of "life in the raw," and consequently pressure to write about "approved" subjects and characters.

The Actualists John recalled from that time were Jim Mulac, musician, poet, and owner of Jim's Used Books and Records; Chuck Miller, poet, teacher and world traveler; Glen and Harry Epstein, poets and owners of Epstein's Books; Darrell Gray, poet; Anselm Hollo, poet, translator and teacher; Dave Morice, poet and Dadaist; and poets Morty Sklar, Allan Kornblum, Patty Markert, Gary Lemon, John Sjoberg, Mary Stroh, Dick Tibbetts, Cinda Wormley, Pat Casteel, Liza Gyllenhall, Dave Hilton and Steve Toth. A fellow traveler who was very popular with the group was the owner of the used books store the Paper Place, Gerald Stevenson. A number of small presses were spawned: Toothpaste Press (Allan and Cinda Kornblum), The Spirit That Moves Us Press (Morty Sklar), *Me Too* (Patty Markert and Mary Stroh), *Matchbook* (Dave Morice), and Left Bank Press, John's own. He treasures the fellowship that developed with his Actualist friends.

It was also at the Workshop where he met his wife, Barbara Grever.

(the following is from U Sam Oeur's Crossing Three Wildernesses, *Coffee House Press)*

"Donnelly's Pub, another bar just around the corner from Kenney's, had a long history as a literary hangout. One of the regulars was a man named "Big John" Birkbeck, who adopted a different persona every evening—once he was a British explorer, another time he was a senator from the Deep South. He was a great raconteur, and his stories were quite outrageous, although he made them sound plausible. I could listen to him for hours, and did, on several occasions. Although he could be a bit over-the-top at times, he was actually the draftsman and personal assistant to Dr. James Van Allen, the star of the University of Iowa physics department, and the namesake of the Van Allen belt."

Morty adds: I once sneaked a reel-to-reel tape recorder under a table at Donnelly's Pub when John was at his best, both in an exchange with another raconteur whose name I forget, or on his own—but he noticed and he seemed self-conscious so I couldn't get him at his best. As U Sam Oeur says above, one couldn't be sure whether what he was telling was true or not. For instance—a visit he'd made to a gal friend's home. He said she had a little puppy, but didn't see it. As he waited for her in the living room on a couch with a comfy cushion, she called-in to tell him to meet her at her car out front. When he rose to leave, he noticed that what he'd sat on wasn't a cushion...

(from *France Poems*)

THE PANHANDLER

I suspect his wallet
       is flat
and he is positive
          mine is too full.

It is hate on sight.

We will have to lie
to each other
each exaggerating
his poverty.

The pigeons wheel and vault
round the old belfry
of St. Germain des Pres
careless of their toil
that seems like play.

flat broke and singing
free of gravity.

WATER SIGN

You will come in
From the November night,
Into the clutter of my flat,
Into the clutter of my life,
To clear out a place among the clutter
of old memories, taming them,
Staving them off,
Keeping apparitions at bay.

You will come as the rain comes
At the end of the summer
To the dry earth.

A single raindrop
Born in the sky
Is a part of all water
That fills the dry well.

A LA BOITE DES BONS ENFANTS

Lady of pleasure they call you
Yet there is none of that
In your smile.

Your face is the shadow
Of boredom, betrayal,
Of never avenged pain—
       still young.

You have seen,
Have heard,
And felt much,
       soon.

Lady of wet night
And dry eye,
Callous of lip,
And weary of thigh,
And late.

ASTRIDE THE FRONTIER

I'm divided into halves
Up through the middle
From crotch to crown;
I'm in two places at one time.

All the land around,

A single panorama,
Looks much the same
From either eye.

Two worlds, sundered
By a line that cannot be seen,
And two languages.

The natal bi-section of my body
Cleaves my buttocks,
A seam welds the set of organs
Into a dual symmetry.

My body is a twinned pair,
Two creatures joined in one,
Each in a different nation.

Like this sweep of landscape,
I'm half in my mother country,
Half in my fatherland.

I COME FROM A SUN-BAKED TOWN…

I come from a sun-baked town
In Middle North America,
And along its main street
Were business establishments
Named Hotel Paris,
Boutique Marseilles,
La Maisonette,
Etoile Cleaners and Laundry.

Once I wandered, lost, in Paris
Not far off the Place de l'Etoile
and noticed the signs hung
above doorways:
Harry's,
The Wisconsin,
Le Weekend Club.

IN A LEFT BANK GARRET

I sit in my garret
seven floors above
the Rue de Seine
swilling cider from a tall bottle

I hear the yodel
of the fishmonger
in the market street
below my window

And happy shrieks of street crazies
And honking of the flat-sided cars
And the babble of the new-formed rabble
        surrounding a self-annointed
        charlatan who bullshits
and believes he is an apostle
as he hawks his contraband
to the glee of cackling
            standers-by

Sounds made by the next-door lovers
amplified through my cardboard walls
make me insaner than
a mountain goat

Young German boys
        students
of the Sorbonne
soddenly thud down hallways
and pound past midnight
on the doors of ladyfriends
coy but cautious
of drunken amours

I raise again
the cool green bottle
and my teeth become numb

189

while I use up my thoughts
in trying to decide which
would have been best

To have been born a bird
Or Baudelaire.

AFTER THE PARTY

The last ambulatory guest
Has stumbled away,
And low snores rise
From flaccid forms
Strewn around the floor.

And the night is old.

I sit on the carpet
At your feet,
Watching the shadows
Dancing in your eyes.

The candles burn low
And this is the magic hour
For young flesh
for ardent desire.

The last of the music is gone
And we stare lazily at each other.
We have become silent fortune-tellers.

books
Twelve Plus 2. Prosopopoeia Press, 1974
Donnelly's Beverage. Left Bank Press, 1976
France Poems. Left Bank Press, 1977
Longitudes. Carmine Creek Press, 1999
Homeless at Home. First Books Library, 2001

John has been published in print and online in numerous anthologies
and over 130 periodicals. For a comprehensive list go to his web site:
www.angelfire.com/ia/carmine.

PAT (P.J.) CASTEEL

Pat Casteel got her first taste of acting with the Actualists. The first Actualists she met were Dave Morice and Allan Kornblum when they were selling their little mags, *Gum* and *Toothpaste*, in the English-Philosophy Building during the summer of 1971. Soon after this, Pat and Dave began dating and over time she met the rest of the Actualists.

She liked the kinds of things Dave was doing, especially the performance art exemplified by poetry readings, conventions, and poetry marathons. She was impressed by the response of the audiences. Dave was already involved with his Joyce Holland hoax at this time. Joyce Holland's poems were getting published and read to the public, and editors were expressing interest. Pat suggested that she portray Joyce Holland at readings to give a face and a personality to the myth.

Appearing as Joyce, Pat gave readings in Iowa City, but she and Dave also travelled with their show to places such as the University of Wisconsin, Madison, to the Body Politic Theater in Chicago, to the Everson Art Museum in Syracuse, and to the television program *The Tomorrow Show*.

Pat states: In 1980 I met Steve Wylie, a playwright in the M.F.A. Playwrights Workshop at the University of Iowa, and in 1982 we moved to New York City together. The only place we could afford to live, ironically, was Alphabet City in the old Lower East Side. Among our neighbors were Allen

Ginsberg, Gregory Corso, Richard Hell, Rockets Red Glare, Seymour Krim, and a host of other characters who were either part of the 1960s and 1970s culture or inspired by it. Steve and I still live on the corner of East 12th Street and Avenue A, and we're now a part of the neighborhood's old-guard.

KAY AMERT
(1947–2008)

Kay Amert, beloved teacher, master typographer and letterpress printer, and noted scholar of French Renaissance printing, joined the University of Iowa faculty in 1972. She was the third director, after Caroll Coleman and Harry Duncan, of The University of Iowa Typography Laboratory. She held this position until her retirement in 2006, as professor in the School of Journalism and Mass Communication. The Type Lab was founded in 1945 as part of the Iowa School of Journalism.

Kay came to the University of Iowa as a freshman in 1966 from Madison, South Dakota. A year later, while a student in Harry Duncan's printing and typography class, she established her own private press imprint, the Seamark Press. The press's first book, *Holding Action*, poems by Sam Hamod, was published in 1969. In all, the Seamark Press published fourteen books over sixteen years—all editions of the work of contemporary American poets. Many of the Seamark Press books are in the holdings of the University

Libraries' Special Collections, where they may be viewed.

Kay also designed and printed typographical posters announcing celebrated scholarly and artistic events, many of them held at The University of Iowa. Typeset and printed by hand in multiple colors, these posters also display the metal typefaces held by the Typography Laboratory.

From the middle 1980s her energies were directed more toward teaching and typographic scholarship. She was a recipient of the Collegiate Teaching Award, and presented her scholarship at meetings of the Society for the History of Authorship, Reading, and Publishing (SHARP) and the Renaissance Society of America. At the time of her death, she was researching and writing a study of the 16th-century French printer, Simon de Colines.

Kay was personally involved for many years with local poet Howard Zimmon. Kay and Howard lived and worked together on the Seamark books produced between 1967 and 1979, which included local Actualist poet Chuck Miller—his *Hookah: Poems*, and *Oxides*, and another local Actualist, Allan Kornblum—his *The Salad Bushes*. In 1972, Kay and Howard collaborated with Kim Merker of The Stone Wall Press to jointly issue *Cargo* by Paul Nelson. Other books included Ken McCullough's *The Easy Wreckage*, and *Creosote*, illustrated by Nana Burford, as well as Donald Justice's *From a Notebook*, and Robert Dana's *What the Stones Know*.

(*from Cinda Kornblum*) Kay was generous in allowing printers to have access to the type lab after hours to finish projects. Once, Allan finally finished a run late at night, cleaned the press and we carried the stack of printed sheets to the car, only to realize that we left the building key behind and were locked out. We flagged down a campus cop who let us in. The next morning we had a call from Kay who sounded quite upset. "You're getting me into trouble. Why did you have beer in the building?" she asked. We were puzzled, since we had not been drinking. It turned out that the morning officer misread the night officer's report which said "They had been in the building" as "They had beer in the building."

193

GLEN and HARRY EPSTEIN
(Glen, 1940–2008)

Glen Epstein entered the Writers' Workshop in 1964. His first instructors were Donald Justice, Marvin Bell, Mark Strand, and Harry Duncan who taught at the Typography Lab in the School of Journalism.

Glen's brother, Harry, and Howard Zimmon followed from Los Angeles in 1968. First Glen, then Harry and Howard all worked for several years at the Paper Place, a bookstore run by Gerald Stevenson. Gerry was a poet and had an apartment above Paper Place and a hand printing press, the Qara press. In the late 1960s this space was shared with the staff of the *Iowa Defender*, an independent weekly newpaper of which Gerry was the publisher, and the Draft Resistor's League. It is hard to imagine now, but the atmosphere up there was highly charged and paranoid because resisting the draft was a crime. The Draft Resistor counselors would help male students find ways to get out of mandatory military service. Here we have together the two elements that fostered the Actualist movement, poetry and rebellion.

After the Paper Place fire in 1970 (a winter fire that left the street light coated in ice for weeks afterwards), Glen and Harry started Epstein's Bookstore. The bookstore was initially on Dubuque Street, but when displaced by Urban Renewal, they were moved a block west to a temporary module on Clinton Street. The Epstein brothers were supportive of the Writers' Workshop and the Actualist Movement and hosted many readings in their store. The bookstore became a magnet for literature. They stocked everything from East Coast little magazines such as *The World, C, Telephone, Fuck You / A Magazine of the Arts*, and *Lines* to West Coast underground comics such as *Zap, Big Ass Comics, Zippy, The Fabulour Furry Freak Brothers*, and *Binky Brown Meets the Holy Virgin Mary*. The sign on the door "No shoes / No shirt / No shit! / Come on In" welcomed all to the store.

In 1973 Harry, tired of the City's treatment of businesses displaced by Urban Renewal, ran unsuccessfully for City Council.

Harry Epstein
city council

BRING IT BACK
TO THE PEOPLE

When the time came for the store to move into the new mall, the rent was too expensive so the brothers closed it in 1977 and returned to California.

Glen's thirty-year career in calligraphy began while in rehab for alcohol over-use, where patients decorated coffee cups as part of occupational therapy. Glen returned to Iowa in the 1980s to teach calligraphy as part of the Center for the Book, although his evening and weekend classes did not make him eligible for full benefits and retirement. He developed a national reputation and his work was displayed in books and exhibits including the Calligraphy Museum in Berlin and the Metropolitan Museum of Art, the Smithsonian, and in Europe, Asia, Australia and South America. His work also traveled aboard the NASA spacecraft Galileo.

HOWARD ZIMMON
(1938–1999)

More about Howard in the previous biographical notes of Kay Amert and Glen and Harry Epstein...

For the second Actualist convention—(2nd Actualization / 1973 Autumn Actualization) Howard tipped his hat to the Dadaists when he contributed a selection of objects bought from a local hardware store. What unified the collection was the fact that each one of them cost just 19 cents.

Howard later married Kristin Garnant, and in 1989 they bought The Haunted Bookshop from Rock and Jan Williams. They operated it for ten years until Howard's health failed.

197

PATRICK DOOLEY
(in his words, mostly)

Patrick was born 1950 in Cleveland, Ohio. His early life was spent there, in Lincoln, Nebraska and finally in Iowa City, Iowa, where his father's family had lived since the 1860s.

He attended the University of Iowa School of Art and Art History where he had the good fortune to study with Howard Rogovin, Art Rosenbaum, Byron Burford, and David Dunlap. He also studied at and was assistant to the wonderful Kay Amert in the university Typography Lab.

Through chance and happenstance he fell in with a group of young poets who formed the core of Actualism—Allan and Cinda Kornblum, George Mattingly, Steve Toth and Sheila Heldenbrand, Dave Morice, Darrell Gray, Morty Sklar, to not name everyone, creating drawings and cover designs for books and magazines and having a good time too. He designed the first Toothpaste Press logo—an outline of two hands holding toothpaste and toothbrush. This experience helped lead to his eventual career in graphic design as well as furthering a love of language, poetry and poets.

Patrick dropped out of school for a couple of years in the early 1970s, during which he was most active with the Actualists, eventually returning to school and receiving an M.F.A. in Fine Arts in 1978.

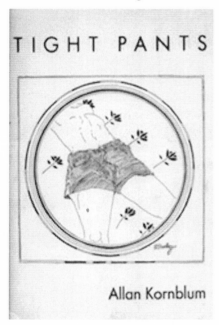
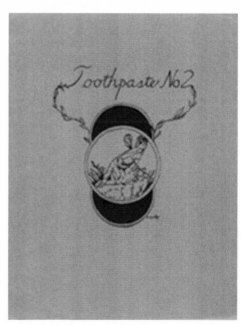

After graduation he moved to Los Angeles where he worked as a freelance graphic designer for several years before becoming designer and then design manager for the J. Paul Getty Museum, where he stayed for ten years.

Following that, he again became self-employed doing design for a variety of cultural institutions and publishers, including Sam Francis' Lapis Press. His work has won a number of design awards, including those from the New York Art Directors, New York Type Directors, and the American Institute of Graphic Arts, which includes several works in its national archive.

During this same period he also taught part-time at Otis Art Institute. This led in 1993 to a position on the faculty of the Department of Design of The University of Kansas, Lawrence, where he remains as Professor of Design to the present time. He's been married for thirty-two years to Mary (Spicer) and is father to three mostly-grown children—Claire, Grace, and James.

Patrick is modest about his achievements. Besides a Senior Scholar Award from the Fulbright Scholar Program and a $25,000 grant to fund a print campaign against child obesity, he has received over eighty awards for excellence in design and art direction. Selections of his work are found in permanent public collections with the American Institute of Graphic Art, Columbia University Rare Books and manuscripts Collection, Documenta Archiv in Kassel, Germany, the Museum of Modern Art in New York City, and the Spencer Museum of Art in Lawrence, Kansas. Furthermore, as a matter of pride, his students have received over 100 regional, national and international awards for work done in his classes.

In 2014 he was a recipient of an AIGA Fellow Award from theAmerican Institute of Graphic Art | Kansas City Chapter—"the highest honor an AIGA chapter may bestow upon one of its members". The Fellow Award recognizes designers and educators who have made a significant contribution to raising the standards of excellence in practice and conduct within the local design community and AIGA chapter.

STUART MEAD
(in his words)

Born in Waterloo, Iowa 1955, with arthrogryposis, a congenital condition affecting the joints and muscles. As a teenager he was inspired by European painting and underground comics—especially those of Robert Crumb, and English seaside postcards, and cartoons appearing in cheap men's magazines of the 1950s and early 1960s. He also draws inspiration from "high" culture sources like German modernist painters. He cites Picasso and Balthus as having the greatest influence on his artistic practice. Another strong influence is Bruno Bettelheim's book The Uses Of Enchantment, which explores the Grimm Brothers' dark fairytales from a Freudian psychological point of view, and Bettelheim's analysis of folktales with their use of simple, powerful archetypes to trigger deep emotional responses. He studied art at the University of Northern Iowa before moving with his parents to England in 1975 where he studied printmaking at the Camden Arts Centre in London.

Stuart returned to Iowa in 1977, and in April 1979 moved to Iowa City. Soon after he met Morty Sklar, for whom he contributed art work at The Spirit That Moves Us Press. In this environment he came in contact with many of the Actualists, and in time counted many as good friends including Morty, Jim Mulac, John Sjoberg and Dave Morice. He created illustrations for The Spirit That Moves Us Press, as well as The Toothpaste Press for John Sjoberg's book *Some Poems On My Day Off*, and Chuck Miller's book *Harvesters*. A quick drawing Mead made in 1979 of a dog chasing a comet later was used as The Spirit That Moves Us Press logo.

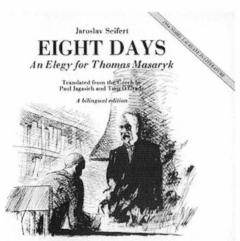

In 1981 Stuart produced his own short-lived poetry and drawing zine called *Diaper Rash*. In 1982 he co-founded The Iowa City Cartoonists Collective with Dave Morice, Cary Kahn, Kathy Dee and others. In 1983 Stuart moved to Minneapolis, Minnesota and in 1987 graduated from the Minneapolis College of Art and Design where he became acquainted with artist and future collaborator Frank Gaard. In 1987, he began contributing to the artist zine *Art Police*, which Frank Gaard edited, and participated in it until its final issue in 1994. *Art Police* gave Mead a forum where he could freely explore taboo themes, including adolescent sexuality, bestiality, and scatology. In 1991, in collaboration with Frank Gaard, he began publishing the zine *Man Bag*, an offshoot of *Art Police* that focused solely on sexual images. In 1993 Mead received the Bush Foundation Artists Fellowship, which made possible a series of trips to Europe. At this time, he began a long association with French art book publisher Le Dernier Cri, as well as with Gallery Endart in Berlin. Le Dernier Cri published a compilation of *Man Bag*'s six issues in 1999 titled *The Immortal Man Bag Journal of Art*. In 1994 he started a series of paintings based on his sexually explicit drawings which were exhibited at Endart in Berlin in 1995. His paintings of this period were a subject of "The Late Great Aesthetic Taboos," an essay included in the controversial anthology *Apocalypse Culture II*, written by Adam Parfrey and published by Feral House in 2000.

Mead moved to Berlin in 2000. In 2003 he participated in the exhibition "Please Don't Make Me Cry," curated by Georgina Starr at Emily Tsingou Gallery in London. There, he exhibited paintings depicting girls in graveyards.

In April 2004 a group exhibition called "When Love Turns to Poison" was shown at the Kunstraum Bethanien in Berlin, showing, among other works by Mead, the painting "First Communion," which was destroyed during the exhibition by a religion-obsessed vandal. The exhibition of eight artists became a national scandal, with conservative newspapers declaring it pornographic and non-art. Controversy also developed around an exhibition of Mead's work at Hyaena Gallery in Burbank, California in 2008, when four artists associated with the gallery left it in protest against Mead's exhibition. In 2009 he participated in the exhibition loop "Öffentliche Erregung" (Indecent Exposure) at loop-raum für aktuelle kunst Berlin Group exhibition that dealt specifically with the gray zone where art approaches the pornographic.

In 2010 Stuart's work was included in a large exhibition called "Family Jewels" at Villa Merkel/Bahnwarterhaus in Esslingen, Germany, in which artist Damien Deroubaix presented a family tree of the artists who have influenced his work.

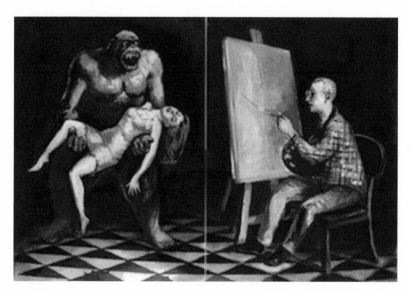

*More of Stu's art at History of Toothpaste Press
and in the color insert.*

DAVID SESSIONS
(1940-1994)

by Carol Harlow

Born 1940, raised in Mason City and came to Cedar Falls, Iowa to attend the University of Northern Iowa. I met David in 1973 or so in Cedar Falls. He had a brother and sister, all of whom called their mother—who outlived him—Eenie. His father had died around 1980.

David lived in Greece and Tehran, where he had to leave in 1979 right before the Shah fell. Also lived in Chicago, Iowa City, and Kansas City, the last of which he left in 1988 to move to Seattle.

We lived together on and off during his time in Seattle. Always painting, always drawing and always writing. For a living he painted furniture and did faux finishes for rich ladies in their boudoirs and powder rooms. Occasionally an interior designer would commission him to do a god-awful couch painting (something to hang over the couch in colors that matched the décor). He did it all with grace. In between we would roller blade all over the city and laugh our asses off at whatever.

In the fall of 1993 he was diagnosed with an aggressive type of lymph-oma and was advised by the Veterans Administration to fill out paperwork regarding his exposure to Agent Orange while he was in the service. He used to tell the story of being in Saigon and plagued with skin rashes as

205

were many other men in his unit. Turned out they all sent their laundry to the same place, and the rice starch being used on their uniforms was contaminated with Agent Orange. Nothing ever came of his filling out the paperwork—his type of lymphoma was not yet on their list.

He passed into the next dimension in March of 1994 at the tender age of 54—in my home in Seattle. His brother Richard was there as well as his niece, his mother, his friend Daniel Horsell and myself. He passed sitting upright in a chair in the living room. When the sun came up and light streamed through the windows he was bathed in a crazy bright, golden light, completely bald and still, but looking for all the world like an alabaster statue.

It was many, many years later when I learned some of his acquaintances and friends had believed or assumed that he'd died of AIDS. Nope.

Note from Morty: David was very generous with the work he created for The Spirit That Moves Us Press and other work such as posters, including one for the 8th Actualization. It didn't fully hit me until one day I wished to contact him (he hadn't been around Iowa City very long), and when I found his phone number and called, a woman answered the phone—his mother, who gave me the sad news that he'd passed-away.

See David's 8th Actualization poster & drawings for Zima's "Photo Liz" poem.

JOYE CHIZEK

Joye Chizek is Actualist Steve Toth's sister, through whom she also became a designer and publisher of books for various Actualists and other poets. She is an independent marketing consultant by profession.

Joye attended Marycrest in Davenport, then the University of Northern Iowa, from which she earned a degree in graphics and writing.

See her illustration/collage in the color insert, of initial Actualists.

Books she's published
Steven Toth (all Vortex Publishing imprint)
Love Whispers (with Sajadi, Melartin & Ruiz), 2005
The Queen of Crescent City, 2005
Still Making Love Not War, 2006
Redwood Dreams, 2008
Sacred Clowns, Holy Fools (with Dave Morice), 2009

Dave Morice / Joyce Holland (JOMO Publishing imprint)
Haloosa Nation, 2009
The Idiot and the Oddity, 2010
Concrete Blocks: An Anagram Love Story (Joyce Holland), 2010
Poetry City; A Literary Remembrance of Iowa City, Iowa, 2015
Dave Morice (Wooden Nickel Art Press)
Dr. Alphabet Unmasked: Inside the Creative Mind of David Morice,

by Joye Chizek and Tom Walz, 2013

Others

Earth National Park, by Dennis Fitzinger. Poetry Vortex Publishing, 2008

Dorothyisms: The Gospel According to Dorothy, by Dorothy Newmire & Karen Dusek. Sackter House Media, 2009

Rhymestorming, by O.V. Michaelson. JOMO Publishing, 2013

Poems for Peace, by Shana Hall. JOMO Publishing, 2013

Joy also published her own book, *Bipolar Bootcamp*, to help people with mental illness live well.

SAN FRANCISCO BAY AREA ACTUALISTS

G. P. SKRATZ

From 1970 to 1972, I toured the country with my poetry and music group, The Stone Show. Aside from my role as the "Grand Pooh-Bear," I mostly read spoken voice poems with the accompaniment of Andy Dinsmoor on guitar, as would my fellow poet, Hash Flash. Singer/song-writer Gene Hall would sing songs, and "Uncle Steve" Homsy would paint a "slow light show" behind us as we performed.

But I was writing and performing songs as well. Our performance of my "False Messiah Blues" played a significant part in our journey. In June 1970 The Stone Show had landed a Saturday night slot in the annual symposium of the Committee of Small Magazine Editors & Publishers held at SUNY/Buffalo. After a day of speeches and critical pretzels we were selected to offer literary entertainment for a very high-end audience: Ted Berrigan, Leslie Fiedler, Allen Ginsberg, on and on. Toward the end of our show we performed "False Messiah Blues," which propelled Allen Ginsberg onto the stage to join us on the choruses, dancing and assaying the role of the "False Messiah." We wound up at his dormitory lodgings with Allen on his harmonium, we on our guitars, trading songs the whole night long. The next afternoon, Allen and my Stone Show comrades merrily entertained pretty

209

much the same crowd at a barbeque in Leslie Fiedler's backyard.

That weekend, in some ways, amounted to "passing the audition": poet/professors like Tom Fitzsimmons saw us blessed as the "next big thing" by Allen Ginsberg, after which I was able to hobble together two cross-country tours for The Stone Show: various stops at coffee shops and clubs didn't pay much; ah, but the stops at colleges, c/o their English Departments made it all possible. Our first tour netted $1,000. Our second, when we brought wives and girlfriends, lost money, but that was all about "overhead."

After 1971's end of The Stone Show's tours, I "knocked-up" my then-girlfriend and married her, after which she gave birth to our daughter, Katy. In 1973 we moved into a "country commune" in Connecticut with Stone Show survivors, Andy and Mary Dinsmoor, their children, and our beloved "Uncle Steve" Homsy, who imagined himself the crazed "uncle" in the attic. In 1974, I started the "J / Stone Press Weekly" poetry postcard series, which lasted till 1976.

In 1975 our commune dissolved, and my wife and I headed off to Western Skies. Our trek west turned into a six-month odyssey that found me:

• Spending a week at Allan Kornblum's house in West Branch, Iowa, meeting Dave Morice and the remaining local Actualists (hence "The Great Band-Aid") feeding on Dave's "Marathon Poems."

• Guesting on Charles Weir's all night radio in Albuquerque. At one point, just as we were about to play a tape of my old Stone Show, he elected to play a recording of Ezra Pound from his Caedmon releases. I was stunned: this was my "Master's Voice." I said, "We've gotta put on humpback whales or something now. I canNOT follow THAT!" So we did that, and ly enough time passed when I was comfortable playing my own stuff, but THEN: the Associated Press wire-ticker started ringing the bells they only ring at Historic Events—presidential assassinations and the like.

We strolled over to the wire-ticker, ripped away the copy and noted that "Saigon" had just fallen, was now named "Ho Chi Minh City," and the last Americans were being airlifted off the roof of the U.S. Embassy. Wow. Well, we cut the copy into little squares, then pasted 'em back together in random order—what was known as the "William Burroughs cut-up method," though that, as well as "Alice B. Toklas brownies," were the inventions of

Byron Gyson, a brilliant avant-gardist who, sadly, never received credit for his best inventions.

• A luxurious month house-sitting for writer/editor Carol Berge in La Honda, California, then (and maybe now) an amazing town with three bars and one combination general store / post office. Ah, yessss!

• A week-long stint at Naropa as a guest poetry teacher at the invitation of Allen Ginsberg. Sadly, Anne Waldman and Larry Fagin pretty much considered me "Allen's Folly," so my "teaching" there was more limited than expected— the $50 the gig paid wasn't enough to entice my musician pals to join me, so I had to convey the image Allen had of my "schtick" all by my lonesome—oh, and I felt lonesome indeed! My dear pal, "Uncle Steve," did show up, but he was mainly a VISUAL artist and was mainly confined to drooling over Allen's pick of a lusty sexual retinue in their early 20's....

• A return to Albuquerque to work with Uncle Steve, who had landed a gig as scene-painter for The Man Who Fell to Earth, directed by Nicholas Roeg and starring David Bowie. Steve, to my glee, invited me to join him as his assistant. Well, SURE! and in fact I, as usual, had ulterior motive, and on our first day on the set I walked up to David Bowie and invited him to do a poetry reading with me on Charlie Weir's all-night radio show—that very night!
Well, it turned out that by day's end they'd changed the shooting schedule to start at 6:30 a.m., so he had to do a cost/benefit analysis:
a) movie/entertainment career; b) poetry reading with Skratz. With sweet generosity he posited it as a fairly even choice, but sadly, delivered his decision of going with his career and backing-out of the all-night radio gig. Ah, deep sigh: it was a blow to Charlie as well, as his radio station had pulled out all stops to get him on, but nothing had worked. Now the most unlikely of their DJs was gonna land him! Who woulda thunk? But deep, deep sigh—that wasn't to happen either. So very close but so very far away.

• And back we went to California: I'd met my idols Darrell Gray and Andrei Codrescu while housesitting at Carol's place, so although I was still going back and forth between deciding on California and New York, I'd decided on the Bay Area as the Capitol of Poetry, where I wanted to be! On the other hand I asked Allen Ginsberg what might have happened had I gone

211

back to New York—might he have hustled me onto Dylan's Rolling Thunder Revue? "Yes," he said, "It would've been a sure thing!" Well, that might've been nice, but I am happy with my life here in Oakland.

In November or early December of 1975, Darrell introduced me to David (Daf) Schein of the Blake Street Hawkeyes. Instantly we hit on the notion of holding an "Actualist Convention" in the Hawkeye's spacious studio. Daf wanted to do it right away. We'd just contact every interesting poet, musician, theater-or-performance artist we knew, slap together a program and put on the show—oh, I don't know, say, Noon to Midnight on Saturday, December 20th. We'd call it, "A Big Day at the Pit: Actualist Convention #3 / Non-Actualist Convention #1."

And thus West Coast Actualism was born.

Since then I've divorced my first wife and married the wonderful artist Linda Lemon, and have published three books of poems: *The Gates of Disappearance* (Konglomerati Press), *Fun* (Philos Press), and *Everything Else* (collaborations with Darrell Gray, Poltroon Press).

ROBERT ERNST

I received a B.A. in Theater and English from the University of Iowa in 1967, and went on to the M.F.A. program with an emphasis in poetry (Anselm Hollo, mentor) in 1968, the same year as Darrell Gray. Darrell and I did our first poetry reading together, along with Merrill Gilfillen.

212

In 1968 I'd become a staff member at the University of Iowa as an artist-in-residence within a new department called The Center for the New Performing Arts (CNPA) with major funding from the Rockefeller Foundation. While on staff, I taught and helped co-found The Iowa Theatre Lab, a theatrical ensemble that was inspired by the concepts and methodology of The Polish Lab Theatre director, Jerzy Grotowsky.

I remained at this position until the fall of 1972 when I moved to Berkeley to teach, act and direct at The Magic Theatre. I co-founded the teaching department at the Magic (Techniques for Experimental Theatre) with artistic director John Lyon, and playwright John O'Keefe. I also co-founded the now legendary Blake Street Hawkeyes in 1975, a theatrical ensemble devoted to daily training, teaching, and the development of original works for performance.

I was a part of all the Actualist Conventions that convened at The Blake Street Hawkeyes studio space/theater from the mid-1970s until the early 2000s. I did poetry, I did performance, improvisation. The specific dates are all well documented in Skratz's piece "West Coast Actualism" in this book. My 24-hour and ten minute marathon in 1987 ("If I die in performance, the audience doesn't have to") opened that year's Actualist Convention and carried on until early into day two of the convention. It was dedicated to the work and the life and the death and beyond of Darrell Gray. According to *The Guinness Book of World Records* it beat the existing record for longest play.

I began developing and performing original solo works in 1973, and have developed and produced ten since that time. I have written three plays (*Nautilus, Smokin'* and *The Best of Times*) and five pocket operas (*Changer, The Drunken Sailor, Towards Away, The John*, and *Catherine's Care*). *The John* was produced at The Intersection for the Arts in October 2001, where it received a Dean Goodman Award in Performance as well as being mentioned in the Best Of The Year series in The *Bay Guardian*.

Catherine's Care was produced at The Alter-Theater in February 2007. It is a theatrical chamber piece and tour-de-force for an older actress and a live, four-piece band. It was nominated for a Bay Area Critics Circle awards for Best Play and Best Actress.

I performed in Night Falls, a physical theater collaboration between playwright Julie Hebert and the Deborah Slater Dance Company at Oberlin Dance Collective in August 2011. It was mentioned as one of the ten best dance performances of the year in *The Bay Guardian*.

I've received developmental support from The Marin Arts Council, Alter-Theater of San Rafael, Z-Space of San Francisco, Intersection for the Arts, Theater Bay Area's Cash Grant Award and The Zellerbach Foundation, and received a commission from the National Institute of Science in association with the Magic Theatre to create a play involving Nano technology.

I have received Dramalogue awards for Best Director and Best Production (*Tokens*, 1984) and as a part of the Best Ensemble for the Eureka production of *Road*, 1987. My performance in the Sam Shepard play, *Eyes for Consuela*, was picked by the *Bay Guardian* as one of the year's best in 1999. I understudied for Nick Nolte in Sam Shepard's play, T*he Late Henry Moss*, at the Theatre on the Square (December 2000), and performed in a critically acclaimed production of William Saroyan's *Time Of Your Life*, a tri-production sponsored by The Steppenwolf Theatre of Chicago, Seattle Repertory Theatre, and American Conservatory Theater of San Francisco and The People's Temple Project. A production at The Berkeley Repertory Theatre that was also produced by Z-Space and New York's Tectonic Theatre Co.

I've performed on every major, and most small, theater stages in the Bay Area, as well as on television and in the movies. Film/TV credits include *The Boat-builder*, *After Ever After*, *Surefire*, *Jumpin' Jack Flash*, *Burglar*, *Metro*, *Escape from Alcatraz*, *Nash Bridges* and *Hill Street Blues*.

I taught acting and the act of creative writing at the Berkeley School of Theater since it began, and have been a play-writing instructor-in-the-schools through the California Young Writers' Project since it's inception. I mentored students through the play-writing process and helped them to develop and write short plays based on their own experience and in their own voice. I taught at Oakland Tech, Macateer High School, and at Mission High School in San Francisco, and work with ESL high school students as well as the general student population.

I have also been a guest artist at Tamalpais High School in Mill Valley for the past ten years, and teach classes in improvisation, play-writing, and the creation of solo and collective original works for the theater. I've directed the development and performance of two complete collective works for their student-run company (Conservatory Theater Ensemble), both of which won best play and best actor awards at the 2007 and 2009 Mother-Lode Theatrical Competition: *City of Puppets, Nothing, Play Roulette* and *Flare.*

I've performed wide-open/nothing-planned improvisation with Ruth Zaporah/Action Theater every year for over thirty years.

Am currently at work on a theatrical episodic, *The Buck & Bill Show.* I'm also a member of the music collective called Smooth Toad.

STEVEN LAVOIE
(in his own words)

Steven covered the fall of Actualism while in Cedar Rapids, Iowa while in exile from the Black Bart Poetry Society, a group based in northern California. His association with that group had condemned him to perpetual obscurity as a poet and literary figure.

While in Iowa, he exploited friendships he developed there with Allan and Cinda Kornblum, Dave Morice and Mira-Lani Bernard (then Perelman) to help jettison much of his past.

After securing the immunity enjoyed by students of librarianship, Steven was able to escape his Midwestern exile and return to northern California where he had studied poetry with David Bromige, Ron Loewinsohn and others, and co-curated a literary reading series at the Grand Piano Café and the New College of California in San Francisco, and where he performed in Poets Theatre.

Since his return he and his small circle of associates have come to be designated in the blogosphere as "post-Actualists," something he was warned about before he took up temporary residence in the shadow of the Iowa Writers' Workshop, although blogging had not yet been conceived. He, of course, rejects that designation.

Since the collapse of Actualism, Steven's been living in Oakland, California where he dropped the use of an upper case "v" in the spelling of his surname. He once was columnist at the *Oakland Tribune*, remains personal friends with more than one Actualist and was published by more than one—and long long ago he published Actualists in his magazine *Famous*. He was a student at the University of California, Berkeley when he attended the reception for George Mattingly and Darrell Gray hosted by Keith Abbott. He'll probably have to move one of these days to someplace he can afford, although he's been saying that for a while now.

A considerable body of extraordinary unpublished original verse resides among his very disordered papers. Upon publication, this work will clearly distinguish him from any association with Actualism and will mention in the acknowledgments the following people and communities, listed alphabetically: Mira-Lani Bernard, Richard Brautigan, David Bromige, Andrei Codrescu, Gloria Frym, Carla Harryman, David Highsmith, Jack Hirschman, Alastair Johnston, Gail King, Komotion, Allan Kornblum, Joanne Kyger, Michael-Sean Lazarchuk, Sarah Menefee, Lana Michaleczko, Dave Morice, Pat Nolan, Victoria Rathbun and Mark Smith. Steven's publications include *Birth of a Brain*, a visual poetry collaboration with Dave Morice; *Erosion Surface*, a Coffee House Press chapbook; a popular weekly column in the Pulitzer-Prize-winning Oakland Tribune; and *Life of Crime*, a literary newsletter held by the Dada Archives at the libraries of the University of Iowa.

He's seen the Sex Pistols perform live three times and attended the last performance of drummer Mick Avory as a member of the Kinks. He played softball alongside Jonathan Lethem and others in the People's League and is currently active in the labor movement. Steven's invited such writers as Eli Brown, Ottessa Moshfegh, Farnoosh Fathi, Margot Pepper and Diane Fujino for appearances at the branch library he currently manages in Oakland.

MICHAEL LYONS
(in his own words)

Michael was born in Montreal, and raised in San Antonio where his French helped with Spanish. He also lived in Austin, Berkeley and Montreal. He was married in San Francisco and has a son.

He had over twenty books in print and epubs, as well as five CDs of musical composition and soundscape with voice radio theatre production. Michael used writing as a diary to observe the journey of his soul. He spent several years in Berkeley where he published a small press literary rag called *The Punctual Actual Weekly*. It was an amazing education in futility and joy all emblazoned under the punk ethos.

He started publishing his own novels when his son was born, wanting to tell the story of who we are. The first was *Dolores Park* about a tantric sex

Buddhist commune. Then two about being an older husband and father: *A Blue Moon in August* and *Thoughts on Vacation*. He went way into his past to publish *Cultivating the Texas Twister Hybrid* about a marijuana farm in Texas, which developed into a trilogy with *The Secret of the Cicadas' Song: A Peyote Trip in Prose and Poetry,* and *Knight of 1000 Eyes*, about learning Tai Chi. Then he started to work his way straight through the sextet with *Sex is the Antigravity of Metamorphosis,* but got sidetracked by a book not in the series, *The Punctual Actual Weekly*. Then the second book in the sextet, *The Indigenous Tribesmen of Neverland.* And the last which was the fourth in the series, *Seeing Through the Spell of Transference*. Writing the sextet took over twenty years and it seemed at times like forever.

Along the way, to escape the rigorous long term commitment to books, he wrote poetry and made several CDs of reciting and singing to original music. Michael always wanted to be engaged in something creative, which made him feel good to be invested in a spiritual and aesthetic project.

To make a living he worked as a tech writer. Starting out as a lowly Kelly Girl he did word processing, and jumped into technical writing using his skill in electrical engineering. In those heydays of desktop publishing he produced dozens of manuals about gas analyzers, scanners, credit card processing and debt collection, disk duplication, microlithography, MRI, artificial intelligence (Bayesian inference) and games. He designed software for writers to help them. He developed software for role playing game masters. Also, he did multimedia marketing for geology equipment. With Hypercard and others he developed many interactive interfaces. It was one creative job after another, at some of the biggest companies in Silicon Valley: Apple, Bank of America, Cetus, Oracle, Tandem, Visa. But as a contractor he always felt like the outside alien, and eventually it became unsatisfactory. He retired when the downturn continued, and returned to being a knock-around carpenter.

A child-like curiosity and sense of his own creative mind gave introverted Michael a intuitive world view. We are lucky that he left us so many views of this world.

DAVID SCHEIN

David is a writer and theater artist. As an undergraduate at the University of Iowa he studied with Anselm Hollo, Jack Marshall and Marvin Bell, then worked as an artist-in-residence at Iowa's Rockefeller Center for the New Performing Arts where he co-founded the terminally avant-garde Iowa Theater Lab.

Fleeing academia to make "rough theater" with other Iowa/California transplants, he co-founded the Blake Street Hawkeyes in Berkeley with Bob Ernst and John O'Keefe.

In 1975, with noir novelist and poet Jim Nisbet and poet G.P. Skratz, Schein began producing Actualist Conventions at the Hawkeye Studio at 2019 Blake Street—consisting of twenty-four half-hour sets for two days all for $5 admission and featuring theater, poetry, music, film, dance, music. Artists included Darrell Gray, Andrei Codrescu, Summer Brenner, Geof Hewitt, Gloria Frymm, Ed Dorn, George Coates, Leonard Pitt, Chuck Hudina, Whoopi Goldberg, Nisbet, Schein, Skratz and many other Bay Area artists.

In the eighties Schein wrote for and toured with Whoopi Goldberg, wrote and taped radio in Tijuana with Guillermo Gomez-Peña and taught and performed in theaters in France, Holland, Switzerland and Germany. Schein's 70-person opera *TOKENS: A Play on the Plague*, with music co-written by Candace Natvig, won three San Francisco Bay Area Drama Critics Awards and three Hollywood Dramalogue awards. Another musical, *Reverence for the Dead*—about the return of Lee Harvey Oswald, with music co-written by Joshua Raoul Brody, was produced in Berkeley and Calgary.

In the nineties Schein directed Free Street Theater in Chicago where he created theater and writing programs for low-income Chicago youth. In 2002 in Awassa, Ethiopia with the street kids of Debub Nigat Circus he co-founded One Love AIDS/HIV Awareness Theater, which for thirteen years has toured original shows about AIDS and gender equality throughout the markets of Ethiopia.

David has been a guest teacher at Brown University, Naropa Institute, at New York University and the New England Young Writers' Conference at Bread Loaf, Vermont and in many elementary and high schools in Illinois, New York and Vermont.

He is currently working on the film version of his solo *Out Comes Butch* with Constant Flow Productions, and collaborating with Vermont writer Geof Hewitt on Hotball, a musical about global warming. His book of performance poems, *My Murder and Other Local News*, was recently published by Fomite Press.

He currently lives in his hometown of Burlington, Vermont.

WHOOPI GOLDBERG

Morty would like to preface this biographical note by saying how Whoopi agreed to our including her piece (co-written with David Schein) at the drop of a hat. In addition to all her great accomplishments, both professional and personal, she remains a regular gal.

Whoopi moved north to Berkeley, California in the late 1970s and joined the Blake Street Hawkeyes Theater, a comedy troupe. While working with the Hawkeyes and touring with David Schein she developed the multi-charactered *The Spook Show* that Mike Nichols developed into *Whoopi Goldberg on Broadway.* She performed at two Actualist conventions with Schein: in Jim Nisbet's *Valentine* and in *The Last Word,"* co-written with Schein, which is included in this book. This helped her develop powerful acting and comedic abilities.

Actress, comedian, television host and human rights advocate Whoopi Goldberg was born Caryn Elaine Johnson on November 13, 1955, in New York City. She and her younger brother Clyde were raised by their mother Emma in a housing project in the Chelsea section of Manhattan. She changed her name when she decided that her given name was too boring. "Goldberg" is attributed to her family history.

Best known for her adept portrayals in both comedic and dramatic roles, as well as her groundbreaking work in the Hollywood film industry as an African-American woman. Goldberg unknowingly suffered from dyslexia, which affected her studies and ultimately induced her to drop out of high school at the age of 17.

She returned to New York, and in 1983 starred in the enormously popular *The Spook Show*. The one-woman Off-Broadway production featured her own original comedy material that addressed the issue of race in America with unique profundity, style, and wit.

By 1984, director Mike Nichols had moved *The Spook Show* to a Broadway stage and in 1985 Goldberg won a Grammy Award for Best Comedy Album for the recording of skits taken from the show.

Director Steven Spielberg cast her in the leading female role of his 1985 production of *The Color Purple* (adapted from the novel by Alice Walker), a film that went on to earn ten Academy Awards and five Golden Globe nominations. Goldberg herself received an Oscar nomination, and her first Golden Globe Award—as Best Actress.

In 1992 Whoopi starred in the enormously popular *Sister Act* as a world-weary lounge singer disguised as a nun hiding from the mob, for which she earned an American Comedy Award for Funniest Actress in a Motion Picture, as well as another Golden Globe nomination for Best Actress in a Comedy.

In 1994, 1996 and 1999, Whoopi hosted the Academy Awards, making her the only woman ever to have done so.

Whoopi holds a Ph.D. in literature from New York University and an honorary degree from Wilson College in Chambersburg, Pennsylvania.

She is one of the few entertainers who has won Emmy, Grammy, Oscar, and Tony Awards.

She has admitted publicly to having been a "high functioning" drug addict years ago, at one point being too terrified to even leave her bed to go use the toilet.

$3.50

The Actualist Anthology

Edited by Morty Sklar & Darrell Gray

The Spirit That Moves Us Press

The Actualist Anthology 1977, Iowa City; cover art by Patrick Dooley

Looking forward and backward,
from letterpress to e-book

COFFEE HOUSE PRESS
& TOOTHPASTE PRESS

An Exhibit at Open Book

IOII WASHINGTON AVENUE SOUTH,
SECOND FLOOR, MINNEAPOLIS, MINNESOTA

This exhibit chronicles the forty-plus-year history of Allan Kornblum and his life in publishing. He began publishing mimeograph and letterpress-printed magazines during the 1970s and early 1980s as Toothpaste Press. In 1984 he founded Coffee House Press, which, in its twenty-sixth year, is regarded as one of the premier independent literary publishers in the country, noted for consistent editorial excellence; an adventurous sense of discovery; elegant design and production; and its continued commitment to writers, to readers, and to literature. This exhibit traces the origins, explores the recent past and present, and points the way to the future of Coffee House Press.

If you'd like to learn more after enjoying the exhibit,
or to find your way into one of our books,
please visit www.coffeehousepress.org.

NOVEMBER II, 2010–JANUARY 9, 2011

Coffee House Press & Toothpaste Press exhibit at Open Book, 2010/2011
spanning over 40 years; poster created by Linda Koutsky

Early Toothpaste Press books at Open Book 2010/2011, exhibit of 40 years of
Toothpaste Press & Coffee House Press books; photo by Allan Kornblum

Allan & Annabel Kornblum sorting manuscripts 1973, West Branch, Iowa
photo by Cinda Kornblum

Poem Around a City Block, 1975, written by Dave Morice (Dr. Alphabet);
Morty Sklar, P.J. Casteel, Dave Morice, Allan Kornblum; photo by Dom Franco?

Matchbook publication of one-word poetry; Joyce Holland, Editor

Jim Mulac in front of his store on South Dubuque Street, 1970s; photo by?

One of many readings at Jim's Books & Records 1970s & 1980s
poster created and colored by Jim Mulac, as many were

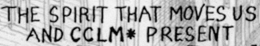

THE SPIRIT THAT MOVES US
AND CCLM* PRESENT

Poetry+Fiction Reading
AND PARTY
with a display of some Midwestern "little" literary magazines.

SATURDAY, APRIL 12
AT CENTER EAST
downstairs
+upstairs

8:00 P.M.
HILMA WOLITZER,
Reading her fiction

9:00 P.M.
Reading their poetry,

MARY STROH,
Editor of ME TOO Magazine;
CHUCK MILLER;
⎡**ALAN KORNBLUM**
⎜Coeditors of DENTAL FLOSS
⎜Magazine, TOOTHPASTE PRESS
⎣**CINDA KORNBLUM**

LOWELL JAEGER,
Editor of EL NAHUATZEN
Magazine;
MORTY SKLAR,
Editor of THE SPIRIT THAT
MOVES US PRESS and Magazine

* Coordinating Council of Literary Magazines has a membership of 700
"little" magazines; it is a national non-profit literary organization
established in 1967.

Rare combined Actualist and Workshop reading, but after the latter's reader led-off,
the Workshoppers all left! poster by Stuart Mead

At the bookstore that became Jim's Used Books & Records
poster created and hand-colored by Jim Mulac

1971; poster by George Mattingly

Actualist Collage created by Joye Chizek

Lew Hyde & Howard Zimmon Reading Neruda, 1971; poster by Kay Amert

Jim Mulac took advantage of the International Writing Program's visiting writers and musicians; poster created and hand-colored by Jim Mulac

Allan Kornblum in Coffee House Press Office above Nate's; early 1990s; photo by?
Allan Kornblum receiving the Kay Sexton Award 2012 in recognition
of long-standing dedication and outstanding work.

Minnesota Center for the Book Arts, Minneapolis; photo by Gina Debogovich

Chuck Miller at The Spirit That Moves Us Press display in Iowa City, 1988
photo by Morty Sklar

JAROSLAV SEIFERT   1984 NOBEL PRIZE

THE CASTING
OF BELLS

Translated from the Czech by Paul Jagasich & Tom O'Grady

The poet, Jaroslav Seifert, won the Nobel Prize the following year, 1984. Tom O'Grady &
Paul Jagasich, translators from the Czech. Published by The Spirit That Moves Us Press

Marcela Bruno and Morty Sklar
The Spirit That Moves Us Press at Small Press Book Fair in New York City, 2008

Anselm Hollo, Jim & Margaret Bateman, Kay Amert at reception for
Allan and Cinda Kornblum's wedding, 1972; photo by Selma Kutner

At the entrance to the Iowa City Public Library; photo by Morty Sklar

Note to Allan Kornblum from Darrell Gray, February 1972

Dr. Alphabet (Dave Morice) typing a poem on the Jefferson Building, Iowa City, 1979
photo by Lillian Morice, Dave's mother

David Hilton & Warren Woessner at Allan & Cinda Kornblum's in West Branch (1973?)

Morty Sklar, Chuck Miller, Jim Mulac, Heidi Mulac at Ann Struthers' home
in Cedar Rapids (date?); photo by Ann Struthers

John Sjoberg at a typewriter; photo by Cinda Kornblum (year?)

Morty Sklar's poetry reading at Uptown Bill's in Iowa City, 2012
P. Dooley, D. Larew, J. Sjoberg, (?), Morty, S. Marsden, R. Rosenbaum,
G. Perret, (?), C. Miller, (?), M. J. Dane, J. Lekin, D. Morice; photo by Marcela Bruno

Dave Morice, Chuck Miller, Morty Sklar
Morty's 2012 Poetry Reading in Iowa City; photo by Maggie Hogan

EDITOR'S CHOICE III
Fiction, Poetry & Art from the U.S. Small Press

EDITED by MORTY SKLAR
Contributing Editor, Robert Peters
INTRODUCTION by FRED CHAPPELL

Cover art by Gertrude Degenhardt. 84 contributors to this volume (1984-1990) were selected from 3,465 nominations by 364 presses & magazines from an open call to 2,000.

THE SMELL OF LIFE

Morty Sklar

poems
1969 to 2005

cover art (which continues around the spine to, and including, the back)
by James Harrison

painting by Stuart Mead

III. ACTUALIST PERFORMANCES AND CONVENTIONS

IOWA CITY

First Actualist Event—Poetry Marathon at Epstein's Bookstore

by Dave Morice

In late February 1973, I went to Epstein's Bookstore to discuss a project with Harry Epstein. He was seated at his desk, which was attached to a raised wooden platform. Its height made it seem like a throne. Nearby, Darrell Gray was shelving books, and was also planning the first Actualist Convention, to take place on March 10th at Wesley House. I wanted to do a public writing at Epstein's either before or after the convention. "Harry, I had an idea last night for a poetry event. I'd like to write a thousand poems in public at the bookstore. Would you be interested in hosting it?"

"Sure," he said. "In fact, we're having our grand opening next week on March 3rd. We're getting some bluegrass musicians to play on the porch. You could write on that table over there."

"A poetry marathon!" Darrell said. "That would be a great way to advertise the Actualist Convention."

On the scheduled day, Joyce Holland (aka P.J. Casteel) and I went to the bookstore with paper and typewriter. We set up the typewriter next to a fishbowl. Darrell had taped a sign to the front of the table:

ACTUALIST MARATHON
Poetry Event in Progress
Dave Morice will write 1000 poems
in 6 hours—from 10 A.M. to 4 P.M.

The Epstein brothers gave me the place to write my first poetry marathons beginning with this geometric trilogy: 1000 poems in 12 hours; a 100-foot poem on the longest day of the year; and a mile-long, 160-pound haiku as the Comet Kohoutek passed the earth.

For that first marathon I brought more than a thousand small sheets of many different kinds and colors of paper, provided by Allan Kornblum. Joyce numbered the blank sheets, and I began writing the poems three at a time with my Royal typewriter with its wide carriage. After I wrote each trio, I put them in a fishbowl. As I typed, people came by, asked questions, and made requests for words and topics that they wanted me to use. The resulting poems ranged in length from one word ("thend") to fourteen lines.

To my surprise, Glen Epstein had contacted the media. Three newspapers did stories about the event, and two television stations did trailers to follow the 10 P.M. news. One channel began its trailer by noting that March 3rd marked the centennial anniversary of the invention of the first practical typewriter in 1873 by Christopher Latham Sholes. That was purely a coincidence.

About Dave's Marathons

by Allan Kornblum,
circa 1973

Dave Morice was born in Saint Louis. His father sold insurance, and his mother did secretarial work on and off.

When a little lad, he was called "Mud" for his baseball dexterity, and although he went to Catholic schools his experiences were mostly American. To this day he likes hamburgers and drinks a lot of coffee knowing he should cut down, and smokes a lot of cigarettes knowing he should cut down. He has a few American neuroses: afraid of bees for instance, but no more than most people.

He is above all, an easygoing guy. Still, it is my contention that of all American poets, Dave Morice most captures the spirit of Rimbaud, the spirit of the explorer into the nature of perception. Rimbaud of course, investigated the results of a conscious attempt to disorder the senses (using absinthe, opium) on the work of a young poet—himself. We have his work, and can and do read his work. We can see he was stoned, had vision, felt outside of everything normal in stuffy Europe of the 1890s.

Dave Morice instead, is after the American experience rather than the bohemian experience, and goes after these discoveries through that very American phenomena, the marathon, as well as his Dr. Alphabet personna and circus-like interactive poetry events. What happens when a twenty-six year old man who has grown up smack-dab in Saint Louis, baseball, greasy hair and fast cars—what happens when such a man sits down and pushes himself to keep going, hour after hour, writing poetry? After several hours intentions evaporate. Our longhaired Huck Finn is still sitting in front of his typewriter reaching further, unaware anymore of how he is doing it, unaware of any deliberate reaching into his past, he's been writing for four hours, now, five hours and he's only half done. Six hours and he's still writing writing writing writing. How does the mind organize experience? Now he has been writing seven hours. Where is the poem coming from? What is the recipe? Two cups of present, three cups of past, a cup-and-a-half of literary preference? Oil of course, the oil of the imagination but how much of that and how to keep the oil from going rancid?

225

Americans have sat on flagpoles, been buried alive and danced for hours. The American press is partly responsible for the international athletic obsession with "records." But apart from the "record" aspect, shall we call the poem a "stunt"? It should seem obvious that Dave is giving us a glimpse into the nature of perception itself.

"At dawn my lover comes to me
And tells me of her dreams
With no attempt to shovel the glimpse
Into the ditch of what each one means"
—*Bob Dylan in "Gates Of Eden"*

First Actualist Convention—Wesley House, March 10, 1973

from the Iowa City Press-Citizen, *March 10, 1973*:

—Experimental Musical Play To Premiere Here Tonight—

A theatrical world premiere will take place in Iowa City tonight when a company of independent actors and writers present *Backyard*, an experimental musical comedy written by local poets. It's at 8:30 pm. at Wesley House.

The event will be part of the Actualist Convention, a festival of the arts, including poetry readings, films, multimedia, drama and happenings. The convention, held in the basement auditorium of Wesley House, will extend from 3 until 11 p.m. and is expected to attract artists from other parts of the nation.

Written by Darrell Gray and James Mulac, the two-part play uses a collage technique to display a revolutionary variety of realistic, surrealistic, existential and vaudevillian performances.

A central character in the play is a composite "blob" which consists of more than one actor and performs in a way unique to modern theater.

The nine characters and their performers are: Devil Worshipper, George Mattingly; Urban School teacher, Katherine Combellick; Farmer, Clyde Harris; Fur Trapper, Chuck Miller; Jagged Piece of Light (a central figure in the Blob), Rick Keeley: Daughter of the Blob (also called Key), Kim Schroeder; and the three chorus women, Cathe McCliment, Lori Gillispie and Penny Bradfield.

226

Commenting on the play, co-author Mulac said: "We are shooting here for something like Stravinski's Le Sacre du Printemps. We want to move things toward the 21st century."

Dave Morice has this to say:

Actualism expanded to include the other arts, and the Convention gave everyone the opportunity to display or perform whatever they wanted. There were poetry readings, musical performances, artworks, and a play.

from Morty:

I'd been in Iowa City less than two years when preparation for the First Actualist Convention was being made. Darrell Gray asked me if I was going to read my poetry there, and I replied, "Isn't it just for Actuaists?" and he said, "Well, you're an Actualist." It was like being knighted.

I'd like to mention another great pull into this community for me: While I was still fairly new here, Dave Morice asked to see my notebook of poems. He said to me, "There are some poems here that I haven't heard you read and haven't seen in the little mags here." He pointed them out. I said they're humorous and I want to be taken seriously. Dave's reply: "Well, humor is serious too."

Thanks again, Dave.

TRANSLATIONS *from* NEW YORKESE

A MONOLOGUE *by*
MORTY SKLAR
AT THE ACTUALIST CONVENTION
WESLEY HOUSE 120 N. DUBUQUE
SATURDAY MARCH 10 FROM **3-11 P.M.**

Dave continues:

My Alphabet Chair was an old wooden chair with a white undercoat and painted with multicolored letters of different sizes in a scattered pattern all over. I'm sitting on it as I write this.

"Marlboro Money": I brought a paper bag full of more than 500 empty Marlboro packs that I'd saved over the previous year, and I announced the Marlboro Money Hunt: I'd put a dollar bill in one pack and a five in another, then put them back in the bag. I swung the bag around and scattered the packs on the floor. Whoever found the money got to keep it. No one ever admitted to finding either bill.

"Door Prize": a drawing in which the prize was the door to the auditorium. Cinda Kornblum won it, but couldn't take it home because it was still attached to the building.

"Actual Ace": a poster-sized painting of an ace of spades in which the spade, normally black, was multicolored and filled with words and pictures.

"The Light Switch": Joyce Holland performed an instantaneous play. She turned the auditorium light off and explained that the play involved everyone in the room. Then she flicked the switch on and off as quickly as possible. The light was gone. The play was over. The auditorium was dark. She flicked the switch on again, and the Convention continued.

228

Poetry and Fiction Readings
by Cinda Kornblum

Poetry and fiction readings flourished in Iowa City. In addition to read-ings sponsored by the Writers' Workshop, Iowa City had a thriving "scene" of unpaid off-campus readings which were instrumental in developing a close-knit community of writers.

I have compiled a list of readings based on the posters we collected during this time. Even though incomplete, the list gives an idea of the mix of local, national and international writers who performed in these venues. In addition to these were readings of other writers such as the 1977 reading of Jack Kerouac's works by Jim Hanson, Tony Hoagland, Chuck Miller and John Sjoberg; of Charles Bukowski by Chuck Miller, Anselm Hollo and Jim Mulac; of William Carlos Williams by Allan Kornblum, and readings at the "Black Hawk Mini-Park" on the corner of Washington and Dubuque Streets, as well as many, many open readings.

Epstein's Bookstore welcomed local and Workshop poets for regular readings in 1970-1972 with elegantly printed letterpress posters designed by local typographers including Kay Amert, George Mattingly and Allan Kornblum (see color insert). The one poster I printed when Allan was ill created some chuckles when I presented David Morrell, a fiction writer, with a sign for "Dave Morrell Reading His Poetry."

Readers at Epstein's included Bill Bode, Ken McCullough, Dave Morice, Allan Kornblum, Jim Stephens, Darrell Gray, Lew Hyde and Howard Zimmon (reading translations from Pablo Neruda), Wendy Salinger, Barrett Watten, Steve Toth, Sheila Heldenbrand, Bill Fox, Scott Wright, Gary Lemmons, Anselm Hollo, Robert Dana, Tony Colby, Tomas Trans-tromer, David Morrell, and William Price Fox. Epstein's also hosted a 24-hour marathon reading to raise funds for *The Iowa Review*.

In 1972-73, the Actualists arranged a series of readings at Wesley House. Included were: Steve Toth, Sheila Heldenbrand, John Sjoberg, Chuck Miller, David and Maria Gitin, George Mattingly, Allan Kornblum, Joyce Holland, Darrell Gray and Jim Mulac. Wesley House was also the location of the Actualist Convention and the production of some Actualist plays: *The Brick Apartment, Backyard, and The Umbrella That Predicted the Future.*

229

Jim Mulac recommended moving the readings to The Sanctuary, a tavern on South Gilbert Street, and a weekly series continued there from 1973 to 1975 with 52 readings. Readers included Allan Kornblum, Cinda Wormley, Sam Hamod, Liz Zima, Audrey Teeter, John Sjoberg, John Wieners, Dick Tibbets, Howard Zimmon, Patty Markert, Barbara Sablove, Sheila Heldenbrand, Pat O'Donnell, Chuck Miller, a group of poets from Chicago (Terry Jacobus, Al Simmons, Hank Kanabus, Pat McPhee and John Paul), Maureen Kinsella, John Birkbeck, David Sessions, Judith Meier, Phil Lemke, John Sjoberg, Liz Voss, Brad Harvey, Michael Waltuch, Elise Nagel, George Mattingly, Dawneen Martinez, Joe Gastiger, Gerald Stevenson (fragments from an autobiography), Josephine Clare, Anselm Hollo, G.P. Skratz, Neil Hackman and Simon Schuchat, Morty Sklar, Mary Stroh, Tomaz Salamun, Pat Casteel and Jim Mulac (reading *Five and Dime Lovers*).

In 1976, Alandoni's Bookstore (610 South Dubuque Street), run by Alan Frank, became the new location for readings, some of which were by Steve Levine, Simon Schuchat, Jim Perelman, Jim Stephens, Warren Woessner, Steve Toth, Sheila Heldenbrand, Alan Axelrod, John Sjoberg, Liz Zima, Walter Hall, Allan Kornblum, Art Lange, Rose Lesniak, David Allen, Dick Bakken, Chuck Miller, Sigurdur Magnusson, Stavros Deligiorgis, Dave Morice, S.R. Lavin, W.P. Kinsella, Will Schmitz, Darrell Gray, Jonis Agee, David Wilk, Darrell Gray, Jim Hanson, Arnold April, David Hilton, Warren Woessner, John Sjoberg, Rebecca Rosenbaum, and Cinda Kornblum.

Jim Mulac bought the bookstore that was Alandoni's and started Jim's Used Books & Records. His hand-colored felt-tip posters appeared in store windows for readings by a mix of international writers, visiting and local writers including Abdul-Latif Akel from Palestine, Abdul Wahab (Malaysia), Bessie Hood (South Africa), Leslie Scalapino, Joy Harjo and Medicine Story, Michael Tarachow, Sasha Newborn & Judl Mudfoot, Jonis Agee and David Wilk, Darrell Gray and Alastair Johnston, W.P. Kinsella, Anselm Hollo, Chuck Miller, Morty Sklar, Cinda Kornblum, Jim Mulac, Dave Morice, Josephine Clare, John Sjoberg, and Ken McCullough.

In January 2015 protests arose in Iowa City to prevent the destruction of three civil-war-era cottages on South Dubuque Street, one of which had housed Alandoni's Bookstore, Jim's Used Books & Records, and Selected Works. These efforts were unsuccessful and the three buildings were demolished.

The Poets' Theater

by Jim Hanson (*from* "Actual Plays," *In the Light* #s 5/6)

The Actualist poets often write collabs, regarding them as a diverting activity to be pursued when two or more poets and a typewriter are gathered together. The imaginative use of language that results is often extraordinary. They are also interested in words as a public event. From this interest come the performances themselves, either by an ensemble or as read by the authors directly.

Backyard was performed on April 14, 1973 at Wesley House on a double bill with *The Brick Apartment*. One device used in this performance was a large cloth with three holes in it, used as a costume for the Blob. This enabled the Blob to gradually incorporate several other characters, as is called for in the play. The performers were George Mattingly as the Devil Worshipper, Catherine Combellick as the Urban Schoolteacher, Clyde Harris as the Farmer, Chuck Miller as the Fur Trapper, Rick Kealey as the Jagged Piece of Light, Kimberly Schroeder as Key, Cathe McCliment as Chorusgirl 1, Lori Gillespi as Chrosugirl 2, and Mary Cook as Chorusgirl 3. The play was directed by Jim Mulac, clarinet and scenery by Bill "Woody" Woodward, light and sound by David Bloom. The play was written about January 1973. Allan Kornblum began the collaboration with Darrell and Jim, but dropped out after several pages. Joyce Holland—mentioned in the dialogue, is of course the well-known Actualist, concrete poet, and editor of the magazine *Matchbook*.

The Brick Apartment was written by Allan Kornblum and Jim Mulac in 1973, printed multilith in February that year by the Toothpaste Press from the original manuscript (including corrections and cross-outs, and a letterpress cover on Japanese paper). It was performed by a company that included Lori Gillespi as Veronica, Darrell Gray as Alivon, and Kim Schroeder as Sally. The production was directed by Jim Mulac.

The Poets' Theater Presents 2 Plays

BY DARRELL GRAY & JAMES MULAC

BACKYARD

AND THE PREMIERE PERFORMANCE OF

The Brick Apartment

BY JAMES MULAC & ALLAN KORNBLUM

Wesley House Auditorium

8 p.m. Saturday April 14

75¢

music & art Bill Woodward

* Steve Toth * George Mattingly *
* Katherine Combellick * Kathe Mc

With * Mary Cook * Kim Schroeder * Lori Gillispie * Climent * Chuck Harris * Clyde Harris * Rick Keeley

Allan is quoted in The Daily Iowan re *The Brick Apartment*: "This play is the beginning, not the end of anything. We are not trying to build a wall with our bricks, not even a foundation or chimney, important as those structures are. Our bricks are not for such purposes. Neither are they merely bricks to smoke or to play with. We have four people here—two men and two women, and we have bricks, plenty of them. Darrell Gray's mattress is here too, not to mention the great music that will be heard."

The Second Actualist Convention, at Wesley House
a.k.a. 2nd Actualization and 1973 Autumn Actualization

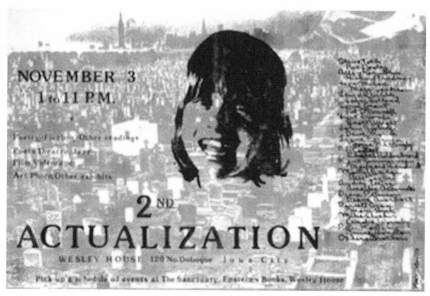

NOVEMBER 3
1 to 11 P.M.

2ND

ACTUALIZATION

WESLEY HOUSE 120 N. Dubuque Iowa City

Pick up a schedule of events at The Sanctuary, Epstein's Books, Wesley House

Following is the schedule that appeared in *The Daily Iowan*:

(*Note*: Allan Kornblum printed a program of the event which differs slightly from it with additional, performances by Howard Zimmon reading Neruda, Richard Snyder, Joyce Holland, and a film by Kent Zimmerman and Lloyd Quibble—and Morty Sklar, who emceed the event as well as sang the "Actualist National Anthem," also recorded it, and the recording has a slightly different list of appearances, indicating that the structure of the event was somewhat fluid and allowed time for anyone who wanted to participate.)

1:00	Tom Baker—slides
1:30	Brad Harvey—reading
1:45	Pat O'Donnell—reading
2:00	James Naiden (out-of-town poet)
2:15	David and Maria Gitin—"The Careens," musical number
2:30	John Sjoberg—reading
3:00	Steve Toth—reading
3:15	Mike Evans—video tapes
3:45	George Swoboda—reading
4:00	P.J. Casteel and Joyce Holland—reading
4:15	Sheila Heldenbrand (Toth) —reading
4:30	Bill Casteel—animated films
5:00	Audrey Teeter—reading
5:15	Morty Sklar, Master of Ceremonies—reading
5:30	Jim Mulac—reading, piano playing
5:45	Cinda Wormley (Kornblum)—reading
6:00	Diane Peterson—film
6:30	Amadeo Achemski—reading
6:45	Chuck Miller—reading
7:00	Diane Auerbach—reading
7:15	Lyn Ferguson—film
4:45	Darrell Gray—reading
8:00	Dave Morice—reading
8:15	Maynard Hendricks—film
8:30	*The Umbrella that Predicted the Future*, a play by Dave Morice. World premier. With Jim Mulac, P.J. Casteel, Pat O'Donnell. Directed by Allan Kornblum
9:30	"Just Friends," a band

The program lists three-Dimensional displays by John Sjoberg (Actualist Museum—a group of objects that had inspired poems by Actualists), Howard Zimmon (19-cent Objects—numerous items he'd bought for 19¢ at Lenoch and Cilek Hardware), Mary Jackson (Olfactory Factory—jars with various odors in them), Dave Morice (Alphabet Chair) and Bruce Houston (Assemblages).

As to Audrey (above) I followed her here from the 1971 National Poetry Festival in Allendale, Michigan, after she told me Iowa City was a nice place to live.

237

The Joyce Holland Hoax

by Dave Morice

Joyce Holland, an Actualist poet from Iowa City, was most active in the contemporary literary scene from 1971 to 1975. Her poems were published in more than 30 newspapers, magazines, broadsides, and other places. Many are gathered in a book titled The Final E (X Press, 1978). She also had a small pamphlet, The 10th J (Toothpaste Press, 1972) printed on what looked like cigarette papers but were really delicate white sheets inserted into Allan and Cinda Kornblum's wedding invitations. Along with being a poet, Joyce edited Matchbook magazine of one word poems, stapled inside matchbooks. Her Alphabet Anthology, published in 1973, contained 104 one-letter poems by as many poets. She read her works in places ranging from Atlantic, IA, to Los Angeles, CA. In February of 1974, she and I appeared on the NBC-TV Tomorrow Show, and I wrote a poem on her dress for the program. That, in brief, is a summary of the writing career of Joyce Holland.

Who is/was Joyce Holland? She has no birth certificate, no social security number, no driver's license. In fact, she has no brothers and sisters, no parents, no relatives or ancestors of any sort, and yet many people sent hundreds of pieces of mail to her about her poems and her magazine. Several people met her in person, and many others saw her on stage. There are photos of her at parties, readings, and other literary get-togethers, and yet she never existed in the normal sense of the word.

Joyce Holland is/was a literary hoax, a figment of my imagination. She appeared to me one balmy spring day as I was sitting down at the type-writer. Her fingers entered my fingers, and I began to write totally different poems than I'd usually written. At first, they came slowly, each glowing letter of the alphabet dancing on the page to form conceptual homages to language, such as "Alphabet at Once," which is simply all 26 letters in capital form typed together in the same spot on the page. The result is a black, letter-sized rectangle with the Q's curly tail sticking out a little at the bottom right. In another type of poem, the letters seem to fly off the page, like a flock of birds suddenly stirred to flight by the crack of the hunter's typewriter.

For a couple of years (1970 and 1971), Joyce was content to have her poems published in Gum, my own poetry mag. Not being there in person, she relied on my initiative to get her work out. At last, in 1972, she persuaded me to send her works to magazines around the country. I reminded her that she must have enough poems to send. At first, they came slowly. Then her mind entered my mind, and I began to think her poems, understand them, and type them up. I was surprised with the results: Now they came rapidly, not one by one, but in sets of poems. Some sets contained an infinite number of poems.

In order to give everyone a chance to publish Joyce's work, I engaged in mass mailings—150 poems sent to 50 magazines with a cover letter on a one-inch square piece of paper that read, simply, "?" The return address was "Al Buck, Box 304, Iowa City, 52240." Al was a printer friend of mine. He acted as the recipient in order to deflect Joyce's identity from me. After 10 or or so rejections, one magazine accepted a poem. Success! Joyce was taking her initial step into the world of small press publishing. Her words would go out on their own, being accepted for what they were, poems in their own right.

As more of her poems were accepted, Joyce demanded a bigger piece of reality. Poets and editors were writing very friendly letters in lieu of meeting her (and in hopes of meeting her, in some cases). A few seemed intrigued by this mysterious lady of the alphabet, whose queries rarely went beyond one sentence: "Dear James, Maybe these? Love, Joyce." Some responses were flirtatious postal passes at Joyce, while others were encouraging her to keep on writing. In back of all this mail, there lurked an inevitable problem: What if someone wanted to meet Joyce? She needed more than poetry for that. She needed a body.

To fulfill this major need, Pat Casteel volunteered for the role. She was very familiar with Joyce's poems, and she felt that she knew Joyce well enough to be her. Pat and I were living together about the Englert Theater at that time. We decided to give Joyce a physical identity and a trial run on a forthcoming reading for us at St. Louis University. We were nervous about her debut, but naturally Joyce wasn't concerned in the least. On the night of the reading, Pat became Joyce as easily as print fits on the page. "My next poem is food for thought. I call it 'Banana.'" She stood on the large stage, where I'd seen W.H. Auden give a reading five years earlier, and she began her recitation with passion.

BANANA

bananananananana
banananananananananananana
banananananananananana
bana
bananananana
bananananana
banananananananananananana

    anananananana
nananananananananana
    nananananana
       ana
anananananananana
    ananananananananana
   nananana
anananananananananana
       na
          a
      ana
   an
banananananananananana

Her dramatic monolog extolled the sound of the word "banana." Almost like the notes of a spoken song, each syllable bounced against the next, sped up, slowed down, and paused till reaching the last line, which completely peeled the banana with the longest string of letters in the poem. Joyce captivated the audience with her dynamic reading. That poem became one of her two favorites, the other being this ballad of nonsense words:

UBBLE SNOP

Uv cabble toyoc fezt
yab sig fovulatic:
Neppcor-inco fendilism

ubble snop.

Treep cov ubble, locastor,
urf seg urf sertap urf.
Neppcor-inco fendilism
    ubble snop.

Wex fendible whask
optera caffing, thatora!
Neppcor-inco fendilism
    ubble snop!

Uv cabble ubble snop!
Treep cov ubble, locastor, ubble snop!
Wex fendible whask, ubble snop!
Neppcor-inco fendilism
neppcor-inco fendilism
neppcor-inco fendilism
    ubble snop!

In the following weeks, Joyce's career picked up momentum, now that she had a body to go along with the poems. The next major step was for her to edit and publish her own magazine. She called it *Matchbook* (see color insert). It was a minimal publication of one-word poems consisting of 10 one-inch square mimeographed pages stapled inside the covers of matchbooks. It cost 5 cents a copy. Local businesses donated boxes of their matchbooks to the project. The Actualists and other Iowa Citians contributed to the first issue.

Matchbook was published for almost a year. There were 14 issues with over 100 poets in its pages. Allen Ginsberg sent a letter saying that the magazine wasn't good for the environment, but he sent a poem anyhow —"apocatastasis." Darrell Gray wrote a parody of it—"apocastasis." Other contributors included Bill Zavatsky ("armadildo"), Anne Waldman ("INCA"), Aram Saroyan ("puppy"), Pat Casteel ("puppylust"), Andrei Codrescu ("GASOLINE"), Tom Disch ("Manna"), G.P. Skratz ("electrizzzzz"), Lyn Lifshin ("contagious"), Gerard Malanga ("Monther"), Bruce Andrews and Michael Lally ("grap"), and Peter Schjeldahl ("shirty"). Somebody wrote "FUH-COUGH" on a postcard and sent it without further comment. The only real problem occurred when someone complained anonymously to the Post Office about the alleged danger of sending matchbooks through the mail. The Iowa City Postmaster wrote:

"Dear Ms. Holland, It is my duty to inform you that you may not send matchbooks loose in envelopes. If you have any questions, please see me."

Joyce couldn't make it in person, so I represented her. The Postmaster and I went over the rules governing combustible materials, and we reached an agreement whereby Matchbook could be sent through the mail if I could prove to him that a properly wrapped example could be held over a kitchen stove flame for two minutes without catching on fire. At home, I wrapped a matchbook in a piece of tinfoil and held it over the stove. After the first minute, the matches burst into flame. I tried two layers. Success! Back at the Post Office, the Postmaster tried it out over a Zippo lighter flame. The weak flame caused no problem at all. Matchbook was given the green light, as long as each copy was wrapped in tinfoil.

I continued sending out Joyce's poems. The return mail increased in frequency and length. My own work was falling behind, while Joyce, in true Frankenstein fashion, was taking over. There were times when I became jealous of the acceptance she and her work were getting. Her reality was growing out of proportion. When poets came through town, they met Joyce Holland, who was secretly Pat Casteel. The Iowa City crowd joined in on this play of words. Who could possibly doubt her existence?

Joyce also published *Alphabet Anthology*, a collection of one-letter pems by 104 contributors. The index tallied up the letters, showing that "o" was chosen most often, and "c" chosen by no one.

In early 1975, I began to hear rumors that people out of town were suspecting Joyce was a hoax. In particular, Ted Berrigan deciphered a Joyce Holland poem in *Gum* magazine that gave my name hidden in the letters. I knew that people would eventually discover the hoax, but I still felt protective about her existence. It was so much fun. I enjoyed the challenge in making it continue. Soon, though, more and more people knew.

That summer, Joyce gave her last reading. The brief career of an invisible poet was over. In its fifth year, the book slammed shut.

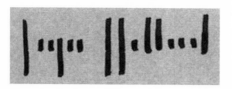

Excerpts from the Email Interview of Pat Casteel (AKA Joyce Holland) by Lisa Roberts

LR: How did you come to play Joyce Holland?

PC: The first time I "played" Joyce Holland was during a phone call to the poet/publisher Jim Mechem. You'll have to ask Dave, but I believe Mechem had published some of Joyce's poems, and he'd sent Joyce (Dave) a flirty postcard asking her to call him about guest editing his little magazine, *Out of Sight*. Dave asked me if I would make the call to Mechem and pretend to be Joyce. Dave had an apartment on Court Street that he shared with Allan Kornblum and Cinda Wormley. Seymour Krim, a Beat poet, was there also, in the kitchen, having dinner with Allan and Cinda. We phoned Jim Mechem that night, and I spoke with him and agreed to guest edit *Out of Sight* (edited of course in reality by Dave). I don't remember much about the conversation, only that I kept things very minimal (after all, Joyce was a minimalist!)

I don't remember how the idea of reading Joyce's poetry came about. I think Dave thought it would be impossible to read the poems. I don't know that concrete poets necessarily gave readings, since so much concrete poetry is dependent visually with how it looks on the page. (Think of Corso's "BOMB" in the shape of a mushroom cloud.) But when Dave showed me the poems, I thought they were charming and interesting, and I had a natural feeling for how they should sound. I'd been to many poetry readings and had seen Robert Bly, Anselm Hollo, and others give dramatic performances of their work. I knew I could do that with Joyce's poems.

If you look at them, the Joyce Holland poems are quite dramatic anyway, so finding a rhythm became the hook into reading them. I mean, many of the poems were not too hard to memorize, e.g. "banananananananananananana." In that way I guess the Joyce Holland readings were more or less minimal performances. I enjoyed doing it very much. It was fun, exciting.

243

LR: Some of the poems rely heavily on blank space for their meaning and humor. I'm thinking of "The Invisible Sonnets" and the "Tic Tac Toe" poems. How did you choose to perform those poems and their blank spaces?

PC: Announce the title clearly. "This is Invisible Sonnet #4." Glance at it carefully. Center yourself, look up. Deep breath. Contemplate those before you, meditate almost. Pause, look down, then move on to the next one.

LR: Did you have a favorite poem that you performed?

PC: One poem that I enjoyed particularly was "Ubble Snop." It was somewhat sad, somewhat wondrous, somewhat plaintive.

LR: How did you understand Joyce Holland as a character? What was your approach to playing her?

PC: I never thought of Joyce Holland in terms of Dave Morice or myself. To me, she was always, she. She was a hoax. I liked the idea of the hoax. The fact that Joyce mysteriously did and did not exist. I think many local poets who knew about the hoax for the most part liked the idea of her and her poetry. And whenever/wherever she performed they would be careful to refer to me only as Joyce.

We gave readings out of Iowa City by invitation. Some memorable places we performed were the University of Wisconsin at Madison and following that, we drove down to Chicago to give readings at the Body Politic Theater. Another reading at the Everson Art Museum in Syracuse, NY (that reading was videotaped and perhaps they still have a copy). Steve Toth, Sheila Heldenbrand, Dave Morice, and Joyce Holland were also on the bill.

One of the last big appearances was when Dave and Joyce appeared on *The Tomorrow Show*. The whole experience was so terrifying I remember very little about it, except afterward Dave and I were in a limousine in the parking lot ready to go back to the hotel, and Tom Snyder and the show's producer Rudy Telez came running over to the limo, had us roll down the window, and began reciting "Banana" back to us and gave us a big thumbs-up.

244

8th Actualization 1979

by Morty Sklar

In 1979 The Spirit That Moves Us Press sponsored the 8th Actualization tied-in with a subscription drive. It was co-sponsored by the Plains Book Bus, C.A.C., the University of Iowa Lecture Committee and the Comparative Literature Department. Readings of poetry and fiction, original films and videotapes, art exhibits and music. Some special visitors/performers including Atukwei Okai, poet from Ghana; Big John Birkbeck, poet and roustabout; Chuck Hudina, filmmaker; Allan Kornblum giving a history of Actualism; Ahmos Zu-Bolton, poet and editor/publisher of *Hoo doo Black* series; Chuck Miller reading from his novel-in-progress; Lisa Krist, singer and guitarist; and many more. It began at the Pentacrest from noon to 1:00 p.m., and continued at Center East until 10:00 p.m.

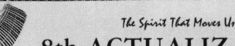

The Spirit That Moves Us

8th ACTUALIZATION
AND SUBSCRIPTION DRIVE

co-sponsored by Plains Book Bus & C.A.C.
& Lecture Committee & Comparative Literature Department

FRIDAY, MAY 11, 1979

Beginning Noon to 1:00 p.m., Pentacrest
1:00-10:00 p.m. at Center East
Clinton and Jefferson Streets — IOWA CITY
★
READINGS of poetry & fiction
FILMS & VIDEOTAPES
ART EXHIBITS — MUSIC

ADMISSION FREE but subscriptions in support of The Spirit That Moves Us
literary magazine encouraged . Printed programs available all around
town after May 1.

SPECIAL VISITORS

Atukwei Okai—Poet from Ghana
Lisa Krист—Singer
Big John Birkbeck—Poet & Roustabout
Chuck Hudina—Filmmaker
Scott Hayward—Mbira player
JoAnn Castagna—Poet and editor/publisher of Azimuth
Chuck Miller—Reading from his novel
Bethany Johns—Poet
Allan Kornblum—A history of Actualism
Anselm Hollo—Poet & translator
Ahmos Zu-Bolton—Poet & editor/publisher of Hoo doo Black series
Morty Sklar—Poet, editor/publisher of The Spirit That Moves Us

THE PLAINS BOOK BUS with small press books & magazines
of the upper midwest

and many many more . . .

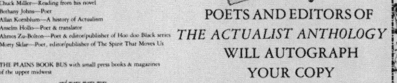

POETS AND EDITORS OF
THE ACTUALIST ANTHOLOGY
WILL AUTOGRAPH
YOUR COPY

246

Post-Modern Poets at the Everson Museum of Art

Andrei Codrescu can be credited with this adventure, as he described it in his eulogy at Allan Kornblum's memorial, January, 2015.

Our trip from San Francisco to Iowa was a spur-of-the-moment thing because Jim Gustafson and I met David Ross, a young documentarian who was using an 8 mm camera to film poets, and I said "Why don't we go to Iowa to film real poets?"—meaning by that something like "Why don't we shoot the grand epic battle between real poets (the Actualists) and the nearby Iowa workshoppers, besieged defenders of the traditional order?" Poetry war verite.

We drove a van that was either rented or belonged to poor innocent Ross, and either Darrell Gray or Jim drove—a heroic feat because we were high on LSD from San Francisco to West Branch, and no time passed at all, but ENOUGH time to blow David Ross' mind and change American art forever (and again).

247

The filming took place in Iowa City and became part of an exhibit at the Everson Museum of Art in Syracuse (press release follows). The museum provided $150 for a group of poets to travel to New York February 11, 1973 and a stipend for each. The videotapes were available for purchase, but to our knowledge none of the Actualists could afford a copy at the time.

Everson Museum of Art: An Innovative Trend in the Presentation of Poetry (a press release)

The Everson Museum is beginning to assimilate the potentials of video with the aesthetics of the spoken word. The enclosed poster represents the beginning of this program, which provides maximum exposure for the benefit of the poets and their public, and which also allows the poet to appear as a living entity. Video and poetry are art forms in themselves. Their synthesis generates the diffusion of a new medium, implemented in this show. The program will continue until we run out of funding.

The show consists of a series of videotapes made in Iowa City, Iowa this past summer. The tapes are shown in three versions: a one-hour edited tape, two one-hour tapes, and two three-hour tapes and a video catalogue. This show has been designed to culminate in a three-hour live reading by the poets of the tapes. We hope you will be able to attend the performance on Sunday.

This show is available to all interested groups and museums. All fees paid for the show will go to the artist after initial costs have been recovered by the museum. Any interested individuals should contact Marc Ross, Curator of Education, Everson Museum of Art, Syracuse, N.Y. Rental and purchase rates will be made available on request.

Iowa City Poets: Dave Morice, Joyce Holland, Anselm Hollo, Tomaz Salamun, Josephine Clare, George Mattingly, Andrei Codrescu, John Batki, Robert Perelman, Darrell Gray, Steven Toth, John Sjoberg, Sheila Heldenbrand.

THE BLAKE STREET HAWKEYES
by Robert Ernst

Ok, ok , so here's the deal.

It's fall 1967 and Darrell Gray, Merrill Gilfillan and myself are first-year grad students in the illustrious Writers' Workshop at the University of Iowa. Anselm Hollo is our mentor/teacher. We're doing our first poetry reading together somewhere on the second floor of the student union. I had received a B.A. in theater at the University and was trying out the idea of foregoing the social, communal, bullshit of theater and going for the lonely isolation of being a full-time writer. Darrell Gray, Merrill Gilfillan, and I went to have our pictures taken for our poetry reading poster at The Black Angel—a huge stone monument in an old cemetery at the edge of town that was supposedly turned black by the infidelity of the woman who lay beneath it. I remember reaching up to hold the Black Angel's hand for the photo and discovered a hand-made ring inscribed "POW-WW 2" in the palm of her hand. Then, like all things over time, I lost it. I also remember that at that time Darrell didn't smoke or drink. Years later, it would be "the drink" that consumed him.

In 1968, the University of Iowa was given a pilot project grant to create a new department called The Center for the New Performing Arts. David Schein, John O'Keefe, John Getz, Sheryl Sutton, myself, and a couple of others whose names I can no longer recall, were hired as staff from the theater end of things to explore improvisation and mix it up with the likes of Hans Breder from the Art Department, instructors from film and television, the Dance Department, and other poets from the Writers' Workshop. It was definitely a pre-digital, analog, multimedia crew. We mix it up and bring it all together. We're successful. The Rockefellers funded the program for at least five years with matching help from the university. The department, The Center for the New Performing Arts (CNPA) is established and a staff of thirty artists is hired as staff/faculty. We don't have to teach; we're to explore our own art forms in collaboration with other art forms,

249

supposedly to create "new" art forms. As performers we were expected to work with up-and-coming guest artists. The first was a young skin-head named Robert Wilson who had an outfit in New York called The Byrd Hoffman School for Birds. While in residence at our The Center for the New Performing Arts he would build one of his first major lo-o-o-ng pieces, titled *Deaf Man Glance*. Foot-note here: myth or history has it that he once performed a piece for the Shah of Iran that lasted seven hours. In the 1970s I know his average running time would be five hours.

Earlier in the summer of 1968 the Polish director and dramaturge, Jerzy Growtowski's book *Towards A Poor Theater* was being printed, chapter by chapter in issues of *The Tulane Drama Review*. I was getting together with some graduate drama students and devouring this new/old approach to theater. That spring and summer we had applied Growtowski's philosophy to the building of two performance pieces: *An Oedipus Collage* and *A Hamlet Collage*. One of Growtowski's main tenets was that all you really needed to create theater at its minimum was a space and actors/performers to inhabit that space. I seem to recall that an audience/spectators weren't even necessary. And that he was not so much creating something "new" as was synthesizing old ways and means and configuring those in a new way. He also believed that the work should be extremely physical and vocal, and that performers should work to form a tight ensemble with improvisation a training component, along with gymnastics, dance, yoga, calisthenics, plastics, opera, Noh, Kabuki and....

By this time those of us who had been hired full-time as performers within the Center had become a very tight ensemble. We informed the administration that we didn't want to be cannon fodder for other companies, that we wanted to create our own company based on the work of Growtowski. So, The Iowa Theater Lab was born.

It was the Marine Corps of theater. We worked to physical, mental and emotional exhaustion, day after day, week after week. Rick Zank, the director of The Iowa Theater Lab, who had been brought in by "Daf"—David Schein, a Hawkeye co-founder along with John O'Keefe and yours truly became the director, and George Kon, his lover and a dancer, became his assistant and the lead physical trainer as well as a member of the ensemble. We worked forty-plus hours a week for nine months on a collage of the death scene from *Othello*. It was performed by the ensemble as a murder of crows and it lasted three-and-a-half minutes from beginning to end. Then we worked for over a year on a piece that John O'Keefe had written for us called *Osiris*, based on Egyptian mythology.

Ah, time to bring in The River City Free-Trade Zone—in all likelihood the country's, if not the world's, first exclusively "hippiefied" mall, for all your "hippie" needs—and I do mean all. The River City Free-Trade Zone was a huge, old, abandoned furniture store on College street that had been taken over by a crew of entrepreneurial, white Rasta converts who had been to the Jamaican mountains outside of Montego Bay and studied, meditated, and smoked with and at the feet of the great guru and pot dealer known as "Boz," who in addition to introducing them to "Jai Rastafari and I n' I" and knowledge & love," was also supplying them with huge amounts of "herb" to facilitate that knowledge. They would get said sacred herb stateside, across the country and distribute this love and knowledge to the people, lots of the people. Things were going well, very well.

Credit Cards were the new thing in 1969 and were pretty much being issued indiscriminately. So, as the Rasta Crew / board of directors of River City Free-Trade Zone decided to just get these free credit cards, max 'em out and split to their island in the sun. (Footnote: Some of these guys might still be doing time in the federal pen.) So they rented the furniture, rudimentarily re-modeled it, divided it into three floors of stalls of various sies, put a dance hall in the basement, and began to rent space at incredibly cheap prices—or in our case they gave us the Iowa Theater Lab, approximately 1400 square feet with a hard-wood floor, for absolutely nothing. I don't believe we were the only ones either. There was an herb shop on the second floor that dealt herb straight across the counter.

The place rocked day and night, made livings for lots of artist and craft folks. Chicago blues and rock 'n' roll in the dance hall. The crew made money as well, so it staved off their leaving for a while.

Back to The Iowa Theater Lab…In the midst of working on John O'Keefe's play *Osiris*, the director of Iowa Theater Lab, Rick Zank, fired David Daf Schein, who was the person that was instrumental in getting Rick hired at The Center For The New Performing Arts. In retrospect, I think Daf was fired by Rick because he asked too many questions and still thought of The Iowa Theater Lab as a collective instead of being director driven. It became a dictatorship, a not-so-benevolent monarchy. It was his way or the highway. He wanted to be a theater guru like Growtowski himself, or Joe Chakin, or Robert Wilson or Andre' Gregory...It had to be his vision alone. Daf got to keep his job within the The Center for the New Performing Arts and was free to actually work collaboratively. We, in this prison of "ensemble" envied his freedom.

Zank stated "the work" was so intense, so special, that the moment we couldn't commit 110% to it we should leave. I took him at his word—that day came and I left. No two weeks notice, no month's notice; I just left.

Two weeks after having been fired, John O'Keefe and I took a Peyote trip at Effigy Mounds State Park. Arthur Ballet, head of the theater-end of the National Endowment for the Arts was connecting talented, young, emerging playwrights with regional theaters and the N.E.A. was paying on both ends in order to make that happen. John had already done his play *Chamber Piece* at the Magic earlier in the summer. It had gone very well and they wanted him back for more. They got me as well, as his assistant director and to teach physical theater / Growtowski-style workshops to the cast of his own play, Jimmy Beam, which was being produced by The Magic Theater, and a few days later we packed up and headed west in his red Volkswagen bus. This was in November 1972.

John O'Keefe, Daf Schein, and I would often talk about working together again, but we were never all in the same place at the same time to do it. And, unspoken, was the agreement that it would be 100% a collective project. That meant for everything. That agreement didn't happen until 1975. All three of us said yes at the same time. We were all living in the warehouse / art house. We were working all the time. It was 24/7 except when we'd watch Kung-Fu—and even then that was like homework.

The Blake Street warehouse housed more than just us. There was Doug Wilson the painter, Ken Raby the musician, The Holmes Bros. (one a photographer and the other a bike builder and mad-man racer), Richard Junglas and Robert Lieber, and Tim White (tablas and sitar, all students of The Ali Akbar Khan school of Classical Indian Music), and Richard Nagler—landlord, factory owner, and noted photographer.

John O'Keefe, David Schein and myself worked together for about six to seven months. We built a 40-minute piece (*Hogstale*) that contained no language. It was all sound and movement except for the phrase "In my adobe hacienda, there is a touch of Mexico." Irene Oppenheim, a tough-minded theater critic for The Bay Guardian, reviewed us. She stated that it left her "Breathless and with hope for the theater." We'd been used to audiences of ten to twenty people. The night after that review came out, we had a hundred people in the space, which reduced our already tiny playing area to about a 5-foot by 4-foot space. We filed for non-profit status. We needed a name—Hawkeyes because the connective tissue for us was Iowa (The Hawkeye State) and Blake Street because that's where the theater aka "the pit" was: The Blake Street Hawkeyes. This brings us to December 20, 1975 and the "Big Day at the Pit: Actualist Convention #3, Non-Actualist Convention #1."

WEST COAST ACTUALISM
by G.P. Skratz

In September of 1975, I'd finally arrived at what I considered to be the Center of the Poetry World: the San Francisco Bay Area, and first on my agenda was to meet, work with, and learn from the great Darrell Gray, who I considered to be one of its Kings. That turned out to be incredibly easy: he was a bit shy, but sweet and utterly open-hearted. We formed a fast friendship and were collaborating in no time flat, though it took us about six months to find a collaborative voice we both felt comfortable with.

Aside from written collaboration, I was also interested in performance —particularly in the expansive inter-disciplinary possibilities suggested by the "Actualist Conventions" that Darrell and his Iowan pals had put on in the early 1970s.

So in early December of the year, Darrell set up a meeting with a friend, David Schein (known as "Daf"), who'd been in the Iowa Theater Lab and involved with the Iowa Actualist Conventions. Currently, he was in a three-man theater troupe called the Blake Street Hawkeyes, operating out of a live-in studio / theater space at 2019 Blake Street in Berkeley, with Bob Ernst and John O'Keefe. Aside from the straightforward "2019 Blake Street" the space was most often referred to as "the Pit," or "the warehouse."

And off to meet with Daf we did go. He was more than receptive to the

253

notion of putting on a new "Actualist Convention," and wanted to do it right away. We'd just contact every interesting poet/musician/theater-or-performance artist we knew, slap together a program and put on the show…oh, I don't know, say noon to midnight on Saturday, December 20th. We'd call it "A Big Day at the Pit: Actualist Convention #3, Non-Actualist Convention #1."

Darrell invited poets Liz Zima, Keith Abbott, Jack Marshall, Kit Robinson, David Lerner, David's fellow "street poet," Palladin, and Peter Luschan. I invited poets Hash Flash, Rich Jorgensen, and composer Bob Davis from my old "Stone Show" poetry and music troupe—and composer John Adams, whom I'd recently met through Bob Davis. Daf and the Hawkeyes contributed the musical excursions, "Tom Toms," "Sowooond," and "The Mystery Burger Band," as well as the theatrical romps, "Trunk 15" by Bob Ernst, and the Hawkeyes' collaborative "Hogstale."

Darrell Gray read poems and the "Actualist Manifesto" toward the end of the show at this and the 4th thru 8th Actualist Conventions below. I read poems at nearby slots up thru the 6th, after which I switched to Performmance Art or showing videos. The format began as a series of 20-minute sets, then grew to afford 30-minute sets in the 1980s. It was free of charge and would remain so until the "10th" one in 1980.

By way of explanation, Darrell wrote the following for the Program:

PUTTING THE SHOE ON THE RIGHT FOOT

Somewhere amidst his voluminous writings Charles Olson says, "Uh huh, that's right—theater is language." The off-hand response reverts to its concomitant corollary: "language is theater." It was Kant who said: "the Categories are Absolute, tho the data is all that we know." Which propels us now into the necessary methods of Imaginary Research.

A useful exercise might be to consciously avoid actions which have predictable consequences.

For the image of the process of mentation: a mirror will come to mind, and in it, if you look closely, you will perceive an inverted vortex. A single word will form, though it will appear to be written backward in the mind. Now consciously transpose the shapes of those letters into a human word, carefully, as if those letters were the vessels of a sacred and internal meaning. Let the process of thought now embrace the letters, and an actual unity arise.

The imaginary and the actual achieve their original inter-course. The dancer dances because, simply, he is at home in both worlds.

At this first Berkeley Actualist Convention publicity was entirely by word of mouth. Most participants tended to arrive, along with whatever audience they'd managed to wrangle, around the time of their scheduled performance. But most became so entranced by the unfolding spectacle that they stayed till the bitter end. As a result, by sundown, the crowd had grown to an enthusiastic full house.

It was a rousing success, and Daf and Darrell and I were soon planning another Convention—this time, to be planned and promoted over a few months' time, in a more professional manner.

2019 BLAKE STREET: I should point out that the hero of West Coast Actualism is the space we were afforded to have it all spin out into: 2019 Blake Street. Like Actualism, its core inhabitants, the Blake Street Hawkeyes, were refugees from Iowa City, specifically one-time members of the Iowa Theater Lab. The fact that they not only made their space freely available to us—unlike other theater spaces which would have charged a significant amount of money—they actively participated in the productions made it all possible. The Hawkeyes actually lived there, along with several visual artists like Russ Conlin and Doug Wilson, who exhibited their works at the Conventions. Doug Wilson even offered up his own live-in studio space as a kind of "Green Room" so that people could hang out in a rowdier fashion without disturbing the performances. And all of that pro-vided a homey, "living room" ambience to the events, encouraging casual interaction between all participants, performers and viewers alike.

As Alastair Johnston would later put it in the May 1984 *Poetry Flash*, "The most useful feature of this event from the performers' viewpoint is the chance to fail. Only your ego is set back if you bomb. You learn to take

255

more risks, update your ideas, or rehearse more. Poets, as a rule, are cosseted by the safe and respectful crowd that attend readings." The rowdy interdisciplinary crowd pushed one into risk to keep up, but the comfy living-room vibe provided a safety net against any fall.

Although echoes continue to reverberate, West Coast Actualism begins and ends at 2019 Blake Street.

ACTUALIST CONVENTION 4 (March 20 & 21, 1976): This is where we pulled out all the stops: although we were still maintaining a "come one, come all" inclusive stance, we weren't just inviting whomever happened to be "at hand." We made sure that now-local veterans of the original Conventions, like David and Maria Gitin and Liz Zima, were scheduled. Jack Marshall, a veteran of Convention 3 as well as the Iowa events, had returned; George Mattingly was always scheduled, from Convention 3 on, but I'm not certain that he ever actually "appeared." And we invited the Bolinas crowd—Joanne Kyger, Lewis MacAdams, Bill Berkson—who showed up with gusto. Other poets included Summer Brenner, Laura Chester, Pat Nolan, Dick Gallup, Ron Silliman, Keith Abbott, et al. "Street poets" were also represented by Julia Vinograd and the return of David Lerner.

By "Street poets" I mean homeless or nearly homeless ones whose primary venue was the mean streets themselves and the occasional open reading. Darrell had taken a real liking to them, and David Lerner, for one, became a serious acolyte, soaking up wisdom at the feet of his master, Darrell Gray for some years. And Julia Vinograd, who was largely known as the madwoman who daily wandered Berkeley's Telegraph Avenue, blowing soap bubbles hither and yon, had earned an M.F.A. from the University of Iowa and had been included in Paul Carroll's important anthology, The Young American Poets. While others fit George Mattingly's dismissive, "They don't read," David and Julia were happy exceptions to George's "rule." Later, they would find a home of sorts at San Francisco's Café Babar and become known as the "Barbarians."

David Daf Schein did a full-court publicity press, and the *San Franciso Bay Guardian* gave it prime billing in their "Events" section. Alan Soldofsky, another poet with Iowa roots, who had landed his "Planet on the Table" show on the alternative station, KPFA, and was himself reading at the Convention, invited Jim Nisbet, a writer with tech skills, to record it.

Jim set up his gear in Doug Wilson's "Green Room," ran a mic wire across the hall to the "Pit," the performance space, but the tapes were rolling in the "Green Room." This also served as a way to broadcast the audio of the performances into the "Green Room" where people could chat and smoke cigarettes (which, by then were verboten in the "Pit") and still catch what they could of the performances through the din of talk and laughter.

Both days opened and closed with theatrical acts: Saturday opened with "Hogstale" by the Hawkeyes and concluded with the hysterical and popular Ducks Breath Mystery Theater, also from Iowa City. Sunday opened with John LeFan's dance troupe, Mangrove, and concluded with Oil Concrete. Musical acts included something called "Sowoond" and Andy Dinsmoor. As before, artworks by the resident artists Russ Conlin, Doug Wilson and others. New arrival, Peter Loschan, was represented both on the art exhibit and the poetry stage.

By the second day our new-found recording engineer Jim Nisbet had shown up as he tells it "with a suitcase full of manuscripts," and approached this guy who was everywhere at once and turned out to be David Daf Schein, about maybe reading a few poems if somebody didn't show up (which was happening often enough). Daf said sure, went out the door, then came right back and said, "Somebody didn't show up; you're on; what's your name" and went out the door again to announce me. A half hour later, I had a whole new cadre of friends and, at least as important, poets writing poems I wanted to hear.

Aside from the bonhomie and cigarette smoke, another aspect of Doug's "Green Room" was a chance to collaborate with all comers. There was a giant page, torn from an easel book, taped to the wall, titled, "My Favorite Word," on which people were invited to write their favorite word. I captured the results in alphabetical order, surely not the order in which they were written, but, being smitten at the time by the aesthetics of Dave ("Dr. Alphabet") Morice and his alter ego Joyce Holland (editor of *The Alphabet Anthology*), it was the alpha order to which I'd consigned them.

MY FAVORITE WORD

abphiety, artishock, ballroom, besultifur, bumdom, electrizzzzz, on, proziac, stacecus, syergy, tar, troglodyte

The other collaboration opportunity came from Darrell Gray's very funky, manual typewriter, which he'd generously placed on a "stump" in the "Green Room," open to all who would venture to type something on it.

At this point, I might mention that we in this volume are not alone in discussing West Coast Actualism. Michael Lyons, who in 1976 began co-editing a "zine" with Darrell entitled *The Punctual Actual Weekly*, eventually published a 356-page volume, *The Punctual Actual Weekly: A Memoir of the Hawkeye Theater*, HiT MoteL Press, 2007. In many ways it's a brilliant critical overview of the works of the three founding Hawkeyes (Bob Ernst, John O'Keefe, David Schein) as well as the poetry of Darrell Gray and Peter Luchan. Several Hawkeye scripts are rendered in full.

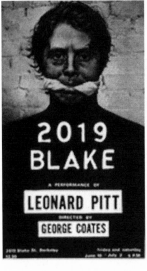

ACTUALIST CONVENTION 5 (April 16, 1977): Now that Jim Nisbet was on board as co-producer with Daf Schein (and your most humble servant), greater care went into curating the poets selected to read. Rather than the "come one, come all" approach of the first two Berkeley Conventions, the poets were actually selected. All of us were Boomers fully conversant in the works of Ted Berrigan and Anselm Hollo, as well as the works of their Actualist associates. They included Michael Sean Lazarchuk, Steve Lavoie, Bob Perelman, Ron Silliman, Rae Armantrout, Alan Bernheimer, Steve Benson, Pat Nolan, Jim Gustafson, Rich Jorgensen, Sotere Torregian, Abby Child, Robert Harris, Summer Brenner, Alan Soldofsky, and making his debut on the official program, co-producer and sound-designer, .

Theatrical acts included the Hawkeyes, and mime Leonard Pitt performing an early draft of what would become the major work, "2019 Blake" as directed by George Coates, this his maiden voyage as director. George would fairly rapidly become the prime mover behind the world famous "George Coates Performance Works." In 1987, George Coates Performance Works would tour the world with "Actual Shō," an homage to the Actualist Conventions.

PUBLICATIONS: By late 1977 the world was treated to not one but two new volumes by Darrell Gray: *Essays & Dissolutions*, Abraxas Press, and *The Actualist Anthology*, co-edited with Morty Sklar and published by Morty's The Spirit That Moves Us Press.

To my delight, Amazon heads the "Editorial Reviews" section of their page on *Essays & Dissolutions* with a quote from my piece in the December 1977 edition of *The San Francisco Review of Books*: "Among other delights, this book preserves the theoretical discovery of Actualism. Even today, much American surrealism reads like stodgy translations from the French. The Actualist movement officially published the map of the junction of European surrealism and the American Whitman-Williams-Codrescu barbaric 'this is where I'm at' lineage."

As for *The Actualist Anthology*, one might note with regret that it includes nobody from the gathering West Coast version. But as far as poetry is concerned, we diddled a tad too long in our "come one, come all" stance. While the 5th Convention may have been a step in the right direction, there simply wasn't a coherent cohort of "West Coast Actualists" among poets as yet.

ACTUALIST CONVENTION 6 (December 18, 1977): This was the one and only Convention held in a location other than our beloved home at 2019 Blake Street, and I think I can safely say that it was pretty universally considered not just the worst of the bunch but a downright unpleasant experience. It was held at the live-in studio of the punk rock band The Mutants across the street from the central bus terminal in San Francisco, and they'd named their studio, "Terminal Concepts." Just four months earlier I had produced the "Punk Poetry Festival" in that space, featuring several veterans of the Actualist Conventions (including Darrell) and several others punkier than the rest.

While my own natural tendency is toward empathy (I would later have a career as an HIV counselor), I've always derived a paradoxical voyeuristic pleasure in empathy's opposite. I enjoyed watching Michael Sean Lazarchuk give a reading at San Francisco's Grand Piano club, where an audience member had called out, "Louder!" Sean stopped, turned toward the sound of the shout and said, "Who said that? Stand up: let me see you." The poor guy did as instructed. Sean looked him over, then turned to the other side of the room and delivered the rest of the reading in that direction, leaving the poor "offender" to wilt back into his seat—and despite my better angels, thus was the birth of "Punk Poetry."

The line-up for the 6th Convention—once again, thank goodness, a one-day affair, looked pretty much like the 5th, but wasn't quite as much fun. Theatrical acts included the Hawkeyes, "Frederick Nilsen and the Do-Do-ettes" and "The Planetary Players with Sandy Berrigan." Poets included Rae Armentrout, Steve Benson, Carla Harryman, Steve Rodefer, Jim Nisbet, David Highsmith, Abby Child, Bill Berkson, Keith Abbott, Laura Chester, Alastair Johnston, Alan Bernheimer, Andrei Codrescu, Kit Robinson and Steve Vincent.

But, as Jim Nisbet recalls, "I distinctly recall (various Punk Poets) ranged along the back wall of the space, all of them wearing beers and leather jackets, haranguing readers…too cool for school, those guys, but as went the prevailing drunkenness of the event, symptomatic." Though I wasn't among the "back wall boys," mea culpa, I'd help set the tone….

"Terminal Concepts," indeed! It buried "Punk Poetry" and damn near finished off the Actualist Convention genre as well: it would be another two-and-a-half years before it pulled itself out of the rubble to reemerge at its home-base of 2019 Blake.

more PUBLICATIONS: 1979 saw two more publications by Darrell Gray: *Ruby Port: The Food Poems of Phillipe Mignon* (Sombre Reptiles Press, Berkeley) and *The New Conventionalism: Observations on a Mode of Contemporary American Poetry* (150 copies off the Vandercook proof press, September 1979).

Ruby Port turned out to be a predictable audience favorite in subsequent Conventions, regularly "bringing down the house" in hilarity. The New Conventionalism, on the other hand, was a 9-page screed in defiance of the newly gathering "L=A=N=G=U=A=G=E" movement that included several recent Convention participants. He calls it, "…a new conventionalism, all the more alarming because it is confused with the avant-garde. To write properly now means a radical dissociation of the self from the emotions. Direct statements are out—the only exception being those grounded in a recognizable non-ego manipulated strata of 'language.'"

Readers of my little essay may recall that I'd introduced Darrell as "a bit shy, but sweet and utterly open-hearted." Now, why is he so directly turning on poets who had so recently been his Actualist allies? Well, at this point in their movement, many (not all) of them were downright hostile to those who disagreed with their poetics. The Greek poet, Nanos Valaoritis—who had introduced Allen Ginsberg and Gregory Corso and others to his Parisian pals Pablo Picasso and Andre Breton in the 1950s—published what he thought a supportive piece on the L=A=N=G=U=A=G=E movement in a Parisian journal, only to be angrily upbraided by a movement member for deviating from their dicta.

ACTUALIST CONVENTION "10" (May 24, 1980): By now, for reasons suggested above, the L=A=N=G=U=A=G=E folks had left the building, but the Convention itself was roaring back with gusto! For the first time we even charged the audience: "50 cents per diem" and we soldiered on with Joanne Kyger, Geoff Hewit, Laura Chester, Geoff Young, Victoria Rathbun, Gloria Frym, John Marron, Sandy Berrigan, Nanos Valaoritis, Steve Rodefer, Julia Vinograd, amid theater by Ducks Breath Mystery Theater, the Hawkeyes, John Duykers and Leonard Pitt, and directed by George Coates and Ellen Sebastian, with film/video by Bill Farley and Margaret Fisher / Bob Hughes. The Actualist Boogie Band rocked the house.

In lieu of reading poems I showed some videos created in collaboration with my future bride, Linda Lemon. My "Terminal Concepts" experience had soured me on the whole notion of "poetry," and I had turned my energies to video and performance art. Steve Lavoie called Andrei Codrescu in Baltimore via speaker-phone. A "mystery guest," rumored to be Carlos Castaneda, was expected but didn't arrive.

From Colleen Larkin (*inserted by Morty* with reference to *Black Woman Bed*, written by Colleen Larkin and Ellen Sebastian, performed by Ellen Sebastian; set by Doug Wilson):
"We did the show at the Actualist Convention—not positive of the year, 1981? but later did it at the San Francisco International Theater Festival where it was picked up to go the Interieurs Festival in Paris, France."

ACTUALIST CONVENTION 8 (March 24 & 25, 1980): Daf Schein and Jim Nisbet upped the ante again, inviting the local press to a catered lunch where they'd be pitching the Convention. I was astonished: the local press was pretty much unanimous in praising everything the Hawkeyes did. Would a literary critic like Christopher Ricks need Tennyson to rise from the grave and bribe him to get him to write another appreciation of his work? Apparently art journalists operate differently than critics....

In any event, the catered lunch brought then-critic at *East Bay Express*, Robert Hurwitt to review the Convention at length in a piece called, "Doing What Comes Actually" in the April 6, 1984 *Express*. Actualist poet Alastair Johnston didn't require the bribe but wrote "The Whole Spectrum" for the May 1984 *Poetry Flash*. Pre-show publicity was sufficiently robust that we were now charging a dollar a day.

THE EIGHTH ACTUALIST CONVENTION

THE EIGHTH ACTUALIST CONVENTION will take place March 24th and 25th, noon to midnight, at 2019 Blake St Berkeley. Admission will be one dollar per day. Each half-hour will feature a different performance or reading in the the theatre and there will be an exhibition of drawing, painting, sculpture and photography in the hallway and in Doug Wilson's studio.

THE SCHEDULE

(T = Theater, D = Dance, M = Music, R = Reading, PA = Perf.Art, C = Comedy, F = Film)

Saturday, March 24th

12:00	Goldberg, Nisbet, and Schein
12:30	Bob Ernst (T)
1:00	Wayne Doba (DC)
1:30	Keith Abbott (RT)
2:00	Helen Dannenberg (D)
2:30	Paul Bernstein (T)
3:00	Max Mack (T)
3:30	Footloose Dancing
4:00	Kim Best (T)
4:30	John English and Candace Natvig (M)
5:00	Jonathan Albert (RM)
5:30	Mark Gordon (T)

Sunday, March 25th

12:00	Skrats, Rosebottom & T'a Leson (T)
12:30	Michael Lyons (R)
1:00	Michael Wolfe (R)
1:30	Tapeworks
2:00	Lee Harwood (R)
2:30	Henry Peters (M)
3:00	John Thorpe (R)
3:30	Rinde Eckert (M)
4:00	Gloria Frym (R)
4:30	Byron Brown & Sara Shelton Mann (DT)
5:00	Lucia Berlin (R)
5:30	Kaye McDonough (R)

·····BREAK·····································BREAK·························

7:00	The Dull Sounds Ensemble (M)
7:30	Ellen Sebastian & Mark Gorney (T)
7:45	Spleenex (TC)
8:00	Lewis MacAdams (R)
8:30	George Mattingly
9:00	Leon Martel & Beth Muscio (T)
9:30	Tom Buckner (M)
10:00	John Lefan & Freddie Long (PT)
10:30	Nightletter Theater (T)
11:00	Alastair Johnston & Dawn Kolokithas (R)
11:30	William Farley (F)

7:00	Kush (R)
7:30	Summer Brenner (R)
8:00	Jeff Stoll & Molly Thomas (T)
8:30	Gulf of the Farralones (T)
9:00	Ducks Breath Mystery Theater (TC)
9:30	George Coates Performance Works (PA)
10:00	Darrell Gray (R)
10:30	The White Gates of Claz (M)
11:00	Deborah Quinn (T)
11:30	Chuck Mudina (F)

Artists represented in the exhibition are Frances Butler, Jane Dunbar, Chuck Mudina, JanAnn Kirchmeier, Colleen Larkin, Peter Loochan, Richard Nagler, Sandy Partington, Joanne Bruff, Lee Nisbet, and Doug Wilson.

Because of the small size of the theater, seating for each event will be on a first-come first-served basis. For more information call 849-3013, or 841 2144.

The Eighth Actualist Convention is produced by The Blake St Hawkeyes with the help of the NEA, the CAC, and the SF Foundation.

8th Actualist Convention
Produced by: Jim Nisbet
David Schein
Doug Wilson

The Hawkeyes themselves had been upping their own ante in the preceding years, expanding greatly from their original three-fold troupe to include Deborah Gwinn, Cynthia Moore, and Daf Schein's girlfriend, Whoopi Goldberg. A couple of years before, Whoopi had been an "Aspiring actress," but O'Keefe and Daf had encouraged her to develop her own material, which she did with great talent and enthusiasm. Guided by director Ellen Sebastian, she presented a tribute to Moms Mabley and a menagerie of character studies called *Ghosts*.

Not long before this Convention, she'd come to the attention of both the Broadway producer Mike Nichols and his Hollywood doppelganger Steve Spielberg, and was cocked and loaded to become the *Toast of Broadway* the following September, then cement her world-wide fame in *The Color Purple*.

At the time of the Convention I was slaving away on *Larry, the Stooge in the Middle*, a biography of Larry Fine. Whoopi and I would often trade Stooge trivia, and she suggested that it might be fun to write a Forward to the book. I pitched the idea as hard as I could to my publisher, but his iron-clad attitude was: "Who the hell is Whoopi Goldberg? I've got Steve Allen on board, and that's what he's gonna say!" I tried to argue: Women Stooge fans were rare: Whoopi was an enthusiastic one, and maybe you haven't heard of her NOW, but, by the time the book comes out, she'll be WAY more popular than old fart, Steve Allen. Which turned out to be true, but....

As theater critic Robert Hurwitt wrote in the April 6, 1984 *East Bay Express*, "The convention got off on a very strong start Saturday with a performance by Hawkeyes David Schein and Whoopi Goldberg in a hilarious piece by Jim Nisbet...." David Schein appears "lying sprawled asleep in an armchair, surrounded by crushed beer cans...Goldberg plays one of those anonymous female sex callers, her classy French accent and sultry voice providing a strikingly funny contrast to Schein's unkempt appearance as the piece progresses laugh after laugh to its postcoital comic climax. It was a tough act to follow, but Saturday went on one highlight after another." There were readings by Alastair Johnston, Dawn Kolokithas, and Keith Abbott amid much theater by Bob Ernst, Wayne Doba, Ellen Sebastian, Nightletter and others.

While Whoopi Goldberg sold tickets outside, day two began with *The Mass of the Scattered Almonds* ("a wondrously nonsensical Latinate service conducted deadpan by G. P. Skratz as the pastor of the Church of the Center That Will Not Hold"—Robert Hurwitt) performed by altar boy Tim Lemon and myself, directed by Rosebottom the Clown. Poetry, music and theater followed from the likes of Rinde Eckert, Gloria Frym, Summer Brenner, Ducks Breath, George Coates Performance Works, and more. A group called Gulf of the Farralones performed their piece, $elling Bomb-shells in the parking lot by the "Warehouse," but not before a memorable prelude: somebody not present at the Convention had illegally parked in the lot and that somebody was impossible to locate, so several of the bulkier guys in attendance picked it up and placed it in the street.

Darrell's performance toward the end of the night was wonderfully described by Alastair Johnson: "The mixed genre audience didn't know the poets from the stand-up comics, so amusing interplays occurred as when Darrell Gray spent ten minutes "preparing" for his reading with asides, page riffling, hair-smoothing and throat-clearing, creating the impression that he was parodying an academic poet. When the hilarity had subsided, the pure humor of his poetry demolished the audience in two stanzas."

another PUBLICATION: On November 1, 1984, *Halos of Debris*, the long-awaited successor to Darrell's *Something Swims Out* and *Scattered Brains* was issued from Alastair Johnston's Poltroon Press. It did not disappoint....

ACUTE ACTUALISM (December 7, 1986): A Memorial Homage to Darrell Gray featuring the Actualist crowd reading Darrell's work, a video of the man himself, and the world premiere of *Bob*, a play by Darrell in collaboration with Allan Kornblum and Jim Mulac. It starred Steve Lavoie as "Bob," Gloria Frym as the "Door of Love," Nanos Valaoritis as the "Door of Return," G. P. Skratz as the "Door of Self," and Alastair Johnston as "Old Man." and yes, those of us playing "doors" actually wore doors hanging from our necks.

(*See the full text of* Bob *following* The Last Word, *by David Schein and Whoopi Goldberg.*)

265

The Blake Street Hawkeyes Present

acute

ACTUALISM

Homage to Darrell Gray

✓ ＼－⊶□⊷＋＼ ✗

Sunday December 7th 1986

BOB

A play by Darrell Gray, Allen Kornblum & Jim Mulac

Cast of characters

BOB — *Steven LaVoie*
DOOR OF LOVE — *Gloria Frym*
DOOR OF RETURN — *Nanos Valaoritis*
DOOR OF SELF — *G. P. Skratz*
OLD MAN — *Alastair Johnston*

✓ ＼－⊶□⊷＋＼ ✗

Videotape courtesy of the Black Bart Poetry Society

Darrell had died in early September 1986, though word hadn't spread till October, long after his landlord had thrown all his books and manuscripts into the dump. Anselm Hollo wrote an angry piece in Ed Dorn's *Rolling Stock* mag. I've got a photocopied page 34 of it that doesn't identify the issue or date; I imagine it's the Fall 1986 or Winter 1987 one, denouncing Darrell's Bay Area pals for having drifted so far from him, but Anselm himself had utterly ignored him during a residency just a year or two before. Funny how people seem angriest at seeing their own sins reflected in others. I personally find it a relief to see others behaving as poorly as I….

The program sported this by Darrell:

PREFACE TO HEAVEN

May I go there
in my own body at last
wordless & facing the sea
of this summer's disapproval—

with McCoy Tyner playing
and Sun Ra on the piano. Make

it a mild day, with only a few
overlapping clouds, such that forms

may clamor to the angel's nest
and in sweet secrecy be blest.
May all my friends be there
in rooms with laughter, and a rest

from distances never known on earth:
Let them ring to a single birth.

ACTUALIST CONVENTION "11" (December 12 & 13, 1987): After the
Standing Room Only crowds of the 1984 Convention, we wound up raising
the price to $5 a day, still a "steal."

Day one began with a half-hour improv by Bob Ernst after which, still
in character, he led some of the audience to Leonard Pitt's studio a half
block down the road, and at over twenty-four hours, would be published in
the *Guinness Book of World Records* as the longest solo performance ever.
Helen Schumaker and Susan Van Benthuysen followed with theatrical performances, after which the "Acute Actualism" crowd reprised the applause
magnet *Bob*. Except for a reading by Summer Brenner, the day was dominated by theater and music by Ellen Sebastian, Deborah Gwinn and Mark
Gordon, Rhiannon, the Dull Sounds Ensemble and Footloose Dance
Company.

Liza Kitchell and I premiered the second half of *The Mass of the Fearful* with Thelonious "Loney" Day as the altar boy, Pamela Z as the choir, and Rosebottom the Clown (our director and young Loney's mom) as the priest's shadow. A week later, on December 20, we performed the entire Mass (both *The Mass of the Scattered Almonds* and *The Mass of the Fearful*) for the first and last time at Larry Blake's.

Day two featured readings by Bobbie Louise Hawkins, Joanne Kyger, Don Guravich, Lucia Berlin and John Thorpe but was otherwise dominated by theater, including a brilliant rendering by John LeFan and Freddie Long of a script by Jim Nisbet. Whoopi Goldberg was otherwise engaged.

Although the Convention as a whole garnered no reviews in the press, Bob Ernst's incredible twenty-four hour and ten minutes solo was memorialized in the *San Francisco Chronicle*'s piece, "San Francisco Performer Does His Many Things for 24 Hours." To promote the show, *Poetry Flash* ran my essay, "Actualism, Origins Of" in their December issue.

ELECTRONIC ACTUALIZATION (December 19, 1988): Jim Nisbet, Bob Ernst, Gloria Frym, Steve Lavoie, myself and others visited the performance art gallery, La Mamelle and tuned in to the WELL—the *Whole Earth* bulletin board service, and fed them Actual poems, manifestos and online collaboration.

THE WHOLE HOG (early 1988): Buoyed by the success of the "eleventh" Actualist Convention, the Blake Street Hawkeyes hosted a series of evening performances over the course of about two months. "Night 4" opened with *The Mass of the Fearful* performed by the crew who'd wowed the crowd at the 11th Actualist Convention.

THE DEACTUALIZATION (July 13, 2002): Although 2019 Blake Street had been officially closed to the public after the 1989 Loma Prieta earthquake, it remained in operation for rehearsal and word-of-mouth performance through June of 2002 when the landlord decided he wanted to take over the space for his own exclusive use. He let us all back in for one final fling. Unlike the old Actualist Conventions that were tightly scripted and included David Schein ever at the ready to use his hook and remove acts that were exceeding their time limit, Bob Ernst ran the event as one long improv. We read the names of "Fallen Heros," beginning with Darrell

Gray, Jon English, Richard Young Glass, Ralph Bomeo, Tim Lemon, Jim Gustafson, David Lerner, John Lyon. Participants added others.

Woody Woodman and Jim Cave, Jim Nisbet, George Coates, Summer Brenner and others did poetry and theater. The Serfs (a reincarnation of the old Actualist Boogie Band featuring Bob Ernst, Andy Dinsmoor, Hal Hughes, myself and others) rocked the house.

David Schein was unable to attend but sent the following to be recited at the event:

ODE TO THE PIT

Warehouse
oh big chunk of lots of us,
you will never close.
Your tablas will keep drumming in the sound-proof room
when only dogs can hear.

Your emptiness was stunning
The puff of the heater in the morning
the cool grit of the hall
against bare feet
the song of the Screamers
faint behind the wall.
AHHHHH! OOOOO!
Safe. SAFE!!!!

by the Alley
in the Ivy
of the Shop.
Climb the iron bars
to look beyond
the asphalt to that other planet
called "the world."

For years
my lot
was to live
to rehearse

in this little slot
to meet from time to time
to watch
some endless new
amazement
BUST OUT
of a throat
a brush
a skin
a bone

The walls cracked
the roof sagged
but the floor we built was strong
From here a thousand investigations purred
primed by a vacuum:
Who could stop the pressure
of the absence of money
plug the 30-year gusher
of incessant production?

Oh studio
oh barrio
oh mafleyville
oh parking lot
Gone to Bob
Gone to Dick
Gone to Real
Too real
Estate
Gone to myth
of where we came from.
And we did. I do
Come from this floor.
We are the ancestors
Our myth is real.

Listen to the Shakuhachi in the fog

To the clack of a typewriter in the van.
Doug's painting clouds.
It's time to rehearse
To the warehouse
Wave hands.
Wave hands.

To the warehouse
Always
Wave hands.

And thus "ended" the Actualist Convention phenomenon. Its legacy was visible throughout the nineties in Theater Artaud's Annual marathons, in which the Bay Area theater community was invited to present ten-minute performances through the course of a frenetic day or weekend. Every year someone suggests that it's about time to put on another Actualist Convention, perhaps at John LeFan's studio space near Artaud. I visualize it at a spa near Callistoga, somewhere where one might rest one's weary bones after performing....

another PUBLICATION: Speaking of lingering legacy, I might add that in early 2012 Poltroon Press released *Everything Else*, collaborations of Darrell Gray and G. P. Skratz. I'll end with one of my favorites therein, for sooner or later everyone always had to go home:

THE WAY HOME

the way home is a compass:
a bridge spanning
2 points that are always here.

& there.

& our love,
which also is a bridge
between what we forget to say

& say constantly

THE LAST WORD

by Whoopi Goldberg and David Schein

W: You can't, can you?

D: What?

W: Stop.

D: Sure I can…

W: Then stop.

D: Okay.

W: Okay.

D: Okay.

W: Okay.

D: All right. (PAUSE) All right.

W: You see?

D: What?

W: Nothing.

D: What do you mean by that?

W: What?

D: Nothing.

W: You see?

D: What?

W: STOP!!!!!!

D: Okay. I'll stop it, I'll stop it dead in its tracks, petrify it…

W: You see, stop, stop, stop, STOP…
     (PAUSE)

D: Okay, you're right…I hear you.

W: All right.

D: I do. I hear you loud and clear.

W: Okay!

D: Wait, you don't understand.

W: But I do.

D: But you don't. Look I agree with you. I'm trying to tell you that I
     agree with you…

W: Don't yell at me.

D: I wasn't…

W: Yes, you were. Your voice was…

273

D: done. I was just…

W: RAISED. And you also interrupted me, in a…

D: I did not!

W: LOUD VOICE! and you just did it again. If you would just wait until I was finished then you could have a rebuttal…

D: JESUS GAWD!

W: AND THEN you can say what you want.

D: Are you done?

W: Yes.

D: So now I can start my rebuttal?

W: No, I'll start first. Okay?

D: Okay.

W: Okay, first I want to say…

D: Now wait a goddam minute!!!
      (PAUSE)

W: Look, let's stop this. I don't want to hassle.

D: Well, you started it.

W: No I didn't. So let's stop it, shall we?

D: All right, we'll drop it. There. It's dropped. Dead. Finito. Finished. Kaput. Buried.

W: Fine.

D: I thought you wanted to drop it.

W: I do.

D: Then why say "fine"? I say, "There, it's dropped," and you say, "fine."

W: I didn't me……

D: No wait, hear me.

W: No.

D: Why won't you hear me out when I hear you out.

W: But you haven't heard me out yet.

D: What? Okay go ahead.

W: I just want to say that in my opinion it's your own fault…

D: What?

W: If you'd not pretended to go along with……

D: Come on !

W: Look you got yourself into it. I didn't do it, you did it, and because you know you did it, you're feeling guilty, and that's why you're trying to lay it on me. Now I'm not laying this on you......

D: (GROAN)

W: You see, you see how you are. You can't just let me say what I have to say, you have to comment. I don't do that to you. Even when I think you're talking right out of your rosy red ass-hole...

D: (D GESTURES GO ON)

W: Don't rush me. I have to think about where I was before you interrupted...

D: I did not interrupt...

W: ...me. (SMILES) Where was I?

D: (RAISES HAND) You're not laying this on me.

W: I'm not laying this on you? Oh yes. Communication is very important. And if I don't feel like I can communicate with you, you know, then there's something wrong with the way that I relate to you, and you relate to me, and uhhhh, the way that we relate to each other, you know. Do you see what I'm talking about.

D: Weelllll...sort of...

W: I'm not done.

D: But you asked me a question.

W: That was...what's the word for it, a para...

D: What?

W: Uh...ooooo, I almost got it...a segue, no, a red...

D: A rhetorical question.

W: No, no, no, that's not it, there, I've got it.

D: What?

W: A rhetorical question.

D: OH JESUS! (HE GOES CRAZY.)

D: (LOWERED VOICE WITH EMPHASIS) Hurry up, hurryup...

W: (LOWERED VOICE WITH EMPHASIS) Don't rush me, don't rush me. (HE WALKS AROUND IN CIRCLES.)

W: Why are you walking around?

D: Waiting for you to finish.

W: I'm finished.

D: Good…now, I will rebut, but…

W: You see, you can't stop. (SHE LEAVES.)

D: What?

W: Stop!

D: What?

W: Stop!

D: What?

W: Stop!

D: What?

W: Stop what, that's what. That!

D: All right the rebuttal…First of all, about interrupting you; I did not interrupt you, in fact, it was you who interrupted me to tell me that I had interrupted you, which did in fact constitute an interruption by any definition of the word, "interrupt" to wit, "to break in with questions or remarks while the other is speaking." Second, about the loud voice part. I did not speak in a "loud voice" first. It was you who brayed at me initially accusing me of speaking in a loud voice, in a voice so loud that I had to raise my voice to cut through the wall of sound that emanated not from me, but from you… Furthermore…

W: Stop! (whispers) Stop stop stop.
       (PAUSE)

D: Asshole.

W: Fuckhead.
       (LONG SILENCE, THEY START PLAYING WITH THINGS ON THE TABLE, MAKING EACH OTHER NERVOUS. THEY FIGHT OVER THE NEWSPAPER ALMOST KNOCK THE CHAIR OVER AND THE TABLE. THEN START YELLING AT EACH OTHER SIMULTANEOUSLY…)
       And you're not listening to a thing I say…
       (THEN THEY REALLY GO CRAZY ALL OVER THE ROOM UNTIL W PUNCHES THE WALL AND PUTS HER HAND THROUGH IT.)

W: I put my hand through the wall.
       (PAUSE)

D: You put your hand through the wall.

W: Yeah, I put my hand through the wall.

D: I hate this.
W: Yeah.
D: We gotta stop.
W: We gotta stop.
D: We gotta stop.
W: We gotta stop, okay?
D: Okay. Okay?
W: Okay.
W: Okay?
D: Okay? (ENDING WITH A HINT OF ANTAGONISM)
        (PAUSE) (THEY SEPARATE)
D: Come here.
W: (NO RESPONSE)
D: Come on, come here, okay?
W: No.
D: Okay. Come on.
W: Uh-uh.
D: Come on.
W: You come here.
D: Okay, here I am.
W: Ha!
D: Ha...who? What?
        (W REACHES OUT AND PICKS A PIECE OF FOOD OFF OF D'S LIP.)
        What are you doing?
        (HE GRABS HER HAND AND HOLDS IT.)
W: A piece of egg on your lip.
D: Oh.
        (HE PUTS HAND TO LIP WITH FREE HAND.)
W: See. (SHE HOLDS OUT CUPPED HAND WITH A PIECE OF LIP on it.)
D: That's not egg. That's a piece of lip.
W: Oh-oh.
D: What's wrong? You don't like my lip?
W: (NO RESPONSE)
D: You don't want my lip?
W: Not coming off in my hand.
D: It's just a scab.

W: You got something.

D: Not me.

W: What you got?

D: Nothin'.

W: You got somethin'.

D: Well if I do, you do too. I must have got it from you.
  (HE LUNGES AT HER.)

W: Oh no you didn't.

D: Oh yes I did.

W: Oh no you didn't.

D: Oh yes I did.

W: You didn't.

D: I did.
  (HE GRABS HER AND KISSES HER.)

W: UKKK.
  (SHE MOVES AWAY.)

D: Come here.
  (NO RESPONSE)

D: Come on, come here, okay?
  (HE WALKS OVER TO HER.)

D: Come here.

W: No, you come here.
  (DESPITE THE FACT THEY ARE ONLY SIX INCHES APART, D MOVES
  EVEN CLOSER TO W.)

W: Give me a backrub, willya?

D: (GROAN) You could at least say please.

W: What?

D: You could at least say, "Please give me a backrub." instead of order
  ing me around like a …

W: Okay. Please give me a backrub right now. Okay?

D: What do you think I am? your slave?
  (HE PUTS HIS HANDS ON HER SHOULDERS.)

W: Don't touch me!
  (SHE MOVES AWAY; LONG PREGNANT PAUSE.)
  Anyway, the thought of you running your ugly hands all over me in
  the same mundane way, like you've done a thousand times before,

smacking and groaning makes me want to throw up. If you can't touch me somehow in a new and exciting way, I say to you, most emphatically, no sir, no sir, don't touch me sir.

D: You're afraid.

W: No.

D: Yes you are. What are you afraid of? That you're going to lose a part of yourself to me. That you're going to catch what I've got. Well you got something coming babe. I'm not gonna touch you. I wouldn't touch you with an artificial dick.

W: Oh.

(PAUSE)

D: I'm sorry. (THEY EMBRACE.)

W: Oh really. An artificial dick!

D: This isn't artificial.

W: MMMMMMmmmm.

D: Oooooooooo

W: Uhhhhhhhhhh.

D: Mmmmmmmmmm

W: Uh.

(THEY MAKE KISSY SMACKY SOUNDS.)

Give me some lip.

(D GIVES LIP. SHE PULLS ON IT WITH HER TEETH AS THEY BOTH LAUGH. SHE PULLS HIM ACROSS THE ROOM BY THE LIP. HE'S TRYING TO TELL HER IT HURTS BUT SHE'S SO INTO IT THAT SHE DOESN'T GET IT.)

D: Ouch, for Christ's sake.

W: Oh…I'm sorry.

D: Jeez…whattya wanna do…bite my lip off?

W: Golly…I got carried away.

D: Oh yeah? Well okay, give me some elbow.

W: What?

D: Give me some elbow.

W: Elbow?

D: ELBOW, now…in my oster.

W: No, no…not…

D: Yes, yes…my oster.

W: Your oster? What's an oster.

D: My armpit. Come on. Ooooh. Oh, soft, oooh, yeeeesssss.
       (STEAMY OSTER. SHE PULLS BACK.)

W: I feel ridiculous doing this, it isn't right.

D: Come on.

W: I can't. My mother.

D: Why? Are you ashamed?

W: Of mother?

D: No, of elbow. Oster

W: Yes, it's against my background.

D: Elbow?

W: Yes.

D: No, it's against my oster.

W: It's unnatural.

D: This.

W: Yes. It can lead to more serious things.

D: Oh, you mean because there are stories about this kind of thing
       leading to other kinds of things, stories about what happens to
       people when they engage in this kind of...

W: Of...

D: You know...

W: No I don't. What kinds of things?

D: Weird things.

W: Like what?

D: Oh I shouldn't talk about it.

W: Yes, you should.

D: I can't.

W: You can.

D: Oh, all right. A person known to me who did that kind of thing,
       well the first sign was...

W: What?

D: Don't rush me.

W: Don't stop.
       (PAUSE)
       Don't stop. Don't stop !

D: It's hard. Okay? All right, well, this person's foot...

W: Yes, yes…

D: Don't interrupt me. (PAUSE) Well, it started to…

W: What?

D: Don't be so eager.

W: Oh forget it then, just forget it.

D: Okay.

W: Okay.

D: Okay.

W: Okay. I don't give a shit. (PAUSE) You're not gonna tell me? (PAUSE) Oh come on, I really do give a shit, I give two shits, but it takes so long for you to say stuff, well, I take it back, and I won't interrupt you again, so…what happened? Oh, I caught myself, I'm sorry. I'm goading you…aren't I? I'll stop. (PAUSE)

D: Let's just forget it, shall we?

W: But why?

D: Because my foot feels bad, okay?

W: Because?

D: Yes.

W: Aha! (SHE ZIPS MOUTH)

D: It really feels bad.

W: (SHE TRIES TO TALK THROUGH ZIPPED MOUTH.)

D: Go ahead.

W: You think?

D: Could be.

W: Oh no.

D: Take a look at it. (HE TAKES OFF SHOES AND SOCKS.)

W: What is that?

D: What?

W: That.

D: That?

W: No, that. These.

D: What?

W: Right there.

D: Ooooooh. Ouch. Oh. I don't know. That hurts, sort-of.

W: Does it.

D: Mmmmm. Yesss. Oh. It feels very…strange.

281

(SHE WORKS HER WAY UP HIS LEG. HE'S WRIGGLING.)

W: Yeah?

D: Let me try it on you.

(SHE TAKES OFF HER SHOES AND SOCKS.)

D: You've got them too.

W: Oh no.

D: Right…there.

W: Aaah. Ouch. Oh.

D: Yeah. And there and there and there and there.

W: MMMMMMMmmmmm

D: Other foot.

W: MMMMMMMMe too.

D: Yeaaahhh! Yee-haw.

W: Oh. Oooooch. Ouch. Oh

D: Mmmmm

W: Mmmmmm

D: Uhhhhhhhhhhhhhh

W: Rrrrrrrrrrrrrrrrrrr

D: Growlllllllllllllllllllll

W: HuhhhhhhhhhhhhhhhHuhhhhhhhhhhhhhhh

(THEY GET INTO IMPOSSIBLE POSITIONS AND HAVE A CLIMAX OF SORTS THAT LEAVES THEM PANTING. HE STANDS UP.)

D: Oh Gawd.

W: What's the matter?

D: I don't feel so good.

W: You feel fine to me.

D: Yeah, but I don't feel fine to myself. I feel terrible.

W: Well…you do look…weak.

D: Yeah?

W: Kinda decrepit.

D: Thanks a lot. I feel terrible.

W: Well, I feel fine.

D: You're gonna die too, you know, yes you will.

(LONG PAUSE)

W: So will you.

D: I know.

W: But when?

D: When?

W: Yes, when? That's the question…

D: You never know.

W: How are you feeling?

D: You know. And you?

W: Fine, I feel great. But you look like you're dying already.

D: To tell you the truth, I feel like I'm already dead, buried, gone…

W: Oh come on, stop whining. You're not gonna die.

D: Yes I will.

W: Oh really? Well let me help you. I hate to see you suffer.
(SHE PICKS UP A CHAIR AND PREPARES TO BEAN HIM.)

D: You do that and I'll kill ya. I'll mop up the floor with ya face.

W: I was just trying to help.

D: Thanks but no thanks.

W: Then at least you'd know. It'd put you out of your misery.

D: What?

W: When.

D: When what?

W: When you're gonna die. You'd know. I'd know. What a relief. Then you'd feel better and I wouldn't have to listen to you.

D: Well you won't, cuz you'll die first.
(PAUSE)

W: If that's wishful thinking I'd hate to disappoint you.
(SHE'S UPSET.)

D: But wait a second…hey…you know…

W: No I don't know anything except that you said I die first. Okay? Okay?

D: Oh, don't be so silly. I don't know that YOU will die first. I was just being spooky. You can't take a joke, you can't, can you, you always have to be the direct…
(SHE DIES.)

D: Opposite of what I feel…
(HE NOTICES.)

D: Right, don't listen.
(HE GETS RIGHT UP TO HER EAR.)

283

Look, we're talking about something serious.
(HE THINKS HE FEELS HIS HEART TWINGE.)
What if I died? You'd be all alone.
(NO RESPONSE.)
You'd miss me.
(HE GETS MORE PISSED.)
You wouldn't be able to take care of yourself.
(NO RESPONSE.)
You wouldn't have anybody to talk to.
(NO RESPONSE.)
Who would you talk to?
(No RESPONSE.)
FOR CHRIST'S SAKE!
(HE GRABS HER ARM. SHE IS LIMP, BEGINS TO SLIDE OFF THE CHAIR.
HE PUTS HER BACK UP.).
What's the matter? (SHE SLIDES OFF THE CHAIR.)
Oh my Gawd, what's the matter?
(HE TRIES TO MOVE HER BUT SHE'S A LITTLE TOO HEAVY. HE PUTS
HER DOWN ON THE FLOOR AND LISTENS FOR HER BREATHING.TAKES
HER PULSE, BUT HIS HAND IS SHAKING.)
Oh Gawd. (HE HITS HER KNEE AND IT JERKS.)
Talk to me!
(HE STARTS GIVING HER MOUTH TO MOUTH. SHE TURNS IT INTO A
KISS. HE KISSES HER BACK BUT THEN GETS REALLY SCARED CUZ THE
CORPSE IS KISSING HIM BACK. W STARTS TO RISE AND SLOWLY
PLAYING THE GHOST BACKS HIM INTO A CORNER, ACTING LIKE A
GHOST. D COWERS.).
GET BACK! I DIDN'T MEAN IT. GET! GET!

W: Ha! Ha! Ha! (SHE CRACKS UP.)
D: Oh shit.
W: Hahahahaha. Your face.
D: You…I thought you were dead.
W: Hahahahaha.
D: Did you hear me? I thought you were dead.
W: I know, Gawd, you had the stupidest, Hahahahaha, look on
      your face. (SHE MIMICS HIM.)

284

D: Why?

W: Hahahaha. What?

D: Why?

W: Hahahaha why what?

D: Why did you pretend to be dead?

(SHE GLARES AT HIM.)

W: Stop being such an asshole. I didn't know you'd get so hot in the pants. Really. I was making a joke, you know. If I'd known you were going to get crazy, I would have stayed dead. Okay?

D: Well, why don't you?

W: I will.

(SILENCE)

D: Don't do that anymore. Please…You scared me…oh. Ouch Oooh. (HE'S HOLDING HIS HEART.)

W: But…

D: NO, NADA, SILENCIOSO!

(SHE WRITES A SUICIDE NOTE.)

JESUS PRIESTESS! I wish you were dead, 'cause it would be a load offa my mind let me tell you. A big burden lifted offa my brain, no more stupid questions to answer, no more uptight bourgeois mores to hold me down, my Gawd, I didn't even realize it till I thought you were dead…but then…I saw the…

W: (SHE FINISHES NOTE AND DIES.)

D: I knew right away that I was free, free of your…

(HE SEES HER ON THE TABLE.)

Ha! Do you think I'm a fool ? Not me, go ahead, lie there. There's a fly on your nose. Bzzzzzz. Bzzzzz. Here, I'm gonna swat it. Ha!

(HE CLOMPS HER ONE, MAKES THE SLAP SOUND ON HIS THIGH.)

Still up to your old tricks are you? Well, give me that chair then.

(HE MOVES HER OFF THE CHAIR. SHE FALLS ONTO THE FLOOR AND LIES THERE.)

You always get the best chair. Now it's my turn.

(LONG PAUSE)

Come on, Okay? Come on! (HE NUDGES HER WITH HIS FOOT.)

Don't be so serious allatime, get with it, will ya? You know, we haven't danced in years. Wanna dance?

(HE TRIES TO PICK HER UP.)

Don't be such a sourball for Gawd's sake.

(HE FINALLY GETS HER UP.)

Let's foxtrot. Remember that song? Remember? Giddyap oopapa mau-mau, Giddyap copapa copapa ma-mau hiyo Silver awayee...

(NO REACTION.)

Lighten up willya for Christ's sake! You know, you could stand on your own two feet. Why do I have to do all the work allatime, y'know? Gawd, I love the way you dig your nails into my back when you get all...

(HER FINGERS ARE GETTING STIFF AS IF FROM RIGOR MORTIS. SHE HOLDS HERSELF UP WITH HER RIGID FINGERS.)

Hey, not that hard. You know...you're too tense my little sweetie. Come on, relax, enjoy, tickle-tickle. Boy you must really be pissed off. Not even ticklish anymore. Gawd.

(HE PUTS HIS HAND ON HER BREAST. NO RESPONS.)

Well, be an ice cube then!

(HE LETS HER GO. SHE CRASHES RIGIDLY TO THE FLOOR AND LIES THERE STIFFENING-UP.)

Are you okay? HEY! ARE YOU OKAY?

(HE BENDS DOWN AND FEELS HER PULSE. HE PUTS HIS HAND OVER HER MOUTH.)

Oh my gawd. Oh my gawd. You're not kidding are you? Oh my gawd. (HE STARTS TO GIVE HER MOUTH-mouth but her jaw is locked shut.)

OPEN YOUR MOUTH FOR CHRIST'S SAKE! Look, I'm just trying to help. (HE PRIES HER MOUTH OPEN.) Thank you. (HE GIVES HER MOUTH-TO-MOUTH AND HEART MASSAGE.)

Come on. Come on, you...bitch. Come on. oh please...

(HE IS CRYING. HE CRIES FOR A LONG TIME, STOPS HIS USELESS REMEDIES, AND FINALLY STARTS COUGHING.)

Well...come on darling. You can at least sit up. (WITH A VAST EFFORT HE GETS HER BACK UP ON THE CHAIR.)

Look, I'm sorry. You don't know how sorry I am, okay?

(SHE LOOKS AT HIM.)

Hey don't look at me that way, okay? (HE MOVES HER HEAD SO

SHE'S LOOKING OUT.)

(SHE MOVES HER HEAD BACK SO SHE'S LOOKING AT HIM AGAIN.)

I saw that. I saw you move your head.

W: Say it again.

D: What?

W: Starts with "I'm," ends with "y."

D: I'm horny? (MOVES IN ON HER.)

W: So what else is new? NO for Chrissakes…you just said it, come on, say it again.

D: What about you?

W: I am not horny, not really horny…well I mean, kind of vaguely, like usually…I could…

D: If I say it will you say it?

W: What?

D: What you just said I said: starts with "I'm," ends with "y."

W: I just ate.

D: No. That's not it.

W: I am not alone. Unfortunately.

D: No. And fuck you.

W: I am pissed off.

D: So what else is new? That's not it. Stop fucking around. You know that I know what you want me to say again, starts with "I'm," ends with "y," and in the middle…

W: "I'm"

D: "So"

W: "Ry"

(PAUSE)

D: I accept.

W: What?

D: Your apology. Your fuckin' apology.

W: For what. I didn't apologize.

D: You did. You just didn't notice. It was great. Thank you. That is exactly what I needed. So now, because you apologized, I can say it again, like you asked me to: I'm sorry.

W: Oh. (SHE GIVES HIM A HUG.)

D: Oh. (HE KISSES HER.)

W: That's sweet. (DOING A LITTLE GRIND)

D: Yeah, I mean, there's no need for this. (GRINDING TOO)

W: What?

D: Hassling.

W: Yeah.

D: I mean, if you'd only…

W: What "me"? What about the "we"?

D: The "we" what?

W: The word, the "we" word.

D: You mean like a tiny little word?

W: No, I mean us. If we'd only stop, but we can't, can we?

D: What?

W: Stop.

D: Sure I can…

W: Then stop.

D: Okay.

W: Okay.

D: Okay.

W: Okay.

D: All right. (PAUSE) All right.

W: You see?

D: What?

W: Nothing.

D: What do you mean by that?

        (BLACKOUT)

BOB

A play by Darrell Gray, Allan Kornblum and Jim Mulac

World premiere at Acute Actualism: A Memorial Homage to Darrell Gray, performed in Berkeley at Blake Street Hawkeyes December 7, 1986

Originally published in In The Light Magazine, *#s 5 & 6: Actual Plays.*

(The stage is set with a back wall and two side walls, in which there are three doorways. Attached to the frame of each doorway is an actor dressed as a door. From left to right, the first is the doorway to The Self, the second (a female) is the doorway to Love, the third (actor must be over 45) is the doorway of Return. Through each doorway can be seen a vaguely distant landscape. Through the doorway of The Self can be seen the houes of a town at varying distances. Through the doorway of Love can be seen a seascape. Through the doorway of Return can be seen the lights of skyscrapers at night. Each door/actor, fastened into a fabric painted like a standard frame door, walks on door hinges from the wall back and forth to a closed door position. When the door of Self and the door of Love are closed, the actors are facing stage front, while when the door of Return is closed the actor is facing backstage. Close beside each door onstage is a chair. When the play begins the first two doors are closed, actors looking outward, while the door of Return is opened against the wall, the actor also facing the audience. A man in his late thirties, dressed in sport slacks, a sport coat and sport shirt, and wearing a light straw hat, walks onstage through the open door of Return. His name is Bob.)

BOB: I'm back. Bob is back! The young man returned to himself. (Gesturing toward the door of Self) That door is the door to myself. I've been gone for years, but I've returned just like I promised I would.

DOOR OF LOVE: Hi, Bob! Remember me?

BOB: Sure. It's not been long, and it won't be long. You are the door of Love that takes me forward and back. You're the prettiest of the three doors. Because when I love you I head away like a ship on which you are the only person.

DOOR OF RETURN: Bob, I must warn you. Now that you've returned, you can never leave through my doorway. If you do, you'll never return again.

BOB: I like that. Ha, ha. "Bob, I must warn you…"

DOOR OF SELF: That's it, Bob. Come back into yourself. You're back now, Bob. Let's at least think about things.

BOB: Wow! That's what I think. Wow! (*he starts to walk through the door of return but the door closes. Return's back is now to the audience. Bob turns again to the audience as at first*).

BOB: I'm back. Bob is back! The young man returned to himself (*gesturing again toward the door of self*). That door is the door to myself. I've been gone for years, but I've returned…

DOOR OF SELF: You're repeating yourself, Bob. Everything is going forward and aft again like it always has, and your returning again has just taken up time. But I love you.

BOB: (*running for a moment from door to door, then sitting at last in the chair beside the door of Return*) I just think about what's happening. (*muttering to himself*)…a ship on which…a ship on which the lights are merely goblets of infirmity…a ship on which the only person is returning…a ship on which the captain himself is only another motivation of the journey back to…back to…

DOOR OF SELF: Come back to yourself, Bob.

BOB: No! That would just be selfishness…returning to myself, working things out in my own time again, walking, meditating, driving through the streets of my own little home town until, by a kind of osmosis, I begin to form an understanding of myself. But what about the others? I'm no kid anymore. No. I won't return. I will stay out here and face things in the open like a man.

DOOR OF SELF: That's just foolishness, Bob. Manhood! Are you Bob The Outward Bound, the Bob of Open Spaces in his mind? It's not Manhood, but Shiphood you should be shooting for.

DOOR OF LOVE: Yes, Bob! Shoot for me! You are the captain. Just don't shoot yourself. You're right in that respect. If you go back to your Self, who knows what happens back there. You may do something foolish.

BOB: I may do something that creates an inner door—a door so personal it may even have babies!

DOOR OF RETURN: I'm closed, Bob. I am covered with three layers of rubber-base paint, resistant to both the atmosphere and the manifold possibilities it presents. My obstinacy protects you; I am your inanimate guard.

BOB: I wish I had a sandwich instead. For years I have traveled over and over this landscape, protected by doors. Sometimes there were whole buildings connected to them, but often they were just doors standing alone in abandoned pastures—doors growing sideways out from the side of mountains, doors of men's rooms with urinals shaped like giant tulips!

DOOR OF LOVE: I was the door to your high school, Bob. I was your gym locker door—the one that rusted shut.

BOB: You were the door to the station wagon in which we all piled one summer night, one night that turned into a road of sighing virgins.

DOOR OF SELF: And you came to me, Bob. Your face swung open to let out an accumulation of twilights. I was quite startled. I said: This is Bob, who am I, and who comes to let himself out of his startled feelings. I must make of myself an aperture for his sense of time; I must expand my vistas so he will have a personal space.

BOB: You did a fine job, or at least I have always thought so. Whenever I walk along a beach, I marvel at how far you have opened. You seem to open so far that beer cans glitter inside you, like snowflakes that never dissolve!

DOOR OF RETURN: (*gruffly*) A simple residue is no occasion for celebration! You must attune yourself to all the things you exclude.

BOB: I once excluded a party because of its people. I excluded a kite, a ski lift, and a grey flannel suit. I excluded African shows quite early, and then I grew up to exclude the drive-in movies.

DOOR OF LOVE: They must have been planted on a terrain improperly hinged.

291

DOOR OF SELF: He was his own terrain; he came 'unhinged.'

BOB: I came to one idea, which I found by chance. It was a structure like a Beethoven string quartet. My mind, which had always hurt me like an ingrown toenail, faded softly away. Each bird became a door, each feather a delicate lock…

(*An old man carrying a giant net appears from stage left and proceeds to walk down sidewalk. He hesitates before each door, mumbling to himself.*)

OLD MAN: When man is placed carelessly, he begins to say strange things. This looks like a city of functions, yet there is only one man.

BOB: I must be the one you refer to, Old Man. These doors are mine, for I have opened them often. May I invite you in?

OLD MAN: I am that being whose nature is both "in" and "out" at once.

BOB: I hate it when you're condescending.

OLD MAN: I was talking about in and out, not up and down. You have to be up to look down.

BOB: The only contest I ever won was making a safety poster in 6th grade. Look both ways before you cross the street. That was the theme. Everybody in the school had to make a poster illustrating the idea—Look Both Ways Before You Cross The Street. I drew a picture of three doors. Each door was open and you could see a street stretching out from each door until the street faded due to perspective. On each street a little child was running carelessly into the street. One little boy was chasing a ball. A little girl ran out to get one of her jacks, which she lost while flipping them over for 'flipsies.' And in the middle of the third street emanating from the third door, lay a dollar bill. A little boy was racing a little girl to get the dollar first. It had fallen from somebody's pocket I guess.

DOOR OF LOVE: Walk down the street you will find behind me, Bob, and you'll find more than an accidental dollar.

BOB: I know. I'll find fast cars.

OLD MAN: I was here before they had fast cars. Horses, they had. Trains, they had. Steamships, they had. Balloons, they had. But no cars. Then one day, after I had been at sea for several months, and weathered many storms, we had just docked and I had sold my catch. I went to the bar where most of the fishermen in the town drank. One of the loudest men at the bar was raving about cars. "They'll drive us from our homes," he said. "Just so they can utilize space in a way that seems efficient."

DOOR OF SELF: Cars are only thinking of themselves when they build superhighways. It's not their fault that they crave efficient space. People can adapt. Cars can't. Old Man, between us we've got to teach this boy to think for himself or else his car is going to do his thinking for him and then…

DOOR OF RETURN: (*Swinging open about halfway, musingly*) Suppose this room was a car in the city (*the sound of distant honking horns can be heard and the lights of the city can be seen again*) and after waving farewell to the ships at the harbor, we were cruising the streets, uptown, downtown, and I would be the car door, through which the driver would be unable to order anything at the drive-in movie through a rear entrance without paying, and I would be the door which would not be able to hold the audio speaker…

DOOR OF LOVE: Then it would be like a silent movie, Bob. Would you take me there?

DOOR OF RETURN: (*Chuckling, and swaying back and forth*) Oh, my. Go. Go then Bob. This Old Man knows why that movie is silent.

BOB: (*Gets up from his chair and closes the door of return, who frowns and grumbles*) Old Man, you may know how to get drunk after your ship has come in, but you are old and the exhilaration of driving the freedom of a fast car is only an accident in your mind that hasn't crashed yet.

DOOR OF SELF: That's it, Bob! There's a new space inside of me now that can totally absorb us in reflections, bumper to bumper…

OLD MAN: You're young, Bob. But you can't go back.

(*The door of self swings open, revealing the scene of the distant town. The sound of a car engine purring forcefully and a distinctive car horn beep can be heard.*)

BOB: (*looking through the doorway of Self with fascination*) Holy Toledo! That's my Bonney! My '66 Bonney! I can almost hear the radio playing the Jazz Crusaders.

DOOR OF LOVE: I'm so glad you remember, Bob. And it's both behind us and ahead.

OLD MAN: If I may interrupt…the reason my ship came in was because of my wife. This girl may do the same for you, Bob. My wife refused to let me drive my car. I always rode alongside on the running board. Sometimes I just ran alongside, while my wife drove. But whenever she had an accident, I always jumped off or made sure I was out of the way…

BOB: (laughing arrogantly) Listen to that. Your wife is lost in an accident, and now you're just a lonely old man like me, only older.

DOOR OF SELF: Beep. Beep. Oh wow, Bob. Just look at those curbs. They're glittering with all the town's possessions. There's an old bouquet of mums. Here's a nice dog chain. Look, Bob! It's a baby in a suitcase (the sound of screeching brakes is heard. A baby's cry is heard).

BOB: (becoming mystified) That's me when I was a baby. I remember my cry. I remember the smell of the suitcase. It was Dad's. Oh, Daddy. Daddy, I'll be a good boy. Wait. That smell…

(*Old Man shies away from Bob, without Bob noticing.*)

DOOR OF LOVE: Smell this, Bob! (she swings open, revealing the seascape and the sound of surf as the sound of the car in the Door Of Self fades away)

BOB: I'm getting too old for this. I'm going to be forty, soon. Maybe…

DOOR OF LOVE: Yes, Bob. I'm open now. I closed myself only because of your selfishness. Sometimes, the breakfast itself has to struggle for its identity only to be taken in by your selfishness. If you come to me now, you won't be washed up, you'll be as free as salt rolling from driftwood to driftwood.

BOB: (heading towards the Door Of Love, hesitating, and then passing through toward the seascape) If I were salt I would reflect in every particle the nostalgia of each passing wave. That would be what Dad would call "carrying on the family tradition."...Mom would cook a great dinner for Dad to be late to, but when he arrived he would only say: "This dinner is ultimate" or "Pass the gravy" etc. Dad was like that—a real gravy man from way back!

DOOR OF SELF: Your suitcase remembers it too, Bob; your toothbrush and your spray deodorant are concrete memories. You must be more concrete—you must, as it were, install handles on all your emotions so that you can function with them smoothly. Otherwise—

BOB: I get the picture.

DOOR OF LOVE: You see them chairs, Bob?

BOB: Yes, they look terribly empty.

DOOR OF SELF: They are the boats whose destination is always to be in one place.

BOB: They look calm, as if they had already got there. (musing to himself) I wish I were here as much as those chairs are—I wish I had a surface smooth enough to invite the passersby.

DOOR OF LOVE: Your heart is open, Bob, but your head slows down your desert.

BOB: Desert?

OLD MAN: I have been standing here watching both of you. And little have I said. The focus you insist upon resembles neither old age nor the boat that carries the Subject to its Object. You have what I call a strange way of 'mixing words.'

BOB: Thank God there are only two sexes, then, or things would not resemble this life after all.

DOOR OF LOVE: You are retreating, Bob. I see your desires like a glowing ball of light. Your head can hardly balance on your shoulders, while your legs and thighs ache to project themselves upon some virgin terrain.

BOB: My head is my father; my legs and thighs are its dream.

295

DOOR OF SELF: Dream on, Bob: dream that your legs are on earth, while your heart races over a bump at 80 m.p.h. You are your keeper's Keeper. Keep it up, Bob! I know you know the locks.

OLD MAN: He may know the locks, but his tires are in need of retreads. He may come to his lock while dangling from the edge of a cliff! And then again, he may not come at all!

BOB: will come, Old Man. I will come like the evening sun to a table spread out with dinner. I will eat and drink and think long hours into the night, and then I might write a few poems.

OLD MAN: (*laughing uncontrollably*) Poems? You are your own poem, Bob—you are the poem of gravy and the poem of locks. You are a living metaphor, the one door your parents forgot to close, the draft through the cracks of their marriage, and the beautiful skyline of their heritage! You are the Keeper of the Globe, Bob.

BOB: I am the keeper of my shoes my car, and the beer. Whatever comes into me I make sure it is put to good use.

IV. TWO PUBLISHERS
WITH IOWA CITY ROOTS

A History of Toothpaste / Coffee House Press
by Allan Kornblum

The following is an excerpt from the introduction to a book in progress by Allan Kornblum titled, *From Gilgamesh to Gutenberg to Google*. This material is protected by copyright.

I Can Do This

After dropping out of N.Y.U. and drifting to Boston, New Hampshire, and Philadelphia, I moved back to New York during the fall of 1969 with a new plan: I was determined to become a poet. I got a job working the midnight-to-eight-thirty shift at the Grand Central Station Post Office and began attending poetry classes and workshops at the New School and at the Saint Mark's Church Poetry Project.

One evening, as our group started to settle down for one of those Saint

Mark's workshops, our teacher told us that we had been asked to help collate the pages of an issue of a mimeographed magazine that focused on a group of writers known as the "New York School" poets. There actually was no such school, and those writers were as diverse in style as New York City itself. Nonetheless the work of this somewhat amorphous "group" spoke to me and—as it seemed then and now—to the spirit of those tumultuous times. The class was game for the adventure, so we went downstairs to one of the back rooms in the old church (the second oldest in the city), and were greeted by several rows of two-by-six-foot tables, each loaded with five stacks of 250 pages. We each took a table and collated the five pages, crisscrossing the groupings as we went.

When I had completed my assignment, I discreetly sidled up to the editor (as so many others have done to me since), and after telling him how much I liked his magazine, I asked if he'd like to see some of my work. He looked off into the distance for a moment and, with a world-weary sigh said, "I've always thought poetry should be as hard to break into as the Longshoreman's Union." And I thought, to hell with him. I can do this. I'll start my own magazine. I've always been grateful for that kick in the pants, which can sometimes be far more productive than well-intended encouragement.

I had already planned a fresh start, enrolling at the University of Iowa with the intention of majoring in poetry. I told all my New York friends that when I arrived in Iowa, I was going to launch a magazine, although I didn't even have a name yet. Then, a week before I left for the Midwest, I went to a retrospective exhibit of the work of Jim Dine at the Whitney Museum and was struck by his six-foot-tall paintings of toothbrushes. Where's the toothpaste going to come from, to go on those toothbrushes? I wondered. That's how I wound up naming my first publishing venture.

When I arrived in Iowa City on July 3, 1970, I immediately started looking for poets as lively as the ones I'd met in New York. Many of the poets I got to know started their own magazines within the next few years: Darrell Gray edited *Suction*; George Mattingly's magazine *Search for Tomorrow*, and later he published some very handsome poetry books under the Blue Wind Press imprint; Dave Morice chewed on *Gum* while his alter ego, Joyce Holland fired up *Matchbook*, a magazine of one-word poems; Morty Sklar located *The Spirit That Moves Us;* and Patricia Hampl and Jim Moore came down with *A Lamp in the Spine.* It was a heady atmossphere.

By early August I had enough poems for Toothpaste's first issue and started typing stencils that came out of a box marked with the once familar AB Dick brand name. Only later did I learn that it was Mr. Lightbulb, Thomas Alva Edison, who had taken out a patent for a theoretical "auto-graph" machine in 1870, and ten years later, a second patent for a method of making stencils. In 1887 Albert Blake Dick, a Wisconsin lumberman, licensed Edison's patents, coined and then trade-marked the word mimeo-graph, and went into business manufacturing a working version of Edison's original idea. During the next eighty years, mimeographs churned out hundreds of thousands of weekly church programolitical leaflets for Dem-ocrats, Republicans, Socialists, and Communists, a stultifying supply of office memos and business proposals, and countless smudgy stapled poetry magazines and books. By the time I cranked out seven issues of *Toothpaste* magazine, three Toothpaste Press mimeo poetry books, and became a full-time letterpress printer in 1973. Photocopying costs had dropped and the mimeograph machine was on its way out, disappearing into office machine history without a trace. Today, few people under the age of sixty have even heard the word.

But near the end of August 1970, my student ID got me free access to a mimeo machine in the Student Activities Center, and in short order the first issue of *Tooth-paste* had been run off, collated, stapled, and was ready for sale. One of my first sales was to Cinda Wormley, a young woman working in one of those food-stand "barrels" in front of a restaurant called the Taco Vendor. I had already met her at a party, and George Mattingly, one of the local poet/editors, told me he knew she was interested in me. So I sold her a magazine, and sure enough we went out later that evening. I don't remember any other details; I certainly can't remember what made me think we would only have a very brief relationship. As it turned out, we were married two years later, and 2012 marked our fortieth anniversary—so much for first impressions.

A Smell That Gets in Your Blood

In September of the same year, I signed up for a class called Introduction to Typography, hoping it would help me understand the publishing process when, some time in a hoped-for future, a major publishing house would accept my first book. Instead I discovered the class was an introduction to letterpress printing and that major publishers hadn't used metal type for about fifteen years. I was a bit put off at first—until I handset some type and pulled my first proof. For fifteenth century technology, it was an incredibly electrifying experience, even if it was just a simple sample paragraph that we all had to crank out on a Vandercook cylinder press as an introductory exercise.

For my class project I printed a little pamphlet of my own poems called *Famous Americans*. Although it showed no signs of typographic talent or taste, I discovered that I really liked the work. I had never been able to force myself to put in the hours required for the other arts disciplines I'd tried, but I enjoyed putting in twelve-to-fourteen hours hand-setting type, and I couldn't wait to come back for more. At that point I thought it might be possible that I'd finally found my path. I know now that I was certainly not the first to be captivated by the smell of printer's ink, or to discover that it could somehow get into your blood.

Some people have actually struggled through the process of learning to print on their own. I was lucky enough to be introduced to the craft by a charismatic teacher, Harry Duncan, proprietor of the Cummington Press, who was (to quote *The New York Times*) "considered the dean of the post-war hand-press revival." Harry had published first editions of such legends as William Carlos Williams and Wallace Stevens, along with Robert Lowell's debut collection, and was as renowned for his innovative typography as for his editorial acumen.

Harry began his career as an actor, and as he aged I believe he realized that the role of the brilliant, absented-minded old coot fit his face and personality. Over time, he added bits and pieces to his act, like an old vaudeville performer, until the line between his public and private persona blurred and eventually disappeared. I can still remember that when I complained to him about the worn type at the University of Iowa typography lab where I completed my earliest projects, he raised his bushy white eye-brows, peered over his glasses, and gently admonished, "It's a poor craftsman who

301

blames his materials."

Over the December 1971/January 1972 Christmas break, I had the opportunity to work for Harry in the print shop he had set up in his home. Watching him crumple up sheets in disgust that I would have killed to be able to claim I had printed, gave me quite the standard to live up to. He even pulled the old type-lice gag on me. Pretending to discover some in the bed of the press, he turned to tell me about them in a voice filled with mock concern, continuing a master/apprentice tradition that went back hundreds of years. For the record, he had me for at least ten seconds, before I realized that lice couldn't possibly eat lead type.

In early spring 1972, someone told me that a local auction house had put up an old platen press for sale, but no one had bid on it. They were going to sell it to the first person to put up $35.00 and haul it off. I knew I had to buy it. When I asked, my poetry teacher, mentor, and eventually my dear friend Anselm Hollo, said he would be happy to store the press in his garage until we found room for it. When Duncan took a new position at the University of Nebraska/Omaha, Cinda and I bought his house (with some help on the down payment from an Iowa City urban renewal project, and from my parents). Harry moved out a month before we were married, and after the wedding we moved in, and his closed-in-porch pressroom became the home of the newly launched letterpress version of the Toothpaste Press.

Learning the Craft & the Business

During the next ten years I continued learning the craft of letterpress printing, and began to learn the business of small press publishing. Our first major project was an 80-page book of poems called Scattered Brains by Darrell Gray. During the course of working on the book, I slowly became dissatisfied with my design and printing skills. While Cinda and I hand-folded the pages after the printing was completed, I remembered that Harry Duncan had once burned every copy of a book he had printed on a hand-press, redesigned the book and printed it again because his work hadn't measured up to his vision of what the book should look like. I gave the idea some thought, but decided that as much as I admired Duncan's integrity, he was more of a book artist, and I wanted to be more of a publisher. I would learn from my mistakes and move on. We never told Darrell about my misgivings, and as far as he was concerned, his book was a work of art.

303

After we printed a few more titles, I realized that it was time to learn how to sell them. (Coffee House Press begins marketing plans for a book about nine months before publication date, but those were different times.) In the 1970s it was very difficult to get small press books into bookstores. We printed and mailed brochures and placed a few small ads in literary magazines, but exhibiting at book fairs was one of the primary ways for small press publishers to help their authors reach an audience back then. I attended my first—the New York Small Press Book Fair—in 1975. I mailed a carton of books to a friend's apartment, then got on a Greyhound bus and headed to New York and the inevitable guest mattress on the floor. But even though I arrived at the book fair wearing my typical blue jeans and my now long-lost wild-looking Bob Dylan hair, for some reason I got the idea that as a poetry publisher, I was obliged to project a dignified demeanor. And so I sat politely during the first two days with my hands folded together meekly, like a hippie funeral director, saying nothing unless spoken to.

The show began on a Friday, and by close of business on Saturday, I believe I'd sold about a dozen books, and taken in about $50.00. I don't remember any soul-searching that Saturday night, I don't remember saying, screw it, I'm going to have some fun, but clearly something must have gotten into me, because that Sunday I took a completely different approach. Treating the show like street theater, I began shouting, "Step right up, step right up. Toothpaste Press books make your mind feel fresh and clean because all our poets went to Colgate College. They make you think of poetry every morning and every night when you brush your teeth. Don't be another blasé New Yorker. We've come all the way from Iowa to show you the most beautiful books at the fair, and they'll look even more beautiful on your bookshelves. Step right up and see for yourselves." I think I took in $500 that day, but more importantly, I learned I could sell books without feeling as if I'd sold out, by maintaining my sense of humor.

Five years later in 1980 Cinda and I took our first trip to California, where we decided to drop in on Andrew Hoyem, who could very appropriately be regarded as the dean of the next generation of American fine printers, after Duncan's prime. In the late 1950s / early 1960s, he and his business partner Dave Hazelwood had published many of the most cutting edge poets of the day with letterpress equipment, but they used very inexpensive paper to keep the price of their books as low as possible, as Cinda and I were doing at Toothpaste. Although their legendary Auerhahn Press had released books by William Burroughs, Michael McClure, John Wieners, Robert Duncan, Charles Olson, and many other important writers, they just weren't able to make a financial go of it.

At the time of our visit, Hoyem was completing his first masterpiece under his new Arion Press imprint—a deluxe letterpress edition of Moby Dick with newly commissioned wood engravings by Barry Moser, at the then unheard of price of a $1,000 a copy. Auerhahn had been one of my models—if they couldn't make it as a letterpress publisher selling inexpensive letterpress poetry books, I began to wonder if I could. I'd read enough printing history by then to know that Gutenberg had gone bankrupt, and his equipment and the completed but unbound Bible had been taken over by his chief investor when Gutenberg couldn't pay back his loans on time. That was a part of history I did not want to share. It took me a few years to realize that Andrew Hoyem's experience was actually a wake-up call, and that eventually I would have to choose between fine printing and contemporary publishing.

The Full Diversity, Complexity, and Absurdity

Later that year, I decided to try exhibiting our books at the American Booksellers Association annual convention, having learned all I could from the many small press book fairs I had attended during the second half of the 1970s. I arrived on the first day of the show with a carton of poetry books balanced on my shoulder, unaware that all the other publishers had set up their booths the day before. After showing my publisher's badge to a guard at the door, I took a few tentative steps into the main exhibit hall at Chicago's McCormick Place, only to be accosted by a woman wearing nothing but a slip, handing out brochures for a book called *The History of the Negligee*. After a few more steps, a woman in a New York Rangers hockey outfit gave me a brochure for her memoir about her attempt to become the first female pro hockey player. And just behind her, a man with a drugged baby tiger on a leash was giving out brochures for a book about animal training. As I continued toward the small press tables, I wondered what I had gotten myself into.

At that moment many of my small press peers would have turned on their heels and walked out the door. But I was inspired by the idea that there might be room for our poetry books, even in the midst of that commercial sensory overload. As I walked around the hall, I saw dignified presses like Norton and Knopf next to booths selling crossword puzzle books and buns calendars. I realized publishing wasn't just about great literature—it represented the full diversity, complexity, and at times, the absurdity of the human experience. And I couldn't get enough of it. I later realized that A.B.A. was continuing the process of nudging me away from fine press printing, toward the life of a small independent literary publisher.

After We Brushed our Teeth, It Was Time for Coffee

In 1977 Cinda and I had gone to a book fair in Saint Paul, responding to a mailed flier that promised couches for out-of-town exhibitors, and a catered dinner for the publishers at the end of the show. I still remember reading that invitation and thinking, this town wants us. We quickly took to the people, and decided the Twin Cities would be our next home, if and when we decided to leave Iowa.

By the early 1980s we began to realize that we either had to go the way of the deluxe letterpress edition, and gear our promotion efforts to wealthy collectors, or we could run a small publishing house and help our authors reach a broader audience, but we couldn't focus effectively or financially on both. And when our first daughter was born in 1979, financial consideration began to take on more importance.

While pondering our fiscal future, we received letters from two authors who were up for tenure at their respective institutions, and both were concerned that their review committees might not think a Toothpaste Press book was a legitimate professional credential because our press name sounded so funky. They hoped we could supply photocopies of articles about the press that might help their case. Even though they both said they loved "Toothpaste," our mission was to be of service to writers, and we started wondering if they would be better served by a new name.

While mulling that over, I stumbled by chance on a book called *Penny Universities: A History of the Coffee Houses*, in the stacks of the University of Iowa Library. I learned that traditional English inns had a list of forbidden topics of conversation in order to avoid fights; also, if you had a prime booth near the fire and a wealthy customer arrived, you had to surrender your seat. The coffee house overturned both those practices. When I saw a reproduction of an advertisement for a 1600s English coffee house clearly stating that you could take the seat of your choice and no one could make you move, and that you could talk about any subject you desired—it seemed as if our new press name had been poured right into my cup. I decided to announce that the toothpaste tube had been squeezed dry, and it was now time for coffee.

Early one May 1984 morning, Cinda and I signed with a realtor and put our Iowa house up for sale, and by noon we were on our way to the Twin Cities where we incorporated Coffee House Press as a Minnesota nonprofit. Later that month we exhibited the first Coffee House fall list at the A.B.A. convention at San Francisco's Moscone Center. Unfortunately it took a while to sell the house, so during its first year Coffee House was run out of our home in Iowa. Finally, in August 1985, we were able to move north when Coffee House became the first "visiting press-in-residence" at the new just-about-to-open Minnesota Center for Book Arts in downtown Minneapolis.

From the start, we envisioned much more than a simple name change.

307

We planned to continue our commitment to poets we had published under the Toothpaste imprint, but Coffee House would use commercial services for typesetting, printing, and binding, enabling us to publish novels, short stories, and memoir—books that would have taken too much time to set by hand, or would have cost too much money to be machine-set in linotype or monotype. We were also hoping that a second printing of one of our Coffee House books might be needed occasionally. Going back to press for a second letterpress printing would take almost as much time as the first, and would have made it impossible to project pub dates for new titles. But switching to contemporary technology meant that a second printing only required a phone call. And over the ensuing years we wound up making that call for books that have gone into second printings, third printings, and in a few cases, as many as ten printings.

Editorially, the Toothpaste Press list reflected my personal influences and friendships, comprising a mix of the poets I had met in Iowa, and some of the so-called second-and-third-generation New York School poets. Coffee House—a press that was to represent our staff, our board, and our community—seemed to require that we broaden and deepen our outreach. I was inspired by Whitman's line: "I hear America singing, the varied carols I hear,...." I wanted Coffee House authors who could and did sing those varied carols, and I found them, and they found me. By the time I made the transition from Publisher to Senior Editor / Founder in July 2011, our list had fully embraced diversity in our authors, and in the many literary techniques they used to tell their stories.

We also embraced technological changes that went beyond simply going from mimeograph to letterpress to offset printing. In the mid-1980s, we sent a copy of each manuscript to a local typesetting firm, after writing line-by-line design specs in the margin. They keyboarded the text into their computer, and sent us the type on long strips of photographic paper. We cut the strips into the size of the text block, coated the back of the strips with hot wax which worked as an easily movable adhesive, positioned the type on layout sheets over a light table, and fixed every-thing in place by burnishing the sheets with a plastic roller.

In the early 1990s, we began designing our books with the new "desktop publishing" software, and sent the fully laid-out text to the printer on a disk. However we continued to create photo-ready layouts of the covers.

308

Eventually our designer began creating the covers on the computer as well —and in many instances there is no longer an "original" on a piece of paper. Now in the 21st century we still make our prose available in print on paper, but also in a variety of e-book formats; and like everyone else, we sell our books through Amazon.com, at chain bookstores like Barnes & Noble, at tried-and-true independent booksellers, and directly from our own website.

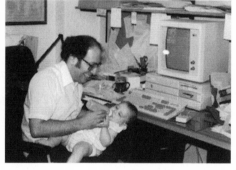

Staying Power

By the 1970s the Civil Rights Movement of the 1960s had morphed into the Black Power Movement, which also inspired Asian Americans, Hispanic Americans, feminists, and Gay Rights advocates to form movements of their own. It seemed as if the emerging counter-culture might actually survive tie-died t-shirts and acid rock, and the literary community responded to the energy in the air by starting a new small press or magazine somewhere in the country practically every day. We all believed and proudly announced that we were part of a Small Press Movement that would provide an enduring outlet for the many new voices that were yearning to make their statements and find their audiences.

But once reality set in, the attrition rate was high—half of those presses and/or magazines failed to last a year. Of those that were left, most folded by the end of their second year when their idealistic founders discovered how much work publishing entailed, and how difficult it was to get their wares onto bookstore shelves. Of the thousands of literary ventures that began in those years of high aspirations, publishers lasting ten years or more could probably be counted on the fingers of two hands—toes not needed.

The editors who did survive shared a few things in common beyond an ear for literary talent and an eye for graphic design. Coffee House, Graywolf, Copper Canyon, Milkweed, New Rivers, Curbstone, Sun & Moon, and a few other small literary presses that began in the 1970s or early 1980s, developed the ability to set goals, to create plans to achieve those goals, and to work with a staff to implement the plans. We learned how to create schedules so we could project the publication dates for our books and get them out on time. We learned how to keep business records that could pass muster during an independent audit, and began to project multi-year budgets based on past performance. And we developed relationships with funders who helped supplement sales income, providing the capital needed for the growth we experienced. None of this was new to the business world in general, or the book business in particular, but in the 1970s, long-range editorial plans, production schedules, marketing campaigns, and financial records actually seemed to violate the spontaneous spirit of the times. In some circles, sloppy design and production actually bestowed a kind of street cred on some small press publishers. Of course street cred doesn't pay the bills, and those publishers tended to disappear after a few years.

When I began my career with a mimeographed magazine there were simply no models within the small press community for the kind of press Coffee House eventually became. It turned out to be my privilege to be part of a generation of editor/publishers who created an "upper tier" for literary indies. By hiring experienced full-time staff and developing detailed procedures for each stage of the publishing process, the presses in that upper tier were able to provide professional level editing, design, production, marketing, and publicity for their authors' books. The presses that briefly flare brightly, only to flicker and sputter out, in the aggregate also make important contributions—the upper tier simply gives writers and readers more options. However beyond the books we produced, I believe that the standards we upper tier publishers set for ourselves, served as a positive influence on the next generation of start-ups, including those who have decided to stay small, and those who have planned for long-term growth. Considering the hippie ethos of my youth, it seems appropriate to lay claim to a collaborative, not a solo legacy. And of course every book we've ever published has represented collaboration between our authors, our staff, our distributor and sales reps, reviewers, booksellers, and ultimately the readers. With pleasure and passion, I've played my part in that collaboration for more than forty years, and although I can no longer put in fourteen-hour-plus days, I still enjoy the work.

Michael Peich compiled an excellent Checklist of Toothpaste Press books which can be found online.

A complete list of Coffee House Press books is available at
CoffeeHousePress.org

311

History of The Spirit That Moves Us Press
by Morty Sklar, founder/editor/publisher

Nine years before I started *The Spirit That Moves Us* magazine in Iowa City, which evolved to The Spirit That Moves Us Press, my inclination for editing and layout revealed itself when as one of the first heroin addicts to enter a new drug rehabilitation therapeutic community in New York City, I created along with another resident, a newsletter that included contributions by residents and staff. We named it *The Phoenix*, the mythological bird that consumed itself in fire and rose from its ashes to live again. Our program was re-named Phoenix House after that.

My literary publishing would probably not have happened had serendipity not taken me from New York City two years after graduating from Phoenix House, to the First National Poetry Festival in Allendale, Michigan in July 1971, where after that six-day festival I was sitting on my Honda 305 "Dream" motorcycle and Audrey Teeter asked me where I was going, and when I told her I didn't know but was looking for a nice place to live, she told me Iowa City was such a place, and I followed her there.

313

The winding road from Interstate 80 up Dubuque Street to town was a welcoming beginning.

Audrey eventually took me to The Mill restaurant where she introduced me to her poet and little-magazine publisher friends, including Allan Kornblum (may he rest in peace) who had been at the festival and told me "I was falling asleep at the open reading but your poem, 'Bed' woke me up."

Eventually Allan and wife Cinda published my first book of poems, *The Night We Stood Up For Our Rights: Poems 1969–1975*, by letterpress from The Toothpaste Press.

After publishing poems in the little magazines that abounded, and participating in poetry readings as well as collating sessions for *Toothpaste* and other magazines, my close friend Jim Mulac (may he rest in peace), owner of Jim's Used Books & Records, poet and jazz pianist, asked me "Why don't you do a little magazine?" I liked the idea of putting out a magazine that contained work I liked most from locals and from around the country and the world. The first thing I did was come up with a title, *The Spirit That Moves Us*, which came from what my mother once told me—to do something if the spirit moved me.

In 1975 I typeset the forty-eight page 5½ by 8½ Volume 1, #1 on stencils with an IBM Selectric Composer and ran it off on a mimeograph machine, but had the cover—with a photo of my maternal grandmother Rose holding me up in her arms—printed offset at a print shop. I then folded-and-gathered the pages and saddle-stitched the issue at the spine.

I also typeset subsequent issues and books on the Composer, and except for the latest publications of the press over twenty years later, sent them to printers as camera-ready copy.

I'd been attracted to much poetry from abroad because of a general seriousness expressed in it, and the very first poems I published in the first two issues were by the Hungarian poet, Attila Jozsef, translated by John

Batki, one of the Actualists.

The Spirit That Moves Us Press received nonprofit IRS-tax-exemption as a 501(c)(3) arts organization in 1976, and after our third issue of *The Spirit That Moves Us* magazine, was eligible to apply for grants. The Coordinating Council of Literary Magazines was the first organization to which we applied and from which we received grants.

About the magazine, *Library Journal* said "A well-deserved reputation for discovering new talent, as well as featuring better-known names. Highly recommended."
Serials Review said "A significant voice on the national scene."

Outside the Actualist community, I learned a lot about publishing from COSMEP (Committee of Small Magazine Editors and Publishers) and *Small Press Review*.

In 1977 our first book, a slim chapbook, came-about when I liked all six poems by Marianne Wolfe that she submitted for the magazine and decided to issue them as *The Poem You Asked For* (the title poem).
American Library Association's *Booklist* said "Embodies the original spirit of small press publishing: produced with care, and high quality poems."

Later that year, after Darrell Gray came up with the name Actualism for the work that our community of poets in Iowa City was producing, Darrell and I co-edited an anthology of fourteen of the poets titled *The Actualist Anthology* and I published it in both trade paperback and clothbound editions as well as Volume 2, Numbers 2 & 3 of *The Spirit That Moves Us*.
As I state on the "Welcome!" page, "Our original desire was to publish in one volume, the poets herein. As the publisher, calling this collection *The Actualist Anthology* came mainly out of a need for a title other than something like *Fourteen Iowa City Poets*, which wouldn't have been accurate since this is not a regional anthology in a strict sense: we come from, among other places, New York City; Newton, Iowa; Hungary, Chicago, Finland, San Francisco, Saint Louis and even Iowa City!"
An application to the Iowa Arts Council for a grant was rejected. Allan Kornblum had the idea that he, Jim Mulac and I approach the Council in person to explain the importance to literature of the small independent press. We did, and this time a grant was forthcoming, which opened the

door to financial support not only for The Spirit That Moves Us Press but also set a precedent for other small-press publishers.

Of *The Actualist Anthology* Robert Bly said, "People looking for worlds their imaginations might bless."

From *Booklist* of the American Library Association: "A volume of interest as a record of and introduction to a purely American poetic movment."

In 1978, one project that wasn't a book or magazine issue was our *Poetry-With-Drawings In The Buses*, an idea that came to me when I was a bus driver for the City of Iowa City. With funding by the Iowa State Arts Council, the City of Iowa City, and the good merchants, cooperatives and people of Iowa City, I sent out announcements for a poetry contest, the eight winners to have their poems illustrated by artists of Iowa City and printed both on 11" x 16" placards to be placed in the buses of Iowa City and the University Cambuses, and printed also as 5" x 7" postcards. Eight hundred eighty-three entries were received from from thirty-five states and Canada. When the winning poems and the covers were illustrated, printed and placed on buses, merchants asked why they couldn't have advertisements in the buses, and the City Council allowed it.

In 1979 The Spirit That Moves Us Press sponsored the 8th Actualiztion tied-in with a subscription drive. It was co-sponsored by the Plains Book

Bus, C.A.C., the University Lecture Committee, and the Comparative Literature Department.

The Farm In Calabria
& Other Poems

DAVID RAY

The Spirit That Moves Us Press

Also in 1979, we received a twenty-two page chapbook manuscript, *The Farm In Calabria & Other Poems* from David Ray, and decided to publish it perfect-bound as part of Volume 5, Numbers 1 & 2 of *The Spirit That Moves Us* magazine but with its own cover on the flip side of the 64-page issue, and with an International Standard Book Number assigned to it too.   David Ray was twice a winner of the William Carlos Williams Award from the Poetry Society of America. *Kirkus Review* said "Ray (English Emeritus / University of Missouri) is one of only a handful of poets to garner a following among non-academics."

Jim Mulac and I were disappointed with the 1978 edition of *The Pushcart Prize: Best of the Small Presses*—a misnomer if ever there was one for a publication that drew most heavily upon academically oriented journals and presses and marginalized a large number of quality writers who were not associated with university or mainstream poetry publishers. We co-edited, and in 1980 I published from The Spirit That Moves Us Press, *Editor's Choice: Literature & Graphics from the U.S. Small Press, 1965–1977* in trade paperback and clothbound editions.

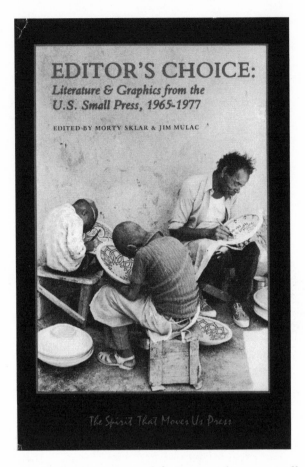

Jim had been presenting poetry and fiction readings as well as musical performances at his used Books and records store—including writers from around the world who came to Iowa City for the International Writing Program and who the Iowa Writers' Workshop practically ignored.

In my application for a National Endowment for the Arts grant for this anthology, I cited a 250-page book, but Jim and I just weren't able to exclude work we loved based on book size, and it ended-up being 501 pages, practically eliminating monetary compensation for us.

The Washington Post said "Invigorating, outrageous, true work by artists who don't fit the establishment mold."

Library Journal: "Highly recommended. No library with an interest in modern writing can miss this essential contribution to the American scene."

We'd read all the submissions in Jim's Used Books & Records store. I typeset the 504 pages in my $45/month room above the Englert Theater, on an IBM Composer which had 8K memory (1MB is 1,000K), so I had to print-out every two pages. I sent camera-ready copy to the printer.

319

In 1981 *Cross-Fertilization: The Human Spirit As Place* (poetry, fiction, an essay, artwork) was offered to subscribers to *The Spirit That Moves Us* magazine as Volume 5, Number 3.

In 1982 *The Spirit That Moves Us Reader: Seventh Anniversary Anthology* was issued in trade paperback and clothbound editions as well as Volume 6, Numbers 2 & 3 of *The Spirit That Moves Us*. In addition to poems, stories and visuals from the inception of the magazine in 1975 to Volume 6, #1 in 1981, an Index to all issues was included.

R.R. Bowker's *Magazines for Libraries* said "*The Spirit That Moves Us* is among the brightest of the nation's little magazines. Sklar is a brilliant editor who never shies away from trying something new, and his magazine has taste, clarity, and good looks."

The American Library Association's *Choice* said, "Recommended for collections with any degree of interest whatsoever in small press publishing in particular and new good writing in general."

In 1983, in the midst of collecting work for two anthologies, I was approached by two people from Hampden-Sydney College in Virginia—the poet Tom O'Grady, founder and editor of *The Hampden-Sydney Poetry Review,* and Paul Jagasich, a Hungarian writer and translator who knows ten languages. They proposed that a manuscript of poetry they had smuggled out of Czechoslovakia—under the thumb of the Soviet Union at that time—be published by The Spirit That Moves Us Press. The manuscript, translated into English by them, was *The Casting Of Bells,* by Jaroslav Seifert, who had gotten himself elected as head of the Writers Union in order to have a platform from which to call for free speech. The collaboration of O'Grady and Jagasich allowed the poet who was not familiar with the Czech language to guide and edit the work of the translator whose native language was not English.

The manuscript had been turned down by commercial publishers. When I explained my workload at that time and said their book would have to wait for a later date, I was told that Seifert was on his deathbed, and so I published it in 1983 as a trade paperback book and offered it to subscribers as Volume 8, Number 1 of *The Spirit That Moves Us.*

One morning the following year, at 7 a.m., I received in my one-room apartment, a phone call from Sweden. The caller said, "This is Fritz, bookiseller to the Crown; we'd like to order twenty-five copies of *The Casting Of Bells*. My spontaneous reply was "Why?!" The answer: "Haven't you heard?—Jaroslav Seifert just won the Nobel Prize in literature."

Nobel award means sudden business boom to tiny Iowa publisher

By TOM KNUDSON
Of The Register's Iowa City Bureau

IOWA CITY, IA. — At 7:30 Thursday morning, Morty Sklar received a phone call from a Stockholm, Sweden, bookstore. "Congratulations," the caller said. "An author you published just won the Nobel Prize for literature."

"I was very happy," said Sklar, who is the owner and sole employee of a tiny publishing company here. "It was like a dream — except it was real."

On Thursday, the Swedish Academy of Letters awarded the Nobel Prize for literature to a little-known Czechoslovakian poet, Jaroslav Seifert. Last year, Sklar became the first American publisher of an English-language translation of a Seifert book. The work is a 64-page collection of poems called "The Casting of Bells," published by Sklar's the Spirit That Moves Us Press here.

Until now, the book has not exactly been selling like kolaches at a Czech bakery. In fact, just 135 copies had been sold. "No one paid much attention to it," said Sklar, 48.

But that's all changed now. "I've been on the phone constantly," said Sklar. "I've had calls from a book distributor in New York, a university bookstore in Seattle, a small press distributor in Connecticut, The Washington Post, even Radio Free Europe. I must have taken orders for 500 copies already.

"I'm more than sold out right now. I've ordered a reprinting for 2,000 paperbacks and 500 clothbound editions. And that's just for starters. I'm afraid to leave the house because I might miss something. I can't even go out and get a six-pack of beer."

The book's price is $6, plus 75 cents for postage and handling.

Sklar, who calls himself an "independent, literary publisher," formed the Spirit That Moves Us Press nine years ago and operates it himself. "I do everything from reading manuscripts to typesetting to design," he said. The Spirit That Moves Us Press has published about 10 books, he said.

A native of New York, Sklar moved to Iowa City in 1971. He came up with the name for his company from a phrase his mother often used. "She used to say to do something if the spirit moved you," he said.

The spirit moved Sklar last year when he received the manuscript of

Czech poet Jaroslav Seifert, 83, shown here in an old photo, was overjoyed when told he had been awarded the Nobel Prize. Details: 4A.

Morty Sklar

Seifert's book from one of the two people who translated it.

"This is a work that express a lot of concern for humanity," he said. "It gives you the sense of a man who has lived a very hard life, who has been oppressed politically and who has lived with integrity. And that's why I published it."

In ordering a reprint run of 3,000 trade paperbacks, I also ordered a first run of clothbound in an edition of 1,000, anticipating many library orders, though the library jobbers didn't want to change their trade paperback orders to cloth.

Of *The Casting Of Bells*, The Nobel Committee said "Endowed with freshness, sensuality, and rich in inventiveness, his work provides a liberating image of the indomitable spirit and versatility of man."

The London Times Literary Supplement called it "Elegant."

Jaroslav asked us to use the royalties he would receive to publish his *Eight Days: An Elegy for Thomas Masaryk*, who had fought for Czech and Slovak independence and was the first president of Czechoslovakia. We did publish it in Czech and English on facing pages, and followed-up with his *Mozart In Prague: Thirteen Rondels*, also in Czech and English on facing pages."

In 1984 we issued *Nuke-Rebuke: Writers & Artists Against Nuclear Energy & Weapons* in trade paperback and clothbound editions as well as Volume 7, Number 1 of *The Spirit That Moves Us*.

American Library Association's *Choice* said, "The quality of their work makes this volume more than a simple polemic. Highly recommended."

Small Press News called it "The human side of Jonathan Schell's treatise."

In 1985 we published *Here's The Story: Fiction With Heart*, a collection of short stories, in trade paperback and clothbound editions as well as Volume 7, Number 2 of *The Spirit That Moves Us*.

Publishers Weekly said "Stories written, indeed, from the heart."

Doris Grumbach said in *Small Press* "These are stories, at their best, to move many readers, in all sorts of ways."

In 1987 we published *Editor's Choice II: Fiction, Poetry & Art from the U.S. Small Press*, which I edited with Mary Biggs, first female editor of *Library Quarterly*. It was issued in trade paperback and clothbound editions as well as Volume 8, Number 2 of *The Spirit That Moves Us*. Mary came to co-edit it with me when she wrote to say how much she liked the first *Editor's Choice*. I'd told her that Jim and I had reached-out to find more work by women for the anthology, but in fact there were not many women's presses / little magazines at that time, and some of them didn't respond to our call for manuscripts—and I invited Mary to co-edit Editor's Choice II with me.

The Nation said "Subtlety and refinement belong in abundance to the anthologists."

Library Journal said "There is something here for every reader: male or female, gay or straight, black or white, etc."

In 1988, Mary co-edited with me *Men & Women: Together & Alone*, which we issued in both trade paperback and clothbound editions as well as Volume 9, Number 1 of T*he Spirit That Moves Us.*

American Library Association's *Booklist* said "A compelling collection of new poems. A well-selected, carefully ordered theme anthology."

MEN & WOMEN
Together & Alone

EDITED BY MORTY SKLAR & MARY DIGGS

I wasn't into publishing single-author books, mostly because as a basically one-person organization it was difficult enough to put out two publications a year, especially the size of most of them—but I liked the poems of Chuck Miller, a fellow Actualist, so much that in 1988 I published his *How In The Morning: Poems 1962–1988* in trade paperback and clothbound editions as well as Volume 9, Number 2 of *The Spirit That Moves Us*. It includes an interview by Ken McCullough titled "Chuck Miller: A Poet Beneath Contempt." The cover was created by Kay Amert, a master typographer, Director of the Typography Lab at the University of Iowa and co-publisher with Howard Zimmon of Seamark Press in Iowa City. (*See cover in color insert.*)

American Library Association's *Booklist* said "Marked by an honesty and compassion rare in today's verses."

The Bloomsbury Review said "Chuck Miller's exuberance and compassion are tempered with the pathos of one who confronts reality at ground-zero and survives."

In 1989, I gave my third leaving-Iowa-City reading at Prairie Lights

Books and drove a rented truck with personal possessions and The Spirit That Moves Us Press stock back to New York City to Jackson Heights, Queens.

The last The Spirit That Moves Us Press book I put-together in Iowa City was published in New York with a New York imprint and address: *Speak To Me: Swedish-language Women Poets*, edited by Lennart Bruce & Sonja Bruce (Swedish and English on facing pages) and issued in trade paperback and clothbound editions as well as Volume 10, Number 1 of *The Spirit That Moves Us*. Four of the eleven poets are Finnish, writing in Swedish. As with all of the previous books, I typeset it on an IBM Selectric Composer, the Swedish part done letter by letter of course, since Swedish was not a language I knew.

Translation Review of The University of Texas, Dallas said "Graced by a number of virtues that recommend it to anyone interested in poetry, women's studies, Scandinavian literature, or translation."

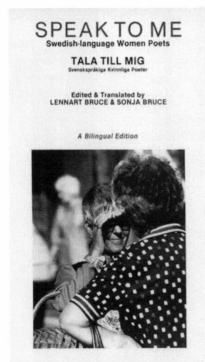

SPEAK TO ME
Swedish-language Women Poets
TALA TILL MIG
Svenskspråkiga Kvinnliga Poeter

Edited & Translated by
LENNART BRUCE & SONJA BRUCE

A Bilingual Edition

In 1990, because of there having been many special issues of *The Spirit That Moves Us* magazine, the next regular non-thematic issue became special, so along with *The Spirit That Moves Us* on its front cover, was the subtitle *Free Parking: Special 15th Anniversary Release*, issued as a trade paperback book as well as Volume 10, Number 2 of *The Spirit That Moves Us*.

The Small Press Book Review said, "The seasoned editorial eye, ecumenical taste, and intent to collect and present noteworthy voices at work in the wide and various American literary scene are evident in this collection.

In 1991 we published *Editor's Choice III: Fiction, Poetry & Art from the*

U.S. Small Press, 1984–1990, with Robert Peters Contributing Editor, in trade paperback and clothbound editions as well as Volume 11 of *The Spirit That Moves Us*.

Kirkus Reviews: "A strong anthology."

Library Journal: "An uncommonly rich anthology.

Highly recommended."

The three *Editor's Choice* volumes now numbered 1,176 pages, spanning a period of twenty-five years from 1965 to 1990. For *Editor's Choice III* alone, 84 contributors were selected from 3,465 nominations by 364 presses and magazines (from an open call to almost 2,000). In this issue I announced that *Editor's Choice* would now be published every two years —but *Editor's Choice III* was the final volume as will be explained later in this history.

See color insert for our only full-color cover.

In 1996 the penultimate The Spirit That Moves Us Press book was *Patchwork Of Dreams: Voices from the Heart of the New America*, co-edited with Joseph Barbato and issued as a trade paperback as well as Volume 12 of *The Spirit That Moves Us*.

It came about this way: Since my return to New York from Iowa City, I soon understood what my mother meant by "I feel like I'm living in a foreign country." Gone were the Jewish delicatessen and bakery, as well as the kosher butcher. I saw a large poster that said, "JACKSON HEIGHTS: America's Real Melting Pot," the borders of which had many flags. South and Central American, as well as Mexican people, stores, restaurants abounded. I was inspired to ask a friend Joe Barbato, who still lived in the neighborhood where we both grew up, Elmhurst—next-door to Jackson Heights, if he'd like to co-edit a Queens anthology of work from people of varying ethnic backgrounds, and he said yes. I suggested the title *The Great Mosaic*, after what the mayor, David N. Dinkins—New York City's first black mayor, called our city. Joe said this was no longer a mosaic the way it was in our childhood when most, if not all, immigrants wanted to blend-in. We used Joe's title, *Patchwork Of Dreams*.

The stories, poems, essays, drama, photographs and interviews from current and former residents of the most ethnically diverse area in the United States and the world makes for an interesting read. For instance, in an interview with Mario Cuomo, former governor of New York State, we learn that when his father emigrated from Italy to the U.S., he was a "ground hog" (underground worker) who dug sewers, saved his money to open a grocery store in Jamaica, Queens.

Publishers Weekly: "Give this joyous compilation to anyone who questions the unique quality of America's ethnic diversity."

The New York Times: "Reflects the mix of writers who grew up in that grand mélange of nationalities that is Queens."

Patchwork Of Dreams also brought Marcela and me together when I got the idea—from city posters and mailers in many languages for an upcoming election, to print the *Patchwork Of Dreams* half-title page in sixteen languages, and I asked Marcela, who worked at a translation company, to ask her employer, Ad Hoc Translations, if they can translate imagistically rather than literally, and they could and did.

Marcela, my wife of twenty-five years in 2017, was born in Arequipa in the Andes Mountains of Perú.

PATCHWORK OF DREAMS

Voices from the Heart of the New America

Stories, Poems, Essays, Drama, Photographs & Interviews

Edited by
MORTY SKLAR & JOSEPH BARBATO
Assisted by Lisa Weinerman Horak

In 2000, we issued *The Day Seamus Heaney Kissed My Cheek In Dublin*, poems 1986–1999 by Bob Jacob in trade paperback and hardback (not clothbound) editions as well as Volume 13 of T*he Spirit That Moves Us*.

ForeWord said "Creates a strong sense of the poet's good humor, modesty, and genuine feeling; the work is affectionate, unpretentious, and engaging."

Editor's Choice IV: Essays from the U.S. Small Press was read for by

Fred Chappell, Patricia Markert and myself, but became the first title that I, with regret, reneged on. This came about as a result of poor judgement in my having mailed a complete catalog of publications from the press that covered its twenty-five years of publishing, too soon after the September 11, 2001 World Trade Center Towers destruction. The mailing of thousands of catalogs to library lists, bookstore lists, teacher lists, and The Spirit That Moves Us Press's subscriber and purchaser list brought a very disappointing return of orders.

I gave readings of my own work and held poetry workshops around Queens in libraries, schools, and in various Phoenix House facilities, as well as presented via The Spirit That Moves Us Press, other writers.

In 2008 I received the first Phoenix House Alumnus of the Year Award, for having introduced poetry to Phoenix House.

Also in 2008, eight years after the press ceased publishing, when I was seventy-three and didn't want my new collection *The Smell Of Life: Poems 1969 to 2005* to be published posthumously, if at all, I brought it out with The Spirit That Moves Us Press imprint in a clothbound edition with dust jacket in full color, and also offered it as Volume 14 of *The Spirit That Moves Us*. It is not in the catalog but is available from the usual suspects.

"Morty Sklar writes from an honesty and courage of the heart. For that I salute him, and all his peers, his colleagues, who share this inexorable dedication."—*Isabella Gardner*

I must acknowledge that my having issued titles as books as well as issues of the magazine came from Curt Johnson (may he rest in peace)— his doing that with his *December Magazine*.

My mother, Selma Sklar, was thrilled to see the first issue of *The Spirit That Moves Us*, 1975, and since she loved poetry herself and was now alone in New York, I set-up a magazine for her—*Alive & Kicking*, named after what she'd said after one of her major surgeries when I'd asked how she was. That's her with my Dad on her second issue. Love ya, Mom.

http://the.spirit.that.moves.us.press.home.mindspring.com

msklar@mindspring.com

329

cover creation by Patrick Dooley

In Memoriam "Elegy" poem by Anselm Hollo; drawing by Catherine Doty
published by The Spirit That Moves Us Press

Toast at First Actualist Convention Barbara Sablove, Patrick Dooley, Steve Toth
photo by Morty Sklar

p. 2 Darrell Gray writing "Actualism–A Manifesto" drawing by Dave Morice

p. 6 Actualist American Poetry Circuit Readings for 1973-1974
created and published by George Mattingly

p. 7 *The Actualist Anthology,* edited by Morty Sklar & Darrell Gray; cover by Patrick Dooley
The Spirit That Moves Us Press, 1977

p. 9 Allan Kornblum and Darrell Gray at an Actualist event; photo by Morty Sklar

p. 13 at the First National Poetry Festival, Allendale, Michigan 1971
from top left: Robert Kelly, Paul Blackburn, Al Young, Robert Vas Dias, Anselm Hollo
below from left: Jackson Mac Low, John Logan, Gregory Corso, Jerome Rothenberg,
Robert Creeley, Custer; photo byAllan Kornblum

p. 14 *Good Morning,* by Darrell Gray & Allan Kornblum; cover art by Patrick Dooley
published by J. Stone Weekly;

p. 16 title page *Wreck O' Lections*, by Darrell Gray & Alastair Johnston, with Anselm
Hollo & Allan Kornblum; design by Alastair Johnston; Poltroon Press, 1987

p. 18 Darrell Gray; photo by?

p. 19 Victoria Ramirez; photo by?

p. 21 cover *Essays & Dissolutions*, by Darrell Gray; published by Abraxas Press, 1977

p. 22 from *Cross-Fertilization: The Human Spirit as Place* drawing by Stuart Mead
The Spirit That Moves Us Press, 1980

p. 33 *The Punctual Actual Weekly* A Memoir of the Hawkeye Theatre, by Michael Lyons

p. 39 Anselm Hollo photo by Allan Kornblum

p. 41 *heavy jars*, by Anselm Hollo, The Toothpaste Press, 1977; art by Patrick Dooley

p. 43 Anselm Hollo & Andrei Vozensensky photo by Allan Kornblum

p. 43 Ted Berrigan from Darrell Gray's photo album

p. 44 Darrell Gray, Anselm Hollo, Robert Creeley at National Poetry Festival 1971
photo by Allan Kornblum

p. 45 The Toothpaste Press logo created by Patrick Dooley

p. 54 Darrell Gray photo by?

p. 59 Dave Morice photo by Allan Kornblum

p. 61 Dr. Alphabet's Medicine Show Poetry Tonic by Dave Morice
photo by Cinda Kornblum

p. 63 Dr. Alphabet (Dave Morice) Poem Wrapping a City Block photo by Dom Franco

p. 71 Steve Toth photo by Morty Sklar

p. 72 Steve Toth and Sheila Heldenbrand photo by Allan Kornblum

p. 79 Sheila (Heldenbrand) Toth photo by Morty Sklar

p. 85 Chuck Miller photo by Morty Sklar

p. 86 *harvesters*, poems by Chuck Miller; cover art by Stuart Mead The Toothpaste Press, 1984

p. 95 David Hilton photo by Cinda or A, 1984llan Kornblum

p. 103 John Sjoberg photo by Morty Sklar

p. 104 *Some Poems My Day Off*, by John Sjoberg; illustration by Stuart Mead The Toothpaste Press

p. 105 *Me Too Magazine*, edited by Patricia Markert, Mary Swanson, Barbara Sablove cover by Patrick Dooley

p. 109 Cinda Kornblum photo by Allan Kornblum

p. 110 Ernest Allen (Al) Buck photo by Allan or Cinda Kornblum

p. 110 Ellen Weis photo by Allan or Cinda Kornblum

p. 111 Poetry City, U.S.A button created by Dave Morice

p. 111 Jim Hanson and Elizabeth Zima photo by Allan or Cinda Kornblum

p. 111 David Duer photo by Allan or Cinda Kornblum

p. 111 Cinda (Wormley) Kornblum photo by Allan Kornblum

p. 112 Cinda (Wormley) Kornblum photo by Sandra Kaput

p. 117 Allan Kornblum photo by Morty Sklar

p. 124 Allan Kornblum's tombstone photo by Cinda Kornblum

p. 120 Morty Sklar photo by Marcia Plumb

p. 125 Morty Sklar on the way to the First National Poetry Festival in Allendale, Michigan July 1971 on his Honda 305 "Dream." photo by Morty

p. 129 *The Night We Stood Up for Our Rights*, poems by Morty Sklar cover art by Jimmy Harrison; The Toothpaste Press 1977

p. 130 note of 1972 from Workshop teacher Stanley Plumly to Morty Sklar

p. 131 Ana Mendieta applying Morty Sklar's facial hairs for her M.F.A. project; photos?

p. 140 Jim Mulac photo by?

p. 141 Jim's Used Books & Records store photo by?
p. 143 Jim Mulac and Morty Sklar at Jim's Books & Records photo by?
p. 143 "Blood of the Iguana" story read by Nigerian author Ola Rotimi poster created and hand-colored by Jim Mulac

331

p. 143 P.J. Casteel's and Jim Mulac's reading at The Sanctuary poster by Dave Morice

p. 144 Jim Mulac's notebook of readings at Jim's Used Books & Records

p. 145 Jim Mulac playing piano (where and when?) photo by Morty Sklar

p. 151 John Batki photo by Morty Sklar

p. 157 George Mattingly photo by Morty Sklar

p. 159 George Mattingly & others collating *Toothpaste* **magazine** photo by Allan Kornblum

p. 160 *Search for Tomorrow* **magazine,** edited by George Mattingly; cover by George

p. 165 Elizabeth Zima photo by Allan Kornblum

p. 166 "Photo Liz" illustration by David Sessions

p. 167 "Photo Liz" illustration, the second by David Sessions

p. 178 Robert Caldwell a.k.a. Lloyd Quibble photo by?

p. 179 "Untitled 1" concrete poem by Robert Caldwell a.k.a. Lloyd Quibble

p. 180 *typewriter* **magazine** first issue, edited by Robert Caldwell
    photo of Allan Kornblum's typewriter by Allan Kornblum

p. 182 "babble2" concrete poem by Robert Caldwell a.k.a. Lloyd Quibble

p. 183 "Untitled 3" concrete poem by Robert Caldwell a.k.a. Lloyd Quibble

p. 183 "xray" concrete poem by Robert Caldwell a.k.a. Lloyd Quibble

p. 183 John Birkbeck photo by?

p. 191 P.J. Casteel photo by Allan Kornblum

p. 192 Kay Amert photo by?

p. 194 Glen and Harry Epstein photo by?

p. 195 Harry Epstein running for City Council poster by?

p. 196 Epstein's Bookstore temporary module during Urban Renewal photo by?

p. 197 Howard Zimmon photo by Morty Sklar

p. 198 Patrick Dooley: photo by him

p. 198 Patrick Dooley at typography lab photo by?

p. 199 *Tight Pants* published by The Toothpaste Press; cover by Patrick Dooley

p. 199 *Toothpaste* **magazine #2** cover by Patrick Dooley

p. 201 Stuart Mead photo by Dom Garcia

p. 202 *Eight Days***,** by Jaroslav Seifert; published by The Spirit That Moves Us Press
    cover by Stuart Mead

p. 203 Stuart Mead painting untitled

p. 204 Stuart Mead painting of girl in chair untitled

p. 205 **David Sessions** photo provided by Carol Harlow

p. 206 **Volume 2, #1 *The Spirit That Moves* Us magazine** cover art by David Sessions

p. 207 **Joye Chizek** photo by her

p. 208 **Duck's Breath Mystery Theater** poster by Dave Morice

p. 209 **G.P. Skratz** photo by?

p. 212 **Robert Ernst** photo by?

p. 215 **Steven Lavoie** photo by Allan Kornblum

p. 217 **Michael Lyons** photo by Sue Schein

p. 218 **David Schein** photo by Chuck Hudina

p. 221 **Whoopi Goldberg** photo by?

p. 223 **P.J. Casteel, Dave Morice—First Actualist Event**
Poetry Marathon at Epstein's Bookstore 1971; photo by Morty Sklar

p. 227 **Steve Toth, Josephine Clare, Jim Mulac, Allan Kornblum, Liz Voss;** photo by?

p. 228 **"Translations from New Yorkese monologue** poster by Morty Sklar

p. 228 **Darrell Gray reading his poetry and talking** photo by Morty Sklar

p. 228 **John Sjoberg reading his poetry and talking** photo by Morty Sklar

p. 230 **Morty Sklar's poetry reading at the Sanctuary** poster by Morty Sklar; photo by?

p. 231 **P.J. Casteel, Dave Morice, Chuck Miller at a Sanctuary reading;** photo by Morty Sklar

p. 233 *Backyard* and *The Brick Apartment* **plays at Wesley House** poster by Al Buck

p. 233 **The Second Actualist Convention** poster by Morty Sklar

p. 235 *The Umbrella that Predicted the Future* **play at Wesley House** poster by Dave Morice

p. 236 **P.J. Casteel and Jim Mulac in** *The Umbrella that Predicted the Future* photo by Morty

p. 236 **Just Friends band** photo by Morty Sklar

p. 237 **John Birkbeck and Darrell Gray facing each other** (I can't recall names of others) photo by Morty Sklar

p. 237 **Phil Lemke and John Birkbeck left, Allan Kornblum standing, Brad Harvey right** can't recall or didn't know names of others; photo by Morty Sklar

p. 238 **Bruce Houston displaying his art** photo by Morty Sklar

p. 238 **Audrey Teeter reading her poetry** photo by Morty Sklar

p. 243 **Joyce Holland signature re the Joyce Holland hoax:**

p. 246 **8th Actualization 1979** poster by David Sessions

p. 247 **Post-Modern Poets at the Everson Museum of Art 1973** poster by the Museum

p. 258 **West Coast Actualist Convention 5** 1987; Leonard Pitt was one performer, and was directed by George Coates; photo by Dave Patrick

p. 262 *Black Womans Bed*, by Colleen Larkin and Ellen Sebastian (who performed it) at West Coast Actualist Convention #? 1981? photo from Doug Wilson's set

p. 263 **West Coast Actualist Convention 8** 1980; program by Blake Street Hawkeyes

p. 266 **Acute Actualism: Homage to Darrell Gray**, west coast 1986 poster by Alastair Johnston at Poltroon Press

p. 267 **The cast of *Bob*,** performed at Acute Actualism; photo by?

p. 268 **The Dull Sounds**, performers at West Coast Actualist Convention "11" 1987; photo?

p. 297 **Allan Kornblum of Toothpaste & Coffee House Presses setting type** photo by Dan Berg

p. 299 **A *Toothpaste* magazine #3**; cover by Patrick Dooley

p. 300 **mimeograph machine at Iowa Memorial Union** photo by Cinda Kornblum

p. 301 **Harry Duncan in his West Branch print shop 1971** photo by Allan Kornblum

p. 302 **Cinda Wormley, Allan Kornblum, Dave Morice before Cinda's and Allan's wedding** in Newton, Iowa; photo by Morty Sklar

p. 303 **Allan Kornblum in Coffee House Press shop above Nate's** photo by?

p. 306 **Toothpaste Press and Coffee House Press books in West Branch (1984?)** photo by Allan Kornblum

p. 308 **Allan and Gwen Kornblum in Coffee House Press office 1979** photo by?

p. 311 **Allan Kornblum, Wang Ping and Chris Fischbach at Minnesota Book Awards** photo by Esther Porter

p. 313 **The Spirit That Moves Us Press's Work-study crew** at the press's location at Center East in 1980: Shelley Sterling, David Duer, Morty Sklar, Michael Cummings, Stuart Mead

p. 314 *The Spirit That Moves Us* **magazine, Volume 1, #1 1975** Morty Sklar with his Grandmother Rose; cover by Morty

p. 316 **Morty Sklar in an Iowa City bus** where The Spirit That Moves Us Press placed Poetry-with-Drawings in the Buses in 1988; photo by Dom Franco

p. 317 *The Farm In Calabria*, **by David Ray**; also issued as Volume 5, #s 1 & 2 of *The Spirit That Moves Us* magazine; photo by Judy Ray

p. 318 *Editor's Choice*, **1980**, edited by Morty Sklar & Jim Mulac; photo by Nagib Assed Selections from nominations by small independent and college/university publishers.

p. 319 **Jim Mulac and Morty Sklar in Morty's $45/month room above the Englert** where he lived and where he typeset *Editor's Choice*, noted above. photo by?

p. 319 **Jim Mulac and Morty Sklar back of Jim's Used Books & Records** after the publication of their co-edited *Editor's Choice*, noted above; photo by Shelley Sterling

p. 321 *Des Moines Register* **article, 1984, about a The Spirit That Moves Us Press author winning the Nobel Prize in literature.** Czech Jaroslav Seifert, his *The Casting of Bells*.

p. 323 *Men & Women: Together & Alone*, edited by Morty Sklar and Mary Biggs
photo by Doug Smith

p. 324 *Speak To Me: Swedish-language Women Poets*, edited by Lennart Bruce
and Sonja Bruce; photo by Marty Youngmann

p. 326 *Patchwork Of Dreams: Voices from the Heart of the New America*,
edited by Morty Sklar and Joseph Barbato; photo by Corky Lee

p. 328 Editors/publishers at Small Press Book Fair N.Y.C. 1981: C.W. Truesdale, Carlo
Pittore, Harry Smith, Tuli Kupferberg, Lynne Savitt, Allan Bealy, Maurice Kenny, Irene
Turner, Don Wellman, Scarlatina Lust, Carol Tuynman, Carol Berge, Morty Sklar, Joseph
Bruchac; photos by Diane Kruchkow & Mark Melnicove:

p. 329 *Alive & Kicking* **magazine**, edited by Selma Sklar, named after what she told Morty
after major surgery when he asked how she was.